DOCTOR WHO
THE
TIME-TRAVELLERS'
GUIDE

The man with all time and space at his fingertips - the first Doctor, William Hartnell, with the leader of the Elders (Frederick Jaeger) in 'The Savages' (1966).

DOCTOR WHO THE TIME-TRAVELLERS' GUIDE

By arrangement with BBC Books,
a division of BBC Enterprises Ltd.

PETER HAINING

W.H. ALLEN · LONDON
1987

The
Time Machine

An Invention

By

H. G. Wells

London

William Heinemann

MDCCCXCV

The 'father' of Time Travel, H. G. Wells, and the title page of the first edition of his famous novel (1895).

THE ORIGINAL TIME TRAVELLER

'Would you like to see the Time Machine itself?' asked the Time Traveller.

And therewith, taking the lamp in his hand, he led the way down the long, draughty corridor to his laboratory. I remember vividly the flickering light, his queer, broad head in silhouette, the dance of the shadows, how we all followed him, puzzled but incredulous, and how there in the laboratory we beheld a larger edition of the little mechanism which we had earlier seen vanish before our eyes. Parts were of nickel, parts of ivory, parts had certainly been filed or sawn out of rock crystal. The thing was generally complete but the twisted crystalline bars lay unfinished upon the bench beside some sheets of drawings, and I took one up for a better look at it. Quartz it seemed to be.

'Look here,' said the Medical Man, 'are you perfectly serious? Or is this a trick – like the ghost you showed us last Christmas?'

'Upon that machine,' said the Time Traveller, holding the lamp aloft, 'I intend to explore time. Is that plain? I was never more serious in my life.'

The Time Machine (1895)

*The TARDIS dwarfed
by one of the
enormous Jagorath
Star Cruisers.*

Typeset by Phoenix Photosetting
Printed and bound in Great Britain
by Mackays of Chatham Ltd
for the Publishers, W.H. Allen & Co. PLC
44 Hill Street, London W1X 8LB

ISBN 0 491 03497 0

Design Cecil Smith
Additional research David Howe

This book is dedicated
to the memory of
ROBERT HOLMES and
PATRICK TROUGHTON
now with the Time Lords
and sadly missed

Also by Peter Haining:

Doctor Who: A Celebration
Doctor Who: The Key to Time
The Doctor Who File

CONTENTS

INTRODUCTION

The TARDIS – A Passport to Time and Space

The TARDIS on the Barnet By-Pass in 1981 where the last original Police Box had once stood.

The one constant feature throughout the three decades of *Doctor Who* has been the TARDIS. Doctors have come and gone as a result of each new regeneration, companions with even greater frequency, and though a few of the monsters such as the Daleks and Cybermen have cropped up almost regularly – only the remarkable Time Travel Machine itself has sailed serenely, if somewhat erratically, on. Its chameleon circuit may remain firmly lodged in the shape of a London police box, and it has certainly had its fair share of narrow escapes; but unfailingly it remains the dream machine in which we all ride to excitement and unexpected places in space and time.

It is the core of the Doctor's adventures, in fact without it he would be as confined to one time and one place as his audience. It also epitomises the dream of Time Travel which has intrigued the mind of mankind for centuries; and now with the enormous advances in space science and technology, it has at last become a serious subject for discussion and even detailed research. One day, perhaps, Earthmen may reach into the vast uncharted realms of Time as we are just now beginning to do into Space.

Entering the Doctor's Time Machine - Jo (Katy Manning) in the TARDIS in 'Colony In Space'.

The mythology which surrounds the TARDIS has, of course, grown irresistibly throughout the twenty and more years of *Doctor Who*. Originally conceived as the unlikely means of transport for the cranky and irascible first Doctor, it has since been shown to play a vital role in the lives of each and every one of the seven Doctors.

Seven may be a lucky number – but luck is not one of the features built into this Time Machine. It flies by the most advanced power system and is controlled by highly sophisticated computers – yet, the reader may be surprised to learn, its origins lie in the primitive science of the late Victorian era and the imagination of a former student turned writer. For, as you will discover in the pages of this book, the inspiration for the TARDIS – and to a degree the Doctor himself – is to be found in the novel *The Time Machine* by H.G. Wells which he began writing in 1888 and finally completed in the year 1895.

This pioneer novel – the first to describe someone travelling backwards and forwards in time under their own control and not by the winds of chance – began as a serial for an amateur magazine, *The Science Schools Journal*, entitled 'The Chronic Argonauts'. Then, when the young Wells turned to fiction and displayed a facility for fantasy tales, it was those self-same pages which he utilised as the basis for *The Time Machine*, the first of his series of now famous major scientific romances, of which *The Invisible Man* (1897) and *The War of the Worlds* (1898) are equally highly regarded.

Years later, in the twentieth century, the still undiminished power of Wells' story grabbed the imagination of the young Sydney Newman, and had such an impact on him that he took it as the basic premise for what is now the most famous and long running science fiction serial on television anywhere in the world!

There is an interesting twist of fate about the association of *The Time Machine* and Newman's television programme. For just as the year 1888 will mark the centenary of the birth of the story, so will *Doctor Who* mark twenty-five years on the screen!

The appearance of the TARDIS, both inside and out, is now so familiar as to need no explanation. But how a machine that is so small on the outside can contain such a vast number of passageways and rooms – not to mention a power unit deep in the interior – is a constant source of amazement to each new generation of viewers. The BBC Production Office, in fact, even has a specially prepared handout on the TARDIS which explains this apparent anomaly:

'The TARDIS,' it says, 'is an acronym for Time And Relative Dimensions In Space. Its special facility of appearing smaller on the outside than its internal dimensions was demonstrated when the Doctor held two cubes of the same size, one close to his eye and the other far away. Naturally, the cube nearer seemed larger than the distant cube.

The TARDIS's principle enables both cubes to occupy the same space at the same time thus accommodating the anomaly.'

Should you doubt this, I can only suggest you try it for yourself!

I have in my earlier book, *Doctor Who: A Celebration* (1983) discussed the working of the TARDIS and also the principles of Time Travel in some detail, so I do not propose to cover the ground again here. But as this is a Guide to the Doctor's worlds of space and time – and what is to be found therein – there are just a few more unusual tit-bits of information about his spacecraft which I should like to add. Some of these, I venture to suggest, may surprise you!

The TARDIS which appeared in the very first story, 'An Unearthly Child', back in November 1963, was not, as many have supposed, a new prop built especially for the series, but a police box that had already been in use for some years in the weekly police drama, *Dixon of Dock Green*! This box, in fact, remained in use until 1976 when it finally collapsed as a result of extreme wear during the making of the story of 'The Seeds of Doom'.

The TARDIS inside itself in the Cloister Room in the story of 'Logopolis'.

A simpler model made of lighter material and with a flat roof was then built by the BBC and made its debut in 'Masque of Mandragora' that same year, putting in excellent service for the fourth Doctor until January 1980 when it, too, was replaced following the story of 'The Horns of Nimon'.

The third version, deliberately made identical to a real police box complete with the original stacked roof, was unveiled in 'The Leisure Hive' in late August 1980, and has continued in the Doctor's not always gentle care to the present day. (The second version, incidentally, made a brief reappearance in 1981 in 'Logopolis' in a scene which was supposed to be on the Barnet By-Pass where the last real police box in the country had stood for some years until its removal in 1981.)

Though it may only be a television prop in reality, I can vouch from personal knowledge of standing in the doorway, that there is an undefinable thrill about gingerly stepping inside. You *know* there is going to be nothing there but a shell – but half a lifetime of watching the Doctor still makes you half-hope you'll magically find yourself in the console room!

But you can *imagine* – which is what has really made *Doctor Who* such a success over the years. And imagination is what I ask you to bring along with you as we travel through the Doctor's many worlds. For here are the planets he has visited, the people and monsters he has encountered, and the spacecraft that he has seen. They are all a tribute to the imagination and creativity of the people who made them – and perhaps even more to the rich tradition of science fiction which inspired the series in the first place.

For like *Doctor Who* itself, the story of Time Travel reaches back into the past as much as it presses forward into the future. And that is where our Guide must first begin . . .

COLIN BAKER

WILLIAM HARTNELL

TOM BAKER

PATRICK TROUGHTON

JON PERTWEE

PETER DAVISON

SYLVESTER McCOY

The world's most
famous Time
Travellers.

The 'father' of
Doctor Who
- Sydney Newman.

King Kojata, a
traveller in time,
from a Russian folk
talk in one of Sydney
Newman's favourite
childhood books,
'The Green Fairy
Book' by Andrew
Lang.

1

THE SCIENCE THAT INSPIRED DOCTOR WHO

The creation of *Doctor Who* owes a great deal to Sydney Newman's love of classic science fiction – and his fascination with Time Travel. For the man who evolved the idea of the eccentric traveller at loose in the galaxies of space and time has recently admitted that it was his childhood delight in sci fi that lead, in the fullness of time, to the hugely successful programme now in its third decade.

Indeed, the show is almost a boyhood ambition come true, for while young Sydney's friends were out playing American football or baseball in his native city of Toronto in Canada, he had his head buried in tales of high adventure not only on the Earth, but underneath the sea, as well as in space and time. And like many children, he dreamed that one day he might share such adventures . . .

Sydney recalls that he was only seven years old when he first became fascinated by books of fairy tales, especially the monsters and giants which populated the vivid folk stories from France and Russia that he liked. He also got enormous pleasure from the long series of books edited by the versatile Scottish man of letters, Andrew Lang (1844–1912) entitled *The Green Fairy Book, The Blue Fairy Book* and so on.

The superb illustrations in these books were a contributing factor in firing him with an early enthusiasm to be an artist, for which he had a natural talent. Later, in fact, he went to art school where he displayed considerable promise, but though he tried to make a living as a cartoonist and commercial artist, it was into television that he

eventually went and made his name. (He does, though, still enjoy painting and making sculptures today.)

Amongst all the books that he read during those formative years, two in particular were to haunt his imagination for years to come: Jules Verne's *Twenty Thousand Leagues Under The Sea* and H.G. Wells' *The Time Machine*.

'I remember that I read an enormous amount of science fiction, in particular the classics, and also the work of such modern masters as Isaac Asimov and Arthur C. Clarke,' he says. 'I was a voracious reader, but I learned to distinguish the good from the bad. I came to believe that good science fiction is basically always about a human being in a crazy or mythical environment.

One of the Doctor's forerunners, Captain Nemo, with two companions meets some strange sea creatures in Jules Verne's 'Twenty Thousand Leagues Under The Sea' (1870). James Mason who played Captain Nemo in the 1954 film version of the story.

The original Master of the World, Robur, from Verne's novel, 'Clipper of the Clouds' (1887), and Vincent Price who played the power mad despot in the 1961 film, 'Master of the World.' Not only does Price bear a striking resemblance to The Master, but he was also, of course, supposed to star as the villain in the ill-fated movie, 'Doctor Who and Scratchman.'

'The best of these environments are the ones that make a comment on our world today – and those are the stories I love the most. Some of the outer space stories don't really reflect our society or any aspects of it and I think that creates a real problem for readers who want to be able to relate to what's going on.'

Sydney does not believe such faults exist in either the Verne or Wells novels, which partly explains their attraction for him.

Twenty Thousand Leagues Under The Sea was first published in 1870, and though Verne cannot be credited with inventing the submarine (the American Robert Fulton had already built the first practicable submarine by then) he was the first to sense its true potential and longevity. Verne (1828–1905) is generally thought of along with H.G. Wells as one of the 'Founding Fathers of Science Fiction' and certainly the series of sixty-five novels he published under the general heading of *Voyages Extraordinaires* (Extraordinary Journeys) – beginning with *Five Weeks In A Balloon* published in 1863 and ending with *Master of the World* in 1904 – is full of exciting stories and the most remarkable scientific prophecies from the first Moon voyage to satellites and even cybernetics!

Though, incidentally, it is true to say that when Sydney Newman devised *Doctor Who* he had no plans to include a character like Robur, the power-mad despot who invents a flying machine to enslave the world and features in *The Clipper of the Clouds*, 1887, and the aforementioned *Master of the World*, there is a strong parallel to be drawn between him and the Doctor's great enemy, the Master. And I think the reader might also agree, after looking at the accompanying

Prototype of the TARDIS? The outside and inside of Jules Verne's space machine as pictured in 'From The Earth To The Moon' (1865).

sketch of the machine used by Verne's space travellers to reach the Moon in *From The Earth to the Moon* (1865), that it is not unlike the TARDIS.

Sydney's youthful memory of *Twenty Thousand Leagues Under The Sea* first surfaced to be put to practical use when he was working at the Canadian Broadcasting Corporation in the early fifties.

'I was looking for ideas for children's television and decided to base this new series on the Jules Verne story,' he says. 'It was about a group of kids in diving suits and the adventures they had under the sea. I remember it was all shot through a little fish tank about two inches thick with all the actors moving very slowly behind it! I think some of the lessons I learned there were carried through to *Doctor Who*.'

The most memorable figure in *Twenty Thousand Leagues Under The Sea* – indeed in perhaps all of Verne's novels – is Captain Nemo, the colourful master of the submarine, the *Nautilus*, and a man who has suffered injustice at the hands of the British colonial power. As a result of this he has become a fighter on behalf of other oppressed people's causes, and very much a man of ingenuity and action. A prototype of the Doctor, one might almost feel!

The second classic, *The Time Machine*, was to be even more

The youthful H. G. Wells at the time he wrote 'The Time Machine' - and his own sketch of the kind of monster that mankind would ultimately evolve into!

influential. Herbert George Wells (1866–1946), the science teacher turned writer, came to international fame with his very first novel, *The Time Machine*, which appeared in 1895. It was not, though, his first published work for he had previously written several impressive short stories and some remarkable essays. 'The Man of the Year Million' (1893), for instance, predicted that mankind would eventually evolve into creatures of enormous intelligence with huge heads and tiny bodies. These descendants of mankind would outlive the Sun, he said, living immersed in nutrient fluids beneath the surface of the planet. In another essay, 'The Living Things That May Be', he discussed the possibility of silicon-based life.

The Time Machine also evolved from some earlier essays speculating on time travel, 'The Rediscovery of the Unique', and the serial 'The Chronic Argonauts'. The book recounted the invention of a flying machine which takes its inventor, called, enigmatically, 'The Time Traveller', on a journey into the far future – approximately the year 80,2701 – where the human race has divided into two species, the pleasure-seeking Eloi and the sinister, savage Morlocks, who are locked in a battle for survival. The traveller is able to help the gentle Eloi overcome their tormentors but at the cost of the Eloi girl with whom he

A 1950 magazine publication of Wells' famous novel - and Rod Taylor starring in the film version made in 1960.

has fallen in love. At the close of the narrative, the man sets out again in his machine and is heard of no more. Whether Wells ever planned further adventures for his time traveller we shall sadly never know . . .

According to one authoritative source, the idea for *The Time Machine* so captivated Wells that he completed the 35,000 word novel in just a fortnight! And once it was published he was established as a writer for the rest of his life.

Although Wells' later novel, *The War of the Worlds* (1898) about the invasion of Britain by aliens from Mars, may be considered his most famous book, *The Time Machine* excited a great deal of interest among readers and actually inspired one Victorian, a Mr Robert W. Paul, to try and make a Time Machine of his own!

Apparently Mr Paul approached H.G. Wells for his help on this project, and although the busy author was unable to offer anything practical, the inventor did lodge his plans at the Patent Office in London. There is, though, no further information on this scheme – nor of Mr Paul himself. In fact, the silence is so profound as almost to suggest he achieved his objective and sped off into the future – or past – never to return!

Fifty years on, Wells' book was still weaving its magic spell around readers like Sydney Newman, not to mention television companies. (Curiously, the story was not turned into a cinema movie for the first time until 1960 when George Pal, who earlier made *The War of the Worlds* (1953), directed a version with the American actor Rod Taylor unlikely cast as the traveller!)

In what can be seen now as a curiously prophetic twist of fate, it was the BBC who first brought *The Time Machine* to the small screen in 1949. It was, in fact, the world's first TV science fiction production, and starred Anthony Nicholls in an hour-long adaptation which went out live from Alexandra Palace. As unfortunately no copy exists of this landmark production, it is impossible to judge accurately its content or quality: but more of this later.

Sydney Newman had never forgotten the book either, and it was still there at the back of his mind when, in December 1962, he was hired by the BBC on a five year contract to make the Corporation's drama the best on television. Prior to this he had learned the business with CBC from 1952 to 1958 (finishing as Head of Drama) and then come to England to work for ABC TV (the forerunner of London Weekend Television) where he had master-minded such shows as *Armchair Theatre*, *The Avengers* and a serial for children, *Pathfinders in Space* in 1959.

Though this Sunday afternoon space serial was clearly a stepping stone to *Doctor Who*, another TV series he devised was to crystallise the idea – aided by his memories of the Verne and Wells novels – as he has also explained recently.

'At ABC I did a series called *Out of This World* with Irene Shubik as the story editor,' he said. 'It grew out of my love for science fiction and we had that great horror actor Boris Karloff introduce and close each story.

'Anyhow, when I went to the BBC they told me they were looking for something to bridge the gap between the afternoon sports programme and *Juke Box Jury*. Some kind of children's drama.

'And what dropped into my mind was H.G. Wells' time machine. I'm not sure precisely how the idea developed, but what I thought was we could have some characters who would travel backwards and forwards in time. They would come into contact with either real historical events or else meet things in the future that were feasible. Everything had to be *possible* – what I didn't want were bug-eyed monsters!'

Sydney was also responsible for dreaming up the multi-purpose flying machine in which his travellers journeyed about space and time.

'The clever thing about the spaceship was that it was to be a very commonplace object, the sort of thing that might be seen by anybody who was watching,' he explained. 'It could have been an old car or something like that – but in the end it turned out to be that old police telephone box.

'I've never actually claimed that the police box was my idea. My only idea was that it had to be the kind of machine that would be ordinary on the outside and absolutely enormous inside. And to drive it would be this old man of 760 years of age, partly senile, who had fled from outer space where his planet had been taken over by some horrible enemies.

'And because he was a bit senile he didn't know how to use the machine properly and that was how he came to be on Earth in the first place. And that situation would lead into the stories of him trying to get the machine back to his planet but always ending up somewhere in Earth's history or in outer space,' he added.

Once Sydney Newman had outlined his idea in a memo to Donald Wilson, the Head of Serials, and brought in Verity Lambert from ABC as the producer of the series, he turned over the realisation of his dream to others. And, indeed, if there is one thing that characterises this extraordinary man and his contribution to television, it has been his ability to pick good people and leave them to get on with an idea. It is something those who have worked for him recall gratefully at every opportunity – and a factor of which he is inordinately proud.

Sydney is also keenly aware of the importance of a strong basic formula for any TV series.

'If there was one thing that made *Doctor Who* successful to begin with it was the amalgam of the past, the present and the future. Not to mention the combination of age and the young. And it's kept going because of the strength of the basic formula – the time and space machine and the characters,' he says.

This strength has, of course, proved itself over almost a quarter of a century with not a few traumas along the way, and though today Sydney bears no grudge at not being able to share in even a part of the world-wide earnings generated by his creation, he does feel he ought to be credited on the programme with the words *Doctor Who devised by Sydney Newman*.

And though he does not think of *Doctor Who* as either the best or most satisfying television series he has made, he is still fond of the programme and would even enjoy being associated with it again.

'Because science fiction has been part of my life for so long, I'm still full of ideas,' he says. 'I have this scheme for changing the programme, and even for what I believe is a clever idea for replacing the TARDIS. Can you *imagine*!'

Indeed, one can! For as we have seen, *Doctor Who* is an extension of Sydney Newman's love of science fiction and two favourite books, *Twenty Thousand Leagues Under The Sea* and *The Time Machine* – which are, of course, only manifestations of even earlier literary works: a fact of which he is also well aware. And before we begin our journey around the Doctor's many worlds, it is certainly worth a trip not unlike one of those enjoyed by the first of his seven incarnations into the past to trace the origins of the unique literary genre of time travel which has inspired a most impressive catalogue of books and television series. . .

The earliest picture of a 'Time Machine' - a late eighteenth century French print of a windmill from which old women emerge as pretty young girls!

2
BACK IN THE MISTS OF TIME TRAVEL

Although H.G. Wells' *The Time Machine* was unquestionably the first novel to give travellers in time mobility and control over their movements – both backwards and forwards – it was far from being the first story on this theme. In fact, what Wells did was to take the idea out of the realms of the fantastical or theological and put it firmly into the mechanical. As Malcolm J. Edwards has written in *The Encyclopedia of Science Fiction*:

'Wells's invention of a time machine revolutionised time travel stories, making it possible for the traveller to venture into other eras selectively and purposefully.'

The earliest time travel story I have been able to trace is *Memoirs of the Year 2500* written in 1771 by a French journalist and playwright Louis-Sebastien Mercier (1740–1814). The tale concerns an eccentric professor's sudden transition into a France of the future where the social conditions are a veritable Utopia. Interestingly, the book was first published anonymously in England and has been said to be influential in generating the French Revolution.

Ten years later, a Norwegian dramatist, Johann Hermann Wessel (1742–1785) created a not dissimilar story in the form of a play, *Anno 7603*. Perhaps because of the technical difficulties of staging such a tale in which the group of time travellers are projected into a lush and highly advanced civilisation, there is no record of it ever having been performed publicly. *Anno 7603* has been claimed in some quarters to be an outspoken plea – considering the times in which it was written – for female emancipation, as the roles of men and women are shown as being reversed.

Both of these stories took the protagonists *forward* in time, and it was not until 1838 that an anonymous British writer had the idea of going backwards. His story, 'Missing One's Coach' told of a time traveller who enters a time warp and finds himself back in eighth-century England where he meets a real person, the great historian and writer, the Venerable Bede (673–735), author of several major works on ancient British history. The two men have an interesting dialogue about the past, during the course of which the man from the nineteenth century tries not to reveal too much of what the future holds and thereby upset the temporal balance. A later publication of this story was illustrated by the pioneer French fantasy artist, Albert Robida (1848–1926), a contemporary of both Verne and Wells. One of his evocative sketches is reproduced here.

Less than a decade later, Edgar Allan Poe (1809–1849), the tragic American genius credited with founding the detective and horror story genres, wrote no fewer than three stories which deal with time displacement: 'A Tale of the Ragged Mountains' (1844) in which a man finds himself in the year 1780; 'Some Words With A Mummy' (1845) a reanimation story in which an Egpytian discloses secrets of the past; and 'Mellonta Tauta' (1849) about a vastly overpopulated future. Other fascinating examples of Poe's 'scientification' – as it has been described – are to be found in 'The Unparalleled Adventure of one Hans Pfall' (1835) about a journey to the Moon, and 'The Man That Was Used Up' (1839) which features a man who is half-human and half-machine. This creature, something like a Cyborg in appearance, might well be considered a predecessor of the Cybermen!

It is highly probable that another American writer, Edward Page Mitchell (1852–1927), was influenced by Poe because he was a journalist on the *New York Sun* which re-published several of the older man's stories. Mitchell's fictions continued where many of Poe's left off, including two on the Cyborg theme, 'The Tachypomp' (1874) about a human calculator, and 'The Man Without A Body' about matter transmission. A less well-known work, though, is 'The Clock That Went Backwards' (1881) in which a timepiece which appears to be broken is wound up and promptly runs backwards, transporting two boys to sixteenth-century Holland. This is without doubt the first time travel story to feature children in the central roles.

The year 1884 also saw another first for time travel stories when a man of the eighteenth century was transported forward to the present day. The story was called 'Pausodyne' and was written by Grant Allen (1848–1899) a Canadian who settled in London and later become notorious for his novel, *The Woman Who Did* (1895) which attacked Victorian hypocrisy about sex. In 'Pausodyne', the man from the past found himself looked upon as a dangerous lunatic in the late nineteenth

One of Albert Robida's sketches for the time travel story, 'Missing One's Coach' written by an anonymous English author in 1838.

century! Allen also reversed this idea in a later novel, *The British Barbarians* (1895) in which a man from the future is horrified by the taboos he finds in Victorian times.

Mention should also be made of Mark Twain's famous story, *A Connecticut Yankee in King Arthur's Court* (1889), which is somewhat unclear about the mechanics of the hero's method of journeying into the past, although it can be argued that his return is achieved by suspended animation. Whatever the case, the tale was very popular with readers, and provided an ideal precursor to Wells' *The Time Machine* which appeared six years later.

Viewed with hindsight, it is curious to find that despite the sensational success of *The Time Machine* it was to be some years before the theme was again explored by writers.

A little diversion, though, occurred in 1898 when the Scottish writer and editor, Robert Barr (1850–1912), who had earlier reviewed the Wells book, produced a novel short story, 'The Hour Glass' in which he humorously suggested that ghosts might actually be time travellers!

Once again, though, it was a Frenchman, Jean Delaire (1870–1939) who sensed the serious possibilities in time travel when he wrote 'Around A Distant Star' (1904). This offered a completely new concept by describing a space machine journeying across the universe at two thousand times the speed of light. Its crew take advantage of this speed to train their telescope back on Earth and pick up light waves generated two millenia before – thereby being able to see Jesus preaching in Galilee!

Time travel also featured in the early work of Murray Leinster (1896–1975), often referred to as 'the Dean of Science Fiction Writers'. Leinster came to public attention with a story called 'The Runaway Skyscraper' written for *Argosy* magazine in 1919, in which a multi-storied office block was hurled back in time to pre-Columbian America. In this tale, the author first developed the concept of a commonplace structure able to move through time – a feature of the TARDIS, of course. The author later wrote two novels about time travellers interfering with the past to ensure the continuation of democracy, *Time Tunnel* (1964) and *Tunnel Through Time* (1966).

Ray Cummings (1887–1957) a contemporary of Leinster and a popular contributor to the American 'pulp' magazines, was perhaps the first man to write a trilogy of time travel stories and to build his reputation upon them. The tales are *The Man Who Mastered Time* (1924), *The Shadow Girl* (1929) and *The Exile of Time* (1931). Unfortunately, the books have not stood the test of time very well and seem out-dated today, though their importance in the development of the genre after Wells – especially in America – should not be overlooked.

Scottish-born John Taine (1883–1960) also wrote a number of time travel stories, including *The Time Stream* (1931), a colourful and far-ranging story of a group of adventurers moving freely about time and space, as well as being full of the contemporary ideas of what forms of life might be found on the remote planets of the universe.

It was, in fact, in the late thirties that time travel really developed as a theme among science fiction writers. It has continued to do so to this day. Among the plethora of stories and novels which have appeared on both sides of the Atlantic, there are certain notable examples which I should just like to mention here.

Jack Williamson (1907–   ), an admirer of H.G. Wells, created the 'Legion of Space' series (1936–1939) about a group of space adventurers led by Giles Habibula moving through various existences and saving human-like worlds from both external and internal threats. In his footsteps, L. Sprague de Camp wrote *Lest Darkness Fall* (1941) in which a time traveller lands in the declining days of the Roman Empire and tries to prevent the terrible future of the Middle Ages.

De Camp was evidently fascinated by the technicalities of time travel for he also wrote one of the earliest practical essays on the subject entitled, 'Language for Time Travellers' (1938). The German-born rocket scientist and writer, Willy Ley (1906–1969), who was a friend of de Camp, backed up his theories in another landmark article, 'Geography for Time Travellers' published in 1939.

Robert Heinlein (1907–   ), one of the grand masters of modern sf, was the first writer to explore the theme of time paradoxes – asking a question that has been much discussed in relation to *Doctor Who*: 'What if I went back in time and killed my grandfather before my mother was born?' He pioneered this idea in 'By His Bootstraps' (1941) and then worked it again in the superb, 'All You Zombies' (1959), where every character is the same person so that, after a sex change, even the offspring turn out to have the same genes!

A major British contribution has been the 'Dancers at the End of Time' series by the prolific Michael Moorcock (1939–   ). These stories feature a group of all-powerful people who have become obsessed with time travel because they have forgotten the meaning of morality and need to journey to earlier times to rediscover their past. 'Behold the Man' (1966) is also a unique story postulating the idea that there was no Christ until a time traveller volunteered for the job!

There are dozens more examples that could be cited, by such noted writers as Robert Silverberg, Paul Anderson, Harry Harrison, Brian Aldiss and J.G. Ballard, but there are just two other writers whom I wish particularly to mention because of their connection with Doctor Who: Isaac Asimov and Arthur C. Clarke who are Sydney Newman's favourite modern sf writers. Both, not surprisingly, have written time travel stories.

Asimov (1920–   ) a professor of biochemistry and writer, made his reputation with the series of 'Foundation' stories, but in 1955 published 'The End of Eternity', a multi-layered story of time travel and men fighting to achieve the future they desire, which many fans and critics believe to be among his best work.

Arthur C. Clarke (1917–   ) the British fan of science fiction who has grown to be among its best-known modern proponents, is arguably most famous today as the scriptwriter of that classic movie, *2001: A Space Odyssey* (1968). His interest in time travel, though, has been vividly seen in stories such as 'All The Time in the World' (1952) about the speeding up of time, and 'Time's Arrow' (1961) in which the footprints of a dinosaur are found embedded alongside the tracks of a Land Rover in some rocks dating from the *Jurassic* period!

As Sydney Newman has admitted these writers were influential in his

Edgar Allan Poe who created the idea of the half-man, half-machine creature - and two photographs from the making of one of the cybermen stories, 'The Invasion' in 1968.

life, I think a little more of the germinal material which grew into
Doctor Who can be found in their work. The interested reader is invited
to look for himself and see . . .

As I mentioned earlier, it was perhaps a curious twist of fate that the
first story of time travel to appear on TV should be H.G. Wells' *The
Time Machine* which was screened by the BBC in 1949. Television was
still very much in its black and white infancy then, and indeed the sum
total of transmissions on the day the adaptation of Wells' story was
screened, January 25, reads like this: 11 a.m.–12 Noon: Demonstration

Film. 3 p.m.–4 p.m.: *The Flying Deuces* (film). 8.30 p.m.: *The Time Machine* by H.G. Wells. 9.30 p.m.: Light Music. 10–10.15 p.m.: News (sound only). The nation's few tiny TV screens were blank for the rest of the day!

The sixty-minute version of the book transmitted live was very much the brain-child of BBC producer Robert Barr, who was also the adapter and director. A life-long admirer of Wells, he used the limited facilities then available at Alexandra Palace to create a production which naturally enough had to rely on description rather than lavish sets to recreate the world of the far future.

Talking about the production at the time, Barr said: 'H.G. Wells was an amazing prophet – I mean, he wrote about the fourth dimension in *The Time Machine* in 1895 well before Einstein produced his theory about it. I also think that some day man *will* travel in time, far fetched as that may seem to us now . . .'

As George, the Time Traveller, Barr cast Anthony Nicholls (1902–1977), a handsome British stage actor with a fine baritone voice who that same year was to make his name as a film star playing the headmaster in *The Guinea Pig*. (Later he was to become a familiar face on television in such productions as *Scotch on the Rocks* and the long-running series *Hadleigh* and *The Crezz*.) Nicholls was also a great fan of the works of H.G. Wells and brought both authority and a sense of drama to the role, according to contemporary reports. Co-starring were Russell Napier, the Australian-born actor famous for his roles as policemen, and two pioneer BBC character players, George Stanford and Christopher Gill.

The Time Machine itself was a rather flimsy-looking machine not unlike a large sleigh with a control panel of flashing lights and small dials. The 'disappearance' of the machine into the future was achieved by a dissolving shot, followed by a lingering close-up of the Time Traveller's face during which his craft was manhandled by scene shifters to its new setting!

Quite obviously, the production was crude by today's standards, but it does indicate the BBC's early interest in time travel which was to be so triumphantly highlighted almost fifteen years later in *Doctor Who*.

The first television *series* to feature time travel among its stories originated not long afterwards in America in 1952 and was called *Out Of This World*. It should, though, be clearly distinguished from the series of the same title which Sydney Newman made in England a decade later and to which we shall return shortly.

Out Of This World was a curious mixture of science fiction and fact, for interlaced with the 25-minute stories of high drama in space were brief discussions by a leading American scientist, Robert R. Cole, about the actualities of travelling to other worlds and the life forms that might be found there.

This pioneer series was the brainchild of an inventive producer

Anthony Nicholls, the first BBC time traveller, in the 1949 version of 'The Time Machine'.

named Milton Kaye, who also wrote and directed a number of the black and white episodes, including 'Journey to the Past' which took a couple of very mature-looking history students on a whirlwind trip though real American history from the signing of the Declaration of Independence to the building of the first space rockets in the aftermath of the Second World War! A narrator, Jackson Beck, helped the linking of the story and the discussion, and it is a fact that the show was curiously prophetic in a number of statements about man reaching the moon and also studying the remote planets with orbiting satellites. Sadly, though, the public interest was never developed to a high enough degree to achieve satisfactory ratings and the series only lasted one season.

A similar fate also lay in wait for the series with the same title which Sydney Newman launched at ABC TV in London in 1962 with Leonard White as his producer and Irene Shubik as story editor. This was certainly a more ambitious project than its predecessor – the stories were each fifty-minutes long and as Sydney Newman has mentioned the narrator was the great horror movie veteran, Boris Karloff.

Newman's personal taste in science fiction was evident in the series which included stories by Isaac Asimov ('The Little Robot') and time travel adventures like 'Pictures Don't Lie' by Katherine MacLean. A young writer destined to become very famous through his association with *Doctor Who* also contributed a story called 'Botany Bay'. His name was Terry Nation.

Despite the undoubted stylishness of this series and the development of characters and plot in the stories, Newman's *Out Of This World* only lasted from June to September 1962, but there were lessons he learned from this failure which he turned into such a triumphant success when he moved to the BBC in December of that same year and shortly afterwards set the wheels in motion for the creation of *Doctor Who* in the autumn of 1963.

In 1965, the BBC launched what they hoped would be science fiction for adults with *Out Of The Unknown*, which remains to this day one of the best remembered early sf series. Despite the fact that producer Alan Bromly and script editor Roger Parkes had only a limited budget for their fifty-minute black and white episodes, they managed to attract some talented writers like Leon Griffiths, Clive Exton and Jeremy Paul while also securing the rights to dramatise the work of many leading sf writers including Isaac Asimov, Clifford D. Simak, John Wyndham and John Brunner.

Time travel cropped up in several episodes – particularly those by Brian Hayles who was already on the *Doctor Who* team of script writers – and ratings for the series was consistently high throughout late 1965, through 1966, and on into early 1967. But then a strange and undoubtedly controversial policy decision by the BBC to include more supernatural stories at the expense of science fiction undoubtedly lead to the show's demise. Among the directors who worked on *Out Of The Unknown* were two other men whose names are now inextricably linked with that of *Doctor Who*: the late Douglas Camfield, and Christopher Barry.

Three years after the successful launch of *Doctor Who* in Britain – though long before it was being shown across the Atlantic in America – the second series to be specifically about time travel was developed in Hollywood by the well-known film maker Irwin Allen, for Twentieth Century Fox Television. This was *The Time Tunnel* about two men taking part in a US Government experiment into time travel which took them in each fifty-minute episode from one famous location to another. Though the stars, the teenage heart-throb James Darren, and Robert Colbert, did make it to the Moon and Mars in the lushly photographed colour production, they were more frequently to be seen present at famous moments in Earth history such as the sinking of the *Titanic* and the Battle of Pearl Harbour. This was quite clearly a device on Irwin Allen's part to be able to use historical news film as a background.

Allen wrote and directed the pilot episode of *The Time Tunnel* which presented the machine in which the two men travelled as an enormous, spiral tunnel which revolved at huge speed to project them either forwards or backwards in time. The men, in fact, had no control over which direction they took, and indeed the military personnel who were supposedly controlling the machine more often than not moved them to the wrong destination instead of back to the present day! The authorities were, though, able to watch the pair's experiences while being helpless to interfere. A similarity to *Doctor Who* is immediately apparent here – in particular that of the omnipotent Time Lords, watching over the errant Doctor's travels in space and time.

A number of leading American television script-writers contributed to the series including Leonard Stadd, William Welch and the talented husband and wife writing team of Bob and Wanda Duncan. However, though *The Time Tunnel* enjoyed a successful period from the autumn of 1966 into early 1967, the production team's seeming inability to develop the stories beyond fairly routine situations caused it to be cancelled after a total of thirty episodes had been made. A measure of its impact may be judged by the fact that two paperback novelisations were written by the leading sf writer Murray Leinster, entitled *The Time Tunnel* and *Timeslip!* both published in 1967.

Timeslip was also the title of a now little-remembered but nonetheless noteworthy series which ATV made in 1970 and which ran for twenty-six episodes into the next year. It was basically a children's drama series about time travel which had been developed by a talented script editor, Ruth Boswell, with her husband, James.

Ruth took her concept – of two young teenage children travelling about in time and becoming involved in a whole series of adventures – to the hierarchy of the ATV Network and was given the go-ahead to develop a season of shows along with a producer, John Cooper. A New Zealander, Bruce Stewart, who had contributed to both *Out Of This World* and *Out Of The Unknown*, was commissioned to write the scripts, and the well-known scientist Geoffrey Hoyle was added to the team to check the authenticity of all the stories. Additional script-writing for some of the later episodes was provided by Victor Pemberton – another name that will be familiar to long-time fans of *Doctor Who!*

STILL from 'Timeslip' in 1970

Cast in the roles of the young time travellers were 18-year-old Cheryl Burfield playing 15-year-old Liz Skinner, and 16-year-old Spencer Banks as 14-year-old Simon Randall. Though the stories hinged very much around this young couple, a fascinating adult character named Commander Traynor appeared in no less than five variations during the course of the series. He was played by Denis Quilley, a leading stage and television actor.

The method by which the children travelled about in space was a time bubble, and to underline the versimilitude of the series, ITV had their science correspondent, Peter Fairley, introduce the first episode to its young five o'clock audience.

'What is a time bubble?' he asked. 'Well, you can't see it, of course, but it might help you to visualise it to think of it as a balloon. Some scientists are now working on the theory that wherever you are, you are at the very centre of the universe, and that the universe is really one giant sphere, and that it has an edge to it. Information about events is flashing constantly back and forth between you and the edge of that sphere, so that at any given moment, you are mixed up in the past, the present and the future, virtually all at the same moment.

'But supposing some little patch of that information – some little patch of history – gets slowed down, and instead of flashing backwards and forwards, it floats, gently, as if in a bubble. It might have collided with some solid object and got temporarily halted in its tracks. Or it might be being slowed down by some mysterious force. Or the edge of the universe might have a hole in it. Well, supposing you could somehow get into that time bubble – that bubble of history – and travel with it. Then you could move backwards and forwards in time at will!'

It was though utilisation of this concept that Liz and Simon moved about in time from the early years of the Second World War to what was, in 1970, the far-flung future of 1990! The series' designer, Gerry Roberts, had to fall back on a number of staple items for his 'futuristic' England, including computers and running tape machines, but did come up with an ingenious imprisoning shield and also a chair which could make anyone sitting in it experience any dream they chose! There were no monsters as such in *Timeslip*, but there were some chilling moments, including the sudden and hideous ageing of a female doctor when she stepped out of her normal time.

William Hartnell in his original costume of the Doctor before filming the first story, 'An Unearthly Child'.

The series ran from September 1970 to March 1971, and though it was not continued thereafter – though a further season *was* hinted at – the independent television programmers obviously considered *Timeslip* good enough to repeat over the same winter period in 1973 to 1974. That apart, the series has remained forgotten to all save a few enthusiasts – but unlike *Doctor Who*, where a number of early black and white shows have subsequently been destroyed – a complete run of *Timeslip* still exists and there are those who would like to see it run again in 1990 to see how the years have aged what was, after all, a contemporary of *Doctor Who* during its first decade.

In recent years, the theme of time travel has cropped up in several of the popular TV series such as *Star Trek, Adam Adamant Lives!* (which of course, was another creation of the Sydney Newman-Verity Lambert partnership), and in one or two of Gerry Anderson's hugely popular animated adventures.

But most recently in America – where *Doctor Who* is now widely screened – a new TV series with strong similarities to the Doctor's adventures has been created. It is called *Voyagers* and concerns the journeys of a 'learned professor' into past history, accompanied by two young companions. Here once again the idea is to introduce young viewers to history in a dramatic concept with the companions being the youthful audience *in situ*.

While I would not suggest that *Voyagers* is a copy of *Doctor Who*, there is no denying the concept is similar. It is, I think, just one more example of the power and influence of H.G. Wells' famous pioneer novel and Sydney Newman's brilliant adaptation of that idea for the medium of television. And long may this influence continue to be felt!

The Council of the Time Lords in session on Gallifrey.

3

TIME AND THE LORDS OF GALLIFREY

Time travel is the greatest possession of the Time Lords of Gallifrey and those who make up the heirarchy of this remarkable planet can be seen to be influenced by its power for either good or evil. Over the years that the Doctor has been pursuing his one man mission for peace and stability in the worlds of time and space, a number of these Time Lords have crossed his path to be revealed in their true colours, while at the same time the chain of command on Gallifrey has also been delineated.

A factor which has made the programme of such abiding interest has been the gradual realisation that Gallifrey and its people do not represent the Utopia we were lead to believe in our early visits to the planet. (Though the very fact he was 'on the run' was clear enough evidence that all was not right.)

Indeed, with each passing regeneration we have seen the world more and more in its true colours and its rulers to be men and women of varying degrees of good and evil. Like many a great civilisation on Earth over the centuries, the Time Lords are beset by the problems of corruption and degeneracy which are always to be found wherever absolute power is concentrated.

With the Doctor and the Time Lords having recently had their most rigorous public exposure since the series began in 'The Trial of a Time Lord', this is surely a most appropriate point at which to take stock of their unique society.

Time travel was initially the dream of a tiny corpus of men: and one in particular, whose presence has haunted the programme. His name

was Rassilon and it was as a result of his research and the self-sacrifice of a solar engineer, Omega, that the freedom to roam unchecked through the enormity of space was finally achieved. Sadly, there is at present no retrievable detailed record of their groundwork in the Archive Tower on Gallifrey, and we are dependent on the scattering of information relayed to us through the Doctor.

The part inventor of Time Travel, Omega (Stephen Thorne) confronts the second and third Doctors in 'The Three Doctors'.

Like the early space-ship pioneers on Earth, Rassilon's driving ambition was to break into a completely new dimension. He wanted to perfect a means of travel which would allow him not only to explore long dead planets, but also flourishing worlds of the present, and even press forward to futures beyond imagining.

As a result of this study, Rassilon concluded that the secret of space travel lay in capturing one of the Black Holes of anti-matter and harnessing this power to drive special time machines about the galaxy. But first a star would have to be detonated to create such a Black Hole.

It was at this point that solar engineer, Omega, came to Rassilon's aid as he wrestled with this problem and also that of building a machine able to withstand the gigantic speeds and enormous pressures of time travel. The price of success, though, was to cost Omega his normal life.

After decades of work, a science which was to be known as transdimensional engineering was perfected. And as a direct result of this, the now-familiar time machine the TARDIS was born, the word being an acronym for Time And Relative Dimensions In Space. The unique feature of this capsule was that it was actually bigger on the inside than it was outside – allowing the outer shell to move while the interior remained in another dimension.

This, the engineers had reasoned quite correctly, would prevent the occupants from growing older or regressing into childhood as the space machine plunged either backwards or forwards in time.

All that remained now was to capture the power of a Black Hole. Omega offered himself to carry out the task of detonating a star (later to be known as the Veil Nebulae) to create the supernova. But in the ensuing explosion, the solar engineer was unexpectedly caught by the mighty forces and flung into a world of anti-matter where he has existed ever since – occasionally attempting to escape by uniting himself with a host body, regardless of the consequences. His reputation as being evil might, therefore, be tempered with the judgement that misfortune caused his original imprisonment, even if his methods of seeking return are invariably unscrupulous.

And so it was left to Rassilon to harness the power of the Black Hole and bring it safely back to Gallifrey for storage in the Eye of Harmony beneath the floor of the Panopticon. Armed with this power, the prototype TARDIS could at last be developed and tested, and in so doing Rassilon qualified himself as the pioneer time traveller from Gallifrey – the first true Time Lord.

The successful operation of several trial machines lead to a range of TARDISes of which the Doctor's is one of the earlier types – a Type Forty, Mark One – though like all the others it is invulnerable to outside attack and protected by force fields. Similarly, it can dematerialise and rematerialise at the operator's discretion – and also possesses the famous chameleon circuit which enables it to take on any suitable appearance. Though, of course, in the Doctor's case, this is stuck in the shape of a now out-dated London police box!

Rassilon's contribution to Gallifrey was not quite finished with the TARDIS, however. For he also developed the Matrix, a huge computer complex into which the knowledge of the whole Gallifreyan race could be stored for future reference. And when his life-spans came to an end at the end of his twelfth regeneration (and thirteenth body) his own mind was fed into the Matrix before his body was laid to rest in a special tomb in the Dark Tower.

But this was not to prove the last anyone heard of Time Lord Rassilon. For as his most recent 'spiritual' appearance in 'The Five Doctors' bore witness he still exerts a potent force.

Today, the TARDIS can be seen as the greatest of Gallifrey's legacies to her citizens, and one that has proved of immeasurable use not only to the hierarchy but also, of course, to the Doctor. . .

Over the years that the programme has been on the air, the Time Lord society has been revealed layer by layer until now we have a clear idea of its delineation as well as knowing something about its leading members. It is a carefully structured society in which religion and technology both have their place in a bureaucratic government.

Heading the hierarchy is the President, who is elected by his or her fellow members of the High Council of Gallifrey, the planet's ruling body which meets in the Panopticon in the Capitol. The Doctor, of course, once proposed himself for this office after the murder of one of the Presidents in the story of 'The Deadly Assassin'.

Second in command to the President is the Chancellor, and among the holders of this office who have appeared have been Chancellor Goth (Bernard Horsfall), revealed as the murderer of the President in 'The Deadly Assassin', Chancellor Thalia (Elspet Gray) in 'Arc of Infinity' and Chancellor Flavia (Dinah Sheridan) in 'The Five Doctors'.

Next in line are the Cardinals, each one heading the Time Lord colleges or chapters among which are numbered the Prydonians, the Arcalians and the Patraxes. The Prydonians, of which the Doctor is one, dress in scarlet and gold robes and are said to be the most devious of the chapters. The Arcalians wear green, and the Patraxes, heliotrope.

These Cardinals demand and receive great loyalty from their chapters and wield a power almost as strong as that of the President himself, though they all admit the ultimate authority lies with the titular head of the Council.

The rest of the ruling body consists of Councillors who are drawn from among the most experienced and wisest Time Lords and Ladies – a notable figure in this respect being Councillor Hedin (Michael Gough) who featured in 'Arc of Infinity'. Other important Time Lords who have come to our attention include Coordinator Engin (Erik Chitty) and Commentator Runcible (Hugh Walters), both in 'The Deadly Assassin'; Rodan (Hilary Ryan), all in 'The Invasion of Time'; and most recently, in 'The Trial of a Time Lord', the Inquisitor (Lynda Bellingham) and the Keeper of the Matrix (James Bree) who was killed and had his identity assumed by the Valeyard (Michael Jayston) in the final moments of the last episode of this dramatic story.

Considerable mystery surrounds the Celestial Intervention Agency who some have argued hold the greatest power and influence on Gallifrey. While the Chancellery Guards unquestionably take care of affairs on Gallifrey, it the highly-secret CIA who deal with all matters beyond the confines of the planet.

The Agency consists of highly trained and intelligent Time Lords who not only police the affairs of others but can also intervene. Only the most senior members of the High Council are involved with the CIA, and it is whispered their loyalty is to a code rather than to the President.

Lastly, of course, there are the ordinary people of Gallifrey. Neither Time Lords nor officials, they are the mass of the population who carry out the whole variety of jobs necessary to support such a society. Without them, Gallifrey would surely grind to a halt.

The fourth Doctor with two of the Time Lord hierarchy, Castellan Spandrell (George Pravda) and Co-ordinator Engin (Eric Chitty) in 'The Deadly Assassin'.

Over the three decades of *Doctor Who* a number of renegade Time Lords have come to our attention – of whom, of course, the Doctor is the most famous! Some of these men and women have been as good-intentioned as he is, but others – most notably, the Master – have been poisoned with evil and greed. Any Time Traveller would find it as well to be armed with information about them all for his journeys.

The first Time Lord introduced into the programme was also the one around whom the greatest mystery still exists. For was Susan Foreman, who appeared in 'The Tribe of Gum' (1963) where she was described as the Doctor's 15-year-old granddaughter, just an ordinary school girl or a Time Lord? Sydney Newman, who created the programme, is in *no* doubt.

'She was originally plotted to be a schoolgirl from *Earth*,' he insists, 'with all the naivety of a young teenager. She was there for the children in our audience to identify with, while the pair of teachers were there for the adults. I was angry when they changed her to a relative of the Doctor because someone thought there might be sexual connotations about an old man flying around with a young girl!'

Carole Ann Ford, who played Susan, says that the original conception was of a much more alien girl than the one who appeared on the screen.

'I wasn't happy with the changes because the part I was offered finally ended up being something quite different,' she says, 'and if I'd known I was going to be asked to do the lady I finished up doing for a year, I wouldn't have been quite so happy to do it.'

Time Lady or Earth Child? The Doctor's first companion, Susan (Carol Ann Ford).

The mystery, in fact, has persisted long after Susan made way for other companions, and when the eighth producer, Graham Williams, still found himself being asked about the matter, he came up with perhaps the most memorable quote.

'We've never quite worked that one out,' he said. 'We can only assume that Time Lords' children are found under a cosmic gooseberry bush. The Doctor is too high-minded to get involved with girls!'

What does remain undisputed is that Susan quite evidently shared the Doctor's fugitive existence *before* he first arrived on Earth, and that she was able to generate moments of good humour from the usually irascible old man. Perhaps her own comment will have to suffice as the

last word on the matter: 'I was born in another Time . . . another world.'

It was not until the second season of *Doctor Who* that the first Doctor met another Time Lord like himself in the story called 'The Time Meddler' (1965) by Dennis Spooner. This was the Meddling Monk, played with great panache by the fine character actor Peter Butterworth. The Doctor was called upon to thwart this rascal's plan to ensure King Harold's victory at the Battle of Hastings and thereby change the course of history.

Dennis Spooner also brought the Monk back again in the last stages of the mammoth twelve-episode 'The Dalek Masterplan' (1966) which was primarily written by Terry Nation. The Doctor had to curb his fellow Time Lord's alliance with the Daleks and stole the directional control of his TARDIS and dumped him on a remote and icy planet.

The first detailed information on the Time Lords was given in the final story of the second Doctor's life-span, 'The War Games' by Malcolm Hulke and Terrance Dicks. This also introduced the War Chief, a devious villain splendidly played by Edward Brayshaw. He was

The most famous Time Lord apart from the Doctor - The Master (Roger Delgado).

responsible for giving some stolen Time Lord technology including a number of SIDRATS – inferior TARDISes – to the followers of the War Lord who were busy recreating Earth wars. He was eventually killed by the War Lord who was himself later tried and executed by the Time Lords.

The most famous of the renegade Time Lords, the Master, made what has proved the first of many appearances – not to mention one regeneration – in Robert Holmes's outstanding story for the third Doctor, 'Terror of the Autons' (1971). According to legend, the Doctor and the Master were once young students together, but while the thirst for knowledge and adventure was to turn one of them into a champion of the oppressed, it made the other a man bent on seeking power for evil ends.

Though a person of great charm and intelligence, the Master has a fatal flaw in the shape of his vanity – which is evident in this very name . . . 'I am usually referred to as The Master' as he liked to announce. He has been played with distinct style and charisma, firstly by Roger Delgado, and more recently by Anthony Ainley. There is no doubt, though, that he is one of the most famous characters in the *Doctor Who* saga, a Professor Moriarty to the Doctor's Sherlock Holmes.

The third Doctor's final story 'Planet of the Spiders' (1974) by Robert Sloman introduced us to the first of the genuinely good Time Lords. K'anpo, played by George Cormack, was in fact the Doctor's mentor on Gallifrey and when the Doctor met him on Earth had assumed the identity of a Tibetan abbot. Cho-Je, played by Kevin Lindsay, was a younger projection of the same Time Lord and was just the person to help the Doctor regenerate after suffering terrible injuries from the spiders of Metebelis 3.

Another Time Lord of the first rank was Morbius who appeared in 'The Brain of Morbius' (1976), a clever variation on the 'monster maker' theme by Terrance Dicks. Morbius had led a treacherous band of outcasts in an attack on the planet of Karn from which Gallifrey receives its supplies of the elixir of life; he paid for this ill-fated expedition with his life. However, his brain survived the disintegration of his body and was then transplanted into a monstrous new one by the mad surgeon, Solon. In a final battle of wills, the Doctor was able to overcome the brain of his former fellow Time Lord. Stuart Fell played the lumbering Morbius Monster with considerable menace.

'The Deadly Assassin' (1976) by Robert Holmes also saw the first appearance of the Time Lord Borusa, who in three further stories spanning the lives of the fourth and fifth Doctor – 'Invasion of Time' (1978) by David Agnew, 'Arc of Infinity' (1982) by Johnny Byrne and 'The Five Doctors' (1983) by Terrance Dicks – rose from the position of Cardinal to Chancellor and finally President. In each regeneration Borusa has been played by a different actor, though each of them has complemented the other in developing his character from ambitious

Time Lord to obsessed fanatic. These men, in order of appearance, were Angus Mackay, John Arnatt, Leonard Sachs and Philip Latham.

'The Deadly Assassin', in fact, marked an important moment in the history of the Time Lords as the scriptwriter, Robert Holmes, has himself explained.

'It was the producer Philip Hinchcliffe's idea that I should explore this place we had never been to before – the home of the Time Lords – in "The Deadly Assassin," ' he said. 'The contract of the Doctor's companion, Lis Sladen, was up just then and we decided to see if we could do a story for him without an assistant, just for a change. It was also the first story, if you discount the Master, that we ignored the "received law" that every *Doctor Who* story had to have a monster. There were no monsters in "The Deadly Assassin" and it was very popular. It did, though, arouse a lot of anger among the traditionalists, but that is something you have to live with.'

Holmes also said that he had been asked by a lot of people whether he based the Time Lord society on a religious order – something like the Roman Catholic Church with its Vatican and Cardinals.

The fourth Doctor with a model of the head of another of the renegade Time Lords, Morbius.

'In fact, I saw it more as a scholastic society,' he explained. 'I mean you have your colleges of learning with Deans and such like. I also began to have doubts then about our view of the Time Lords as wise and remote people only concerned with keeping the structure of time in place. For when I looked back I discovered they had "framed" the second Doctor and got him to do various things for them, and then hauled him up in front of them on trial!

'So I decided there were two sides to them. They had one image that they projected, but there was something else in their make-up which every now and then produced renegades like the Meddling Monk, Omega and, of course, the Master. So they couldn't all be good could they?'

Borusa, who first appeared in 'The Deadly Assassin', was a man of no mean intelligence, a member of the Prydonian college and a former tutor of the Doctor. Indeed, for a time the two men were firm friends, and the fourth Doctor could even take a reproof from the other man that he 'will never amount to anything in the galaxy while you retain your propensity for vulgar facetiousness!' But despite such remarks, a lust for power was growing in Borusa all the time, and his devious and ruthless nature who first revealed in 'Arc of Infinity' when he sanctioned the termination order on the Doctor.

It was in 'The Five Doctors' – and despite all his ploys to outwit the first five incarnations of his former pupil – that Borusa was finally caught out by a mixture of his own cleverness and the intervention of Rassilon who had long expected someone like him to be seduced by the dream of immortality. In fact, the saga of this particular Time Lord underlined the conviction that Gallifreyan society was not as perfect as we had once been led to believe!

The Time Lord with the sinister name but good intentions, Drax (played by Barry Jackson) joined forces with the Doctor in 'The Armageddon Factor' by Bob Baker and Dave Martin (1979). Apart from being the inventor of the giant computer, Mentalis, on the planet Zeos, Drax was also instrumental in playing a crucial part in helping to bring the final segment of the Key to Time series to a successful conclusion.

The first Female Time Lord to appear regularly in the series – since young Susan, that is – was Romanadvoratrelunder, known to one and all as Romana, who made her debut in 'The Ribos Operation' by the ever-imaginative Robert Holmes. She was teamed up with the fourth Doctor in his search for the Key to Time during 1978 to 1979, but following her torture by the evil Shadow, she regenerated into the likeness of Princess Astra of Atrios in Terry Nation's story, 'Destiny of the Daleks'. The two roles were played by Mary Tamm and Lalla Ward

respectively, each developing the character of the Time Lady into quite a match for the fourth Doctor!

Professor Chronotis, a Time Lord living unobtrusively in present-day England as a Cambridge don, has the unhappy distinction of being the only one of his kind filmed for showing on *Doctor Who* and then never screened! He was a main character in Douglas Adams' story 'Shada' which was made in 1979 but never transmitted because of an industrial dispute at the BBC. Played by Denis Carey, the Professor is revealed to be Salyavin, one of the most powerful of the Time Lords, but a man wishing to live in retirement. In return for helping the fourth Doctor to retrieve a missing book of great importance, *The Ancient Law of Gallifrey*, our hero agrees to keep the whereabouts of Salyavin a secret.

The mysterious figure of the Watcher whose presence was sensed during the regeneration of the fourth Doctor into his successor in Christopher H. Bidmead's story 'Logopolis' (1981), may or may not have been a Time Lord. Certainly the figure was something of an enigma, and may even have been a projection of the Doctor himself – as I shall discuss in the next section on Regeneration.

The loveliest of the Time Ladies, Romana (Mary Tamm) with K9.

Mention of Regeneration brings me conveniently to Professor Edgeworth, the ageing scientist, who the sixth Doctor met not long after taking on his new persona in the story of 'The Twin Dilemma' by Anthony Steven (1985). Ostensibly the leader of a party of Jacondan kidnappers, the Professor – played with considerable panache by Maurice Denham – turned out not only to be a Time Lord named Azmael, but one of the Doctor's former teachers from Gallifrey!

Azmael had unfortunately come under the telepathic control of the evil gastropod, Mestor, but with the Doctor's assistance he managed to confront the slug-like villain when the creature announced his plans to implant his consciousness into that of the younger Doctor! In a dramatic finale, Mestor demonstrated his power and left his own body to enter that of Azmael. What he did not realise, however, was that the old Time Lord was actually nearing the end of his thirteenth incarnation – and so Azmael promptly gave up his last life-span, and by so doing took the life of Mestor as well. It was a noble sacrifice, the like of which had not been seen before in the history of the Time Lords.

The next time Lord to be introduced to us was the remarkable lady called the Rani, whom the beautiful feline-looking actress Kate O'Mara made so memorable in 'The Mark of the Rani' by Pip and Jane Baker in 1985. Miss O'Mara was shortly afterwards recruited for the hugely successful Hollywood TV series *Dynasty*, but the Rani returned to threaten the newly-regenerated seventh Doctor. The Rani is showing all the signs of developing into an adversary every bit as fascinating to watch as the Master.

The Rani was, in fact, a renegade Time Lord, named after the Hindu word for Queen, who turned her great intelligence and scientific skills to amoral ways. In 'The Mark of the Rani' she was discovered

masquerading in nineteenth-century England as an old woman stealing chemical substances from the brains of her victims. Into her world came both the sixth Doctor and the Master – and all of them recognised the others' Time Lord origins.

With two of his own kind to cope with, the multi-coloured Doctor had all his resources strained, until he finally managed to trap both these enemies in the Rani's TARDIS.

Finally, there was the appearance of the Valeyard in the dramatic 'The Trial of a Time Lord' sequence (1986) in which Michael Jayston gave an absolutely unforgettable performance as the black-clad Time Lord prosecutor who set out with razor-sharp precision to shatter the image of the Doctor and his achievements in space and time. His mixture of aggressive cross-questioning, clever use of visual evidence, and powerful impression on the Time Lords sitting in judgement on the hapless sixth Doctor, seemed to be leading to only one possible verdict until the dramatic pronouncement by the Master – of all people! – about

The enigmatic figure of the Valeyard (Michael Jayston) whose relationship with the Doctor is now one of the greatest puzzles of the series!

the relationship between the accused and his accuser. The fact that the Valeyard was a future incarnation of the Doctor made up of all the darker sides of his character was a truly stunning revelation!

That the Valeyard is destined to appear again in the journeyings of the Doctor – whether in his seventh or even a later incarnation – would, it seems, be inevitable!

Just as inevitable is the fact that the future will bring us further information about the nature of the remarkable Time Lord society. Each decade has turned further pages in its unfolding history, and more surprises are surely guaranteed!

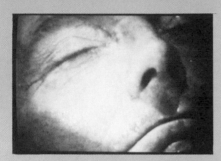

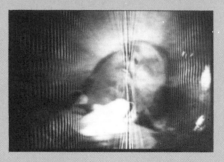
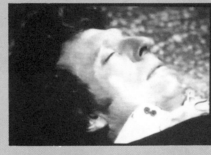

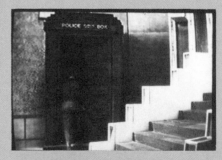

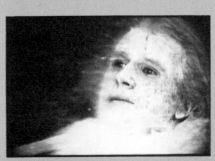

4
REGENERATION – THE MYSTERY OF AGES

After Time Travel, the mystery of regeneration is arguably the most intriguing concept in the history of *Doctor Who*. In simple terms, it has enabled the series to continue through three decades with – so far – seven different actors playing the main role of the Doctor, and at its most complex reveals the man from Gallifrey as a remarkable alien being possessed of a truly magical power.

Without the concept of the Doctor being able to change his appearance and characteristics in a manner wholly acceptable to his viewers, the series could not have continued beyond William Hartnell's illness and departure from the programme. Few other television series have endeavoured to change their leading actors – and fewer still have been able to continue with the total acceptance of its enthusiasts that *Doctor Who* enjoys.

Although the notion of the Doctor's regeneration came initially from a moment of inspiration by the producer of the closing Hartnell stories, Innes Lloyd, and his script editor, Gerry Davis, it has since been evolved into the core of the whole legend. The introduction of each succeeding Doctor has thrown a little more light on the mystery – while at the same time posing still further questions for the future. And such issues can be seen as among the most important in ensuring the interest and attention of viewers . . .

As Innes Lloyd has explained, the idea came – perhaps appropriately and certainly with a hint of fate about it – from a problem of age that was besetting his production team.

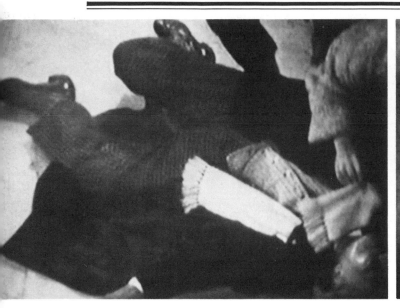
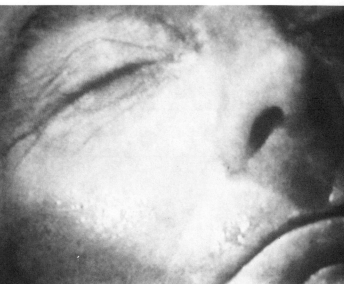

'We were going through a difficult time in the first half of 1966,' he says. 'By this time Bill Hartnell was no longer a young man. He had played the Doctor for three or more years and I don't believe he'd ever really intended staying as long as that. It took a great toll on him and he felt he needed a rest. His wife, Heather, also felt he needed a rest and we were left to decide whether or not to carry on.

'Of course, we had to go to the Godfather of the whole thing, Sydney Newman, to see what he felt. And there was no doubt he was all for going on. So we set out, with the help of Shaun Sutton, to look for a new Doctor, while Gerry and I had to think of a way to introduce him. Because Bill was leaving through age, the idea suddenly hit us that *this* was the key. If the Doctor could travel through Time, why couldn't he also change his personality – be different people in different times?'

Gerry Davis was the man who had to work out the detail of making this crucial change possible, and was aided by his scientifically-minded writer-friend, Kit Pedler, who had initially been recruited to make the science fiction in *Doctor Who* more factually based. The transformation – or regeneration as it later became known – was effected at the conclusion of the powerful story of 'The Tenth Planet' which introduced the second most popular of all the Doctor's enemies, the Cybermen.

Throughout the struggle with the Cybermen, the Doctor had complained about tiredness and even remarked that his old body had had enough. But when Ben Jackson, the cockney merchant seaman, told the Doctor that the battle with the Cybermen was over, he was somewhat taken aback by the answer.

'It isn't over,' the Doctor said. 'It's not over by a long way' – and with those words heralded the change which took place in the TARDIS and introduced the second Doctor, Patrick Troughton.

The charming and affable Troughton has recalled how the

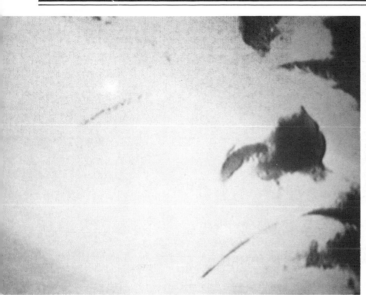
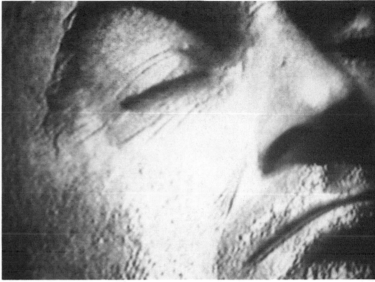

regeneration scene was filmed. 'Billy and I had to lie on the floor at either end of the set. It took nearly all day to perfect the scene and transmogrify Billy into me. It was a really historic moment, I suppose.'

Indeed it was – and one that startled unsuspecting viewers as well as delighting them. The actual change first showed the lined face of Hartnell glowing, then being lost in a blaze of light, and finally emerging in the whimsical shape of Troughton's unmistakable features. This effect was achieved by means of a camera on each actor and the images 'mixed' through an electronic effects generator working in conjunction with the mixing console and thereby 'speckling' one face into another.

The second Doctor was, of course, younger than his predecessor, shorter, and obviously a more spritely and high-spirited fellow. Later, he was to explain that he had known when his original body had reached its natural end and had then drawn upon the powers of his race to renew himself. It was not a process of rejuvenation, he said, but a voluntary process in which he knew he could not continue to exist without a change of body.

To the Doctor himself it might have been as natural a thing to do as breathing – but to *Doctor Who* audiences it was a concept of breath-taking originality which has since been shown to have had an absolutely crucial effect on the show's ability to continue through any change of personnel.

It was not, however, until the second Doctor's last serial, 'The War Games' in June 1969 that the matter of the Time Lord's ability to regenerate was broached again. The new information was provided by two of the programme's most experienced and inventive writers, Malcolm Hulke and Terrance Dicks. Derrick Sherwin, who by then had taken over as producer, remembers the problems created by this next transformation.

'That show was a monster,' he says, 'which, looked on with hindsight, should not have been strung out as long as it was because there really wasn't that much story to it. But we were able to extend it simply by adding an extra War Game every other week. But as a developing saga it really lacked running characters enabling it to hang together. The idea was OK, but never, in my opinion, worked properly.'

One element that certainly *did* work was the introduction of the Time Lords and this, says Derrick Sherwin, was Terrance Dicks' contribution.

'Terry has a very clear and analytical mind which is just what a show like *Doctor Who* needs. He could analyse stories well and plan sequences of events that made sense. In other words, he was a damn good storyteller!'.

Dicks himself has explained what happened in these words:

'Prior to this story there was no explanation about the Time Lords,' he says. 'My recollection is that Derrick Sherwin said to me one day that the Doctor should come from this superior race of beings called the Time Lords – though where he got *that* idea from I have no idea!

'And because it seemed to work in "The War Games" we went on to develop and extend the idea of these people during the Jon Pertwee years. Indeed, whenever we wanted to get the Doctor off the Earth on some mission, we'd have the Time Lords use him as a kind of reluctant secret agent. It was quite a challenge to have the Doctor arriving somewhere in a state of high indignation and then get him involved in putting a stop to some evil-doing!'

The story of 'The War Games' told viewers that the Doctor was actually a renegade Time Lord on the run from his home planet of Gallifrey. And as a result of various 'misdemeanours' – interfering in the activities of other peoples in Space and Time – he was put on trial and found guilty by his peers. His sentence was to be exiled on Earth.

'The time has come for you to change your appearance and begin your exile,' he was told as a parting shot.

Only one puzzling note was struck by this story – Patrick Troughton's claim that, barring accidents, Time Lords could 'live forever'. This was later to be most emphatically refuted!

On Earth, the new Doctor proved to be a very different man in his fresh regeneration – older, taller, and quite changed again in his appearance. Derrick Sherwin explains the thinking behind these changes.

'With Jon Pertwee we wanted a slightly pottier Doctor than we'd had

with Patrick Troughton. He was older than the second Doctor and so
came across with more conviction in the role of a 'dandy'. The idea was
that he would be basically the same character underneath, but
superficially more selfish and less introverted than the Troughton
character.

'Jon, who is really good at comedy, didn't want to be funny with
Doctor Who. So in the end it became a dichotomy between what the
actor *wanted* to be and what we felt he *ought* to be.'

Although the third Doctor was forced to operate solely on Earth, it
was as early as the second of his adventures, 'Doctor Who and the
Silurians' that viewers were given an insight into the 'unearthly' side of
his nature, and in particular the thorny problem of his age. It was little
more than a glimpse, though, for he told his companion, Liz Shaw,

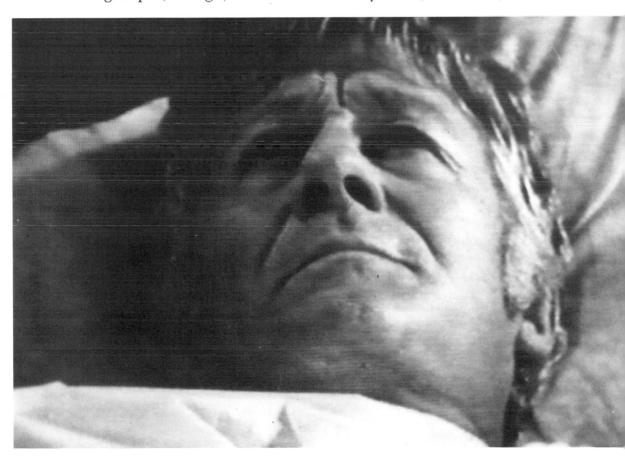

rather enigmatically that he had lived for 'several thousand years'.

The immediate problem this raises, of course, is how *long* is a Gallifreyan's year? An Earth year, we know, is quite different to a year on, say, Venus where a single day lasts for 2,800 hours or the equivalent of 120 Earth days – so what might the period be on the Time Lords' world? This puzzle had to await the arrival of the fourth Doctor to get any nearer a solution.

The story of the Silurians also has vivid memories for Barry Letts, who had just taken over as producer. It concerned just how much of the Doctor's background should be revealed.

'There were a number of people who felt we shouldn't be explaining things like where the Doctor came from and his power of regeneration,' he says. 'The first producer, Verity Lambert, for one, felt that even as far back as the Troughton era when it was shown he came from Gallifrey, the show lost a lot of its poetry and ambiguity. All the mystery that was so much a part of its beginning was now gone.

'That is certainly a valid point of view,' he goes on, 'but I think that although it had been a lovely show when it started, if it had stayed exactly the same it certainly would not have lasted for over twenty years. One of the reasons *Doctor Who* has gone on for so long is that it has developed and moved in a new direction every so often.'

True to his word, Barry Letts, aided by Terrance Dicks – who was now script editor of the series – gave audiences a revealing new insight into the world of the Time Lords in the meeting of 'The Three Doctors', screened early in 1973 to celebrate the programme's tenth anniversary. Once more the topic of regeneration popped up in Terrance Dicks' script about the Time Lord Omega trapped inside a Black Hole.

The story, in fact, established that it was possible for the various 'selves' of the Doctor to come together and act in unison if required, and also that talk of the man from Gallifrey having 'many lives' in the past was meaningless. The earliest of the Doctor's incarnations had, without any doubt, been William Hartnell.

A year later in 1974, a fourth Doctor, Tom Baker, regenerated from Jon Pertwee's body, which had been irreparably damaged by the Crystal of Power on 'The Planet of the Spiders'. In this story, too, we met Cho-Je, ostensibly a Tibetan monk, who reveals himself to be the Doctor's old teacher on Gallifrey, K'anpo, a Time Lord of awesome power who is able to regenerate into *whatever* form he might require and *whenever* he wishes.

K'anpo is clearly a man of far superior abilities to his former pupil, and as events transpire with the Doctor's mind and body injured beyond the point where he can organise his own regeneration, it was as well that he was on hand to accelerate the process. Thanks to his help, the fourth Doctor becomes not only a younger man, but also a more vital and outgoing figure – even a little outrageous.

The explanation of this from the production point of view has been

JON PERTWEE

*The Earthbound third
Doctor dreaming of
journeys to come in
'Doctor Who
and the Silurians'.*

TOM BAKER

The archetypal time traveller and his space machine. The fourth Doctor, complete with telescope for stargazing!

DOCTOR WHO

PETER DAVISON

A rival for the TARDIS! Concorde overshadowing the fifth Doctor and Tegan (Janet Fielding) and Nyssa (Sarah Sutton).

COLIN BAKER

The sixth Doctor found the TARDIS as erratic as ever during his life span.

SYLVESTER McCOY

The seventh Doctor, at his first press call and preparing for new travels through time and space.

given by Philip Hinchcliffe, who had taken over as producer with Robert Holmes as his script editor.

'When I took over *Doctor Who* I had a great respect for the tradition of the Doctor being a moral stereotype and being a figure who fights evil on a galactic scale,' he says. 'But then, in the mid-Seventies, people were more interested in the Doctor being human with all the human frailties. So that, while he might talk about the Time Lords being non-human and unemotional, he was only acting and, underneath, really a far more vulnerable and human figure. The "with one bound he was free" level of storytelling could not apply to him. If he got himself into a corner and he'd got to fight his way out of it by somebody going to the wall – well, they'd go to the wall! His world was such that he could no longer be a boy scout!'

Philip Hinchcliffe wanted, in fact, to remodel the fourth Doctor into very much a man of his time.

'I always thought that Jon Pertwee was the Regency Buck. He belonged to the Swinging Sixties – jumping into fast cars and whizzing off in a swirl of gadgetry like James Bond. What Tom Baker brought to the part was an inability to do all that. For example, he'd fiddle with a screwdriver but it wouldn't always work. He was *fallible*.'

'Robot', the first story to feature the fourth Doctor, was written by Terrance Dicks and script-edited by Robert Holmes, and right at the start added a new dimension to the regeneration story. It illustrated that the process could be unstable and the Doctor himself would have to adjust to his new body.

'A new body's like a new house,' he observes after the change has taken place, 'it's bound to take a bit of time to settle in!'

Paying tribute to Robert Holmes' contribution to the series at this time, Philip Hinchcliffe has observed, 'Bob and I had a deliberate plan to raid the whole genre of science fiction in all its manifestations from the Gothic strain to Sword and Sorcery, but avoiding the earthbound setting of a present day Doctor fighting an invasion from space – which had already been done. What we wanted to do was to take the viewer into a more fantastic scene at a time before that great upsurge of interest in the medium which, of course, happened with *Star Wars* not long afterwards. But *Doctor Who* was ahead of the field, thanks to Bob Holmes and the other writers like him.'

It was in 'Pyramids of Mars', written by Robert Holmes and Lewis Greiffer under the pseudonym of Stephen Harris, that the subject of the Doctor's age was discussed in a more positive way.

In this story which combined ancient Egyptian mythology with unimaginable Cosmic forces, the Doctor stated quite categorically that his age was 749. What he did *not* say was whether this age was in years or centuries – or if, indeed, that was purely the age of his, the fourth Doctor's, body! Though this still did not resolve the problem, it certainly left us closer to his age than 'several thousand years old'.

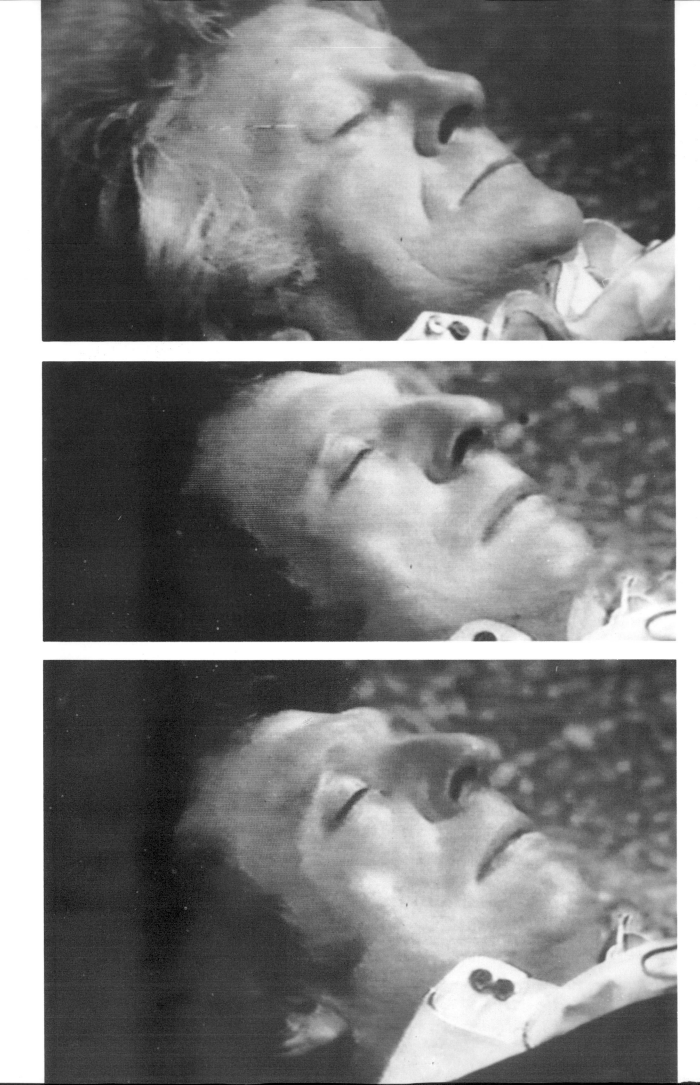

In another, much later, story from the fourth Doctor's era, 'The Leisure Hive' (September, 1980), the Time Lord had quite a nasty shock when he experimented with the machine that had been developed by the Earth scientist Hardin – for it promptly aged him over a thousand years. If such an age *is* possible for each regeneration without the necessity of a new body, we are talking about a life-span for the Doctor (accepting twelve regenerations – or thirteen bodies – as being the maximum number: a point to which we shall come in a moment) of at least 12,000 years.

'The Brain of Morbius' in January 1976 was Terrance Dicks's version of the Frankenstein story complete with a mad scientist trying to put the still-living brain of a high ranking renegade Time Lord executed some centuries earlier into a new body. In it, he also informed viewers about a liquid known as the Elixir of Life, a drug which can give immortality to those who take it and which the Time Lords can use if there is a problem during regeneration.

During the course of a conversation, the fourth Doctor says that the liquid has never been used by his people to prolong life indefinitely, for Time Lords *do* die. Tantalisingly, he does not make clear whether this happens inevitably or by choice. As viewers of this episode will recall, the Doctor had need of a little of the Elixir himself to save his life after the fearsome mind-battle with Morbius's brain.

If the idea of an Elixir of Life was a stunning one – it was nothing to the inference in 'The Hand of Fear', screened in October 1976, that anyone with the power to regenerate might re-emerge in either male or female form! This story, by Bob Baker and Dave Martin, featured Eldred, a Kastrian villain, who had been executed centuries before for his crimes. When his fossilised, though still alive, hand is found on modern-day Earth by the Doctor's companion, Sarah Jane, she is unwillingly made to take it to a nuclear reactor where the energy regenerates it in a female form modelled on her own.

Later in the story, Eldred changes his form to that of a man, and is identified as a silicon-based alien whose own civilisation has been destroyed and which he plans to regenerate back to life. This plan, plus Eldred's ability to regenerate into either male or female, is a surprise to the Doctor, though the alien chides him, 'As a Time Lord, Doctor, you should be *well* acquainted with the process of regeneration!'

The inference is that a Time Lord may choose his sex as well as his body – though, of course, the Doctor is not a silicon-based lifeform – and the story has proved just one of the factors which have caused certain enthusiasts of the programme to suggest a female might well be cast as the Doctor, and even provide a listing of actresses suitable for the part! Indeed, in recent years every time a change of Doctor has been announced in the press, the names of certain female actresses have been very much to the fore – Tom Baker being perhaps the Doctor who most fuelled this possibility with his tongue-in-cheek comment on his retirement, 'My successor? It could even be a woman. There's no reason why the Doctor should always be a man!'

The very next story, 'The Deadly Assassin', was once again the handiwork of Robert Holmes and went far more deeply into the mythos of Gallifrey and the Time Lords than ever its predecessor 'The War Games' had done.

The lavish sets and costuming took viewers into the heart of the Time Lords' empire, and the fourth Doctor's clash with the Master brought another valuable piece of regeneration information to the surface. Arguably, the most important of all.

For here viewers learned that the Master was in his twelfth and final regeneration. In a memorable moment, the Time Lord Coordinator Engin informed his listeners, 'After the twelfth regeneration, *no* plans can stop death.'

At that moment, the Doctor suddenly had a 'life-span' – albeit an enormous one – to which mere human beings could relate. He was not immortal: he had the ability to change, certainly, and even regularly – but not an *infinite* number of times. And if on Earth the number thirteen was considered unlucky and ill-omened, on Gallifrey it clearly spelt the end for a Time Lord.

Even so, in 'The Deadly Assassin', the Master managed to tap into the mysterious power of the Eye of Harmony and escape, apparently set on a new cycle of regenerations. Perhaps, it might be said, producer Hinchcliffe and writer Holmes stepped back at the very last moment from establishing a precedent whereby the end of a twelfth Doctor would also automatically mean the end of *Doctor Who* as a programme!

What this particular story also showed was the first crack in the Time Lords' façade of being an all-powerful and benevolent race. In an interview given later, Robert Holmes explained how this came about.

'I noticed over the years that the Time Lords had produced quite a few galactic lunatics,' he said. 'People like Omega, Morbius and the Master. How did this square with the received notion that the Time Lords were a bunch of omnipotent do-gooders? Could it be that this notion had been put about by the Time Lords themselves? Remember Linx telling the third Doctor in 'The Time Warrior' that Sontaran Intelligence considered the Time Lords 'lacked the moral fibre to withstand a determined assault'? Most damning of all, at the end of 'The War Games', did they not condemn the Doctor to exile for interfering in the affairs of other planets? And yet *who* had sent him on these missions? They had!'

The impact of this story was considerable: confirming the Doctor as a kind of anti-establishment figure who had left his own world because of his disillusionment with the leaders. He would probably never be seen in quite the same light, and his failings certainly never again measured against supposedly superior beings.

It was to be February 1978 before new information about regeneration again figured in a story. By then, Graham Williams had taken over as producer alongside Robert Holmes.

The story in question was 'The Invasion of Time' which was to all intents and purposes a sequel to 'The Deadly Assassin' although this time Gallifrey was presented in a much more substantial way by clever filming on location instead of just studio sets.

The writer was credited as one 'David Agnew' but was, in fact, Graham Williams himself aided by Anthony Read – the reason for this being that he had suddenly found himself faced with one of the typical problems that have beset the series over the years.

'The Invasion of Time' came about because the original script for the slot came in right up against the deadline,' he said. 'And it was quite unworkable. As I remember it featured an amphitheatre in which the audience had been infiltrated with killer cats. So that story went out of the window leaving us just five days to write three hours of television. I don't think Anthony and I went to bed for three days solid!'

The story which resulted from this brain-storming took the Doctor back to Gallifrey where he assumed the powers of President and then apparently turned traitor by allowing an attacking force of Vardons to take control of the planet. In fact, it was only a ruse to gain their confidence and thwart their plans.

The most intriguing element of the plot, however, concerned the Doctor's companion, Leela, who decided to stay on Gallifrey to marry Andred, the Captain of the Guards, and by so doing confirmed that there was a reproductory system on Gallifrey *as well as* regeneration!

There was confirmation of a kind for this idea in the David Fisher story 'The Creature From The Pit', screened in late 1979, which informed viewers that there was a maternity ward on Gallifrey for the raising of Time Lord offspring!

Terry Nation's 'Destiny of the Daleks', in the following season, presented something far more surprising than the return of the Doctor's arch-enemies: a Time Lady changing her body – and for no immediately apparent reason. In fact, it was another case where the brilliant concept of regeneration could be utilised by the programme when a member of the cast decided to leave.

The person involved was Mary Tamm playing the beautiful Romana who, during filming of the preceding story, 'The Armageddon Factor', had announced her intention to depart.

But when her body regenerated in the form of Princess Astra of Atrios played by Lalla Ward there were obvious questions to be asked. *Why* should a Time Lady of approximately 120 years of age in excellent physical and mental condition want to change? And *why* in so doing try three different bodies before she was satisfied?

It seemed therefore apparent from this story that the Gallifreyans had the power to change *whenever* they wished and *however* whimsical the reason might be – though at the cost of a precious life, of course. And if

there was an explanation for having the option of different appearances, then it probably lay in the established fact that every regeneration is followed by a period of instability. Or more basically still, it could just be a matter of choice in much the same way as a viewer might try on a suit of clothes or a dress before finding what he or she wants!

The next regeneration of the Doctor took place in March 1981 when after seven years in the *persona*, Tom Baker handed over the role to the younger and more circumspect Peter Davison. The transformation occurred in the remarkable story of 'Logopolis' by Christopher Bidmead who had taken over the previous year as the new script editor along with a new producer, John Nathan-Turner.

This story, with its central battle between the Doctor and the Master, threw up a puzzling figure in the form of the Watcher who appeared to be another Time Lord – perhaps even a future manifestation of the Doctor himself sent back in time to watch over him.

Throughout the story, the Doctor simply maintains that the figure is an omen of his impending fate. But after the regeneration has taken place, Nyssa feels sure he must have been 'the Doctor all the time'. Neither explanation really solves the mystery – for if the Watcher was a future reincarnation *why* had he not come to the Doctor's aid before? And, more strangely still, *where* did he come from?

'Castrovalva', which began on January 4, 1982, and was also written by Christopher Bidmead, laid emphasis on a point made by earlier stories about regeneration. To be successful, it said, the ritual had to take place in the TARDIS, but, to be absolutely sure, the Doctor must be in the Zero Room. Even so, the fifth Doctor remained unstable for much of this first adventure – and the fact was to have greater relevance when yet another aspect of regeneration was revealed four years later in 1986.

The fallibility of the Time Lords was illustrated again in 'Arc of

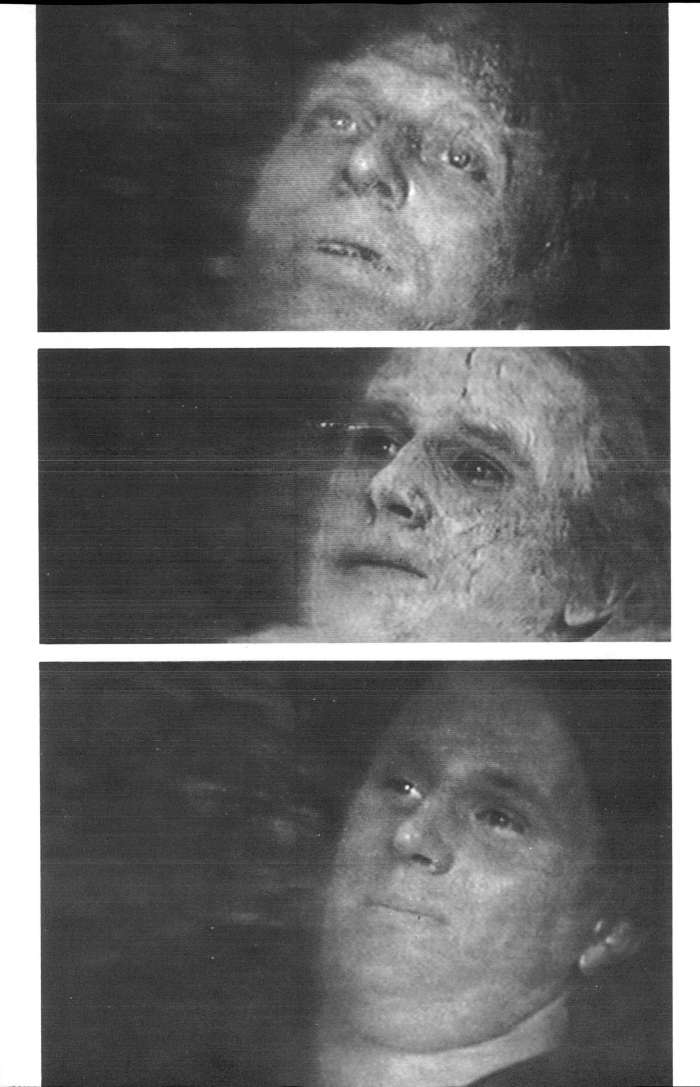

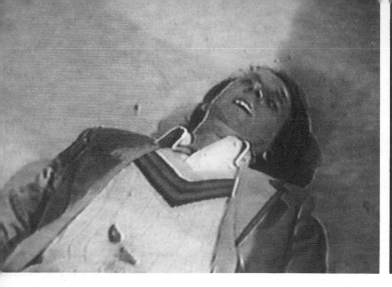

Infinity' by Johnny Byrne, in which the renegade Omega, last seen in 'The Three Doctors' and now consisting of anti-matter, attempted to steal the details of the Doctor's molecular structure so that he could 'bond' with him and achieve a physical existence once again. Learning of these plans, the whole Gallifreyan High Council callously decree that the Doctor must die to prevent such an objective being achieved.

While there has never been a suggestion that *all* the Time Lords are cruel, or even degenerate and corrupt, the instability of some of them was becoming increasingly evident and was very much a feature of the special programme 'The Five Doctors' which Terrance Dicks wrote to commemorate the twenty-first anniversary of the programme in November 1983. In it, of course, Richard Hurndall gave a remarkable performance as a 'real-life regeneration' of the first Doctor!

During the story of 'The Five Doctors' we saw that the Doctor's mentor, Borusa, had become corrupt and was now madly seeking immortality and unbridled power. Even Rassilon, the first of the Time Lords, stood accused of being a leader whose integrity could be questioned. And as for the Death Zone – what truly civilised group of leaders could countenance such a place within their boundaries?

March 1984 saw yet another regeneration with Peter Davison transformed into the colourfully bizarre figure of Colin Baker in 'The Caves of Androzani' by Robert Holmes. The sixth Doctor was soon proved to be as unpredictable as he was querulous.

It was also Robert Holmes who introduced the latest and perhaps most challenging element into the history of regeneration in the serial 'The Trial of a Time Lord'. Sadly, it was also was to prove his last contribution to the series for he died in May 1986 before the programme was actually screened.

For what Holmes and his fellow scriptwriters, Philip Martin and Pip and Jane Baker, showed was that corruption on Gallifrey could spread not just through the hierarchy, but perhaps might even engulf the Doctor himself! And perhaps the cause of this was the very process of regeneration.

Evidence for such an idea was already there, for there was no denying that after many regenerations a Time Lord became increasingly unstable. Borusa was mad after twelve, and the Master in what appeared to be his thirteenth body was acting with the wildest desperation. Even the Doctor in his sixth life cycle – the trial suggested – had tried to kill his companion. The puzzle of the Valeyard and his

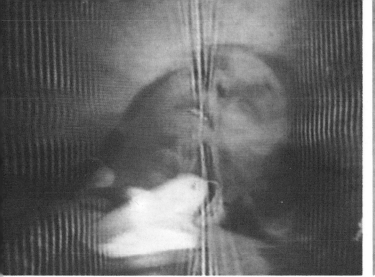 

relationship to the sixth Doctor merely strengthened the conviction that a whole new dimension was opening up for the long running programme.

Regeneration, it is true to say, has been almost as integral a part of the *Doctor Who* programme as the Doctor himself. And with the certain knowledge that he can survive at least six more life-spans, only *Who* knows what the future may hold . . .

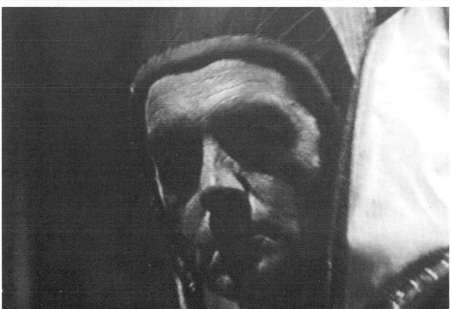

5

A WHO'S WHO OF ENEMIES

Any traveller like the Doctor with the facility to move through space and time is sure, like him, to encounter a great many enemies who wish him nothing but the worst. Villainous humanoids, for example, or dangerous robots and evil monsters of every conceivable shape and size. In these next three sections are described and listed in alphabetical or chronological order the most important foes that the Doctor has met during his journeys over the past twenty-three years. Anyone contemplating following in his footsteps would do well to read, learn and inwardly digest this information, for it has been hard won by the intrepid Time Lord and is an invaluable guide to the perils that lie in wait for the unwary traveller in the vastness of the Galaxy . . .

I Villainous Humanoids

ADRASTA, LADY

Appeared in: 'The Creature From The Pit' by David Fisher (1979).
Played by: Myra Frances

The evil female ruler of the planet Chloris who imposed her will through the carnivorous Wolf Weeds – and also through the monopoly she had of what little metal there was to be found on her world. Lady Adrasta's ruthless dictatorship was finally ended by an enormous creature called Erato, an ambassador from Tythonus who merely wished to exchange metal for the chlorophyll found in abundance on Chloris, but instead found himself imprisoned in a pit. After years of this imprisonment, he was finally released by the fourth Doctor and extracted his revenge on his captor.

BENNETT

Appeared in: 'The Rescue' by David Whitaker (1965).
Played by: Ray Barrett

An unscrupulous murderer who was prepared to take more lives to save his own skin. When his spaceship crashlanded on the planet Dido, he murdered all of fellow passengers, who had found him guilty of a murder. Only one member of the crew, Vicki, was unaware of this and he intended to use her ignorance to protect him when the Earth authorities arrived in the planet. He tried to convince her that a monstrous creature named Koquillion was protecting them from the wrath of the supposedly belligerent Didoi. In fact, Bennett was none other than Koquillion

himself, and when the first Doctor unmasked his crimes he tried to flee from justice but instead plunged over a cliff to his death.

THE BLACK GUARDIAN

Appeared in: 'The Armageddon Factor' by Bob Baker and Dave Martin (1979), 'Mawdryn Undead' by Peter Grimwade (1983), 'Terminus' by Steve Gallagher (1983) and 'Enlightenment' by Barbara Clegg (1983).
Played by: Valentine Dyall

The Black Guardian is the personification of evil and the ways of darkness throughout all of space and time. His mission is to plunge the universe into eternal chaos and he uses human beings and aliens with callous disregard of life to further these objectives. The Black Guardian was first encountered by the fourth Doctor while the Time Lord was searching for the final segment of the Key to Time – but he also reappeared to give even more trouble to the fifth Doctor, including dangerously influencing his companion, Turlough. Having been thwarted twice already, the Black Guardian will be waiting for the third encounter with the Doctor for his power does not diminish and he will exist until he is no longer needed.

THE BORAD

Appeared in: 'Timelash' by Glen McCoy.
Played by: Robert Ashley (Mutation)
Dennis Carey (Old man)

The Borad was an apparently aged and tyrannical dictator who kept his people on the planet of Karfel in total

Bennett (Ray Barrett)
with Barbara
(Jacqueline Hill) and
Vicki (Maureen
O'Brien).

submission by use of a monitoring system, ruthless android slaves and the dreaded Timelash — a time corridor which can thrust its victim into any hostile environment anywhere in space or time. The unfortunate Peri fell into his clutches, and in rescuing her, the sixth Doctor learned that the Borad was not one person but *two* — the fusion of a young scientist and one of Karfel's savage monsters, the Morlox! The Time Lord needed all his guile to defeat the Borad and his plan to populate the planet with mutations like himself.

CAPEL, TAREN

**Appeared in: 'The Robots of Death' by Chris Boucher (1977).
Played by: David Bailie**

Although he was ostensibly another mad scientist with his eyes on world domination, Taren Capel differed from most in that he had been raised from childhood by robots and considered them as his brothers. So it was that he banded together a group of them as 'Robots of Death', with the ultimate intention of creating a society where robots were the rulers and human beings the subjects. However, the fourth Doctor out-thought him by releasing helium into the atmosphere which changed Capel's voice so that the robots did not recognise their master and instead destroyed *him*.

The friend of robots, Taren Capel (David Bailie).

The maniacal General Carrington (John Abineri) with the third Doctor, Liz (Caroline John) and The Brigadier (Nicholas Stewart).

CARRINGTON, GENERAL

**Appeared in: 'The Ambassadors of Death' by David Whitaker (1970).
Played by: John Abineri**

Carrington was an astronaut on the first manned space mission to Mars who encountered an alien species and as a result became xenophobic. When promoted to General of the Space Security Department, this mania developed into an unreasoning fear of alien life forms and he plotted to start a war between Earth and Mars by exposing three ambassadors from the Red Planet as a deadly threat. It was the third Doctor who managed to avert this tragedy and keep the peace between the two worlds.

CAVEN

Appeared in: 'The Space Pirates' by Robert Holmes (1969).
Played by: Dudley Foster

A notorious space criminal who travelled wherever the pickings were richest and was assisted by Madeleine, the daughter of his former partner, Dom Issigri. Caven was the leader of a gang of space pirates who were attacking navigation beacons for the metal Argonite, that they were made of. He was unmasked by the second Doctor when the blame for this crime was at first laid on the wrong man. Caven was finally brought to justice by Madeleine who realised how she had been duped when she discovered that her father was still alive, and being held by Caven's men.

CHASE, HARRISON

Appeared in: 'The Seeds of Doom' by Robert Banks Stewart (1976).
Played by: Tony Beckley

Harrison Chase was a deranged English millionaire botanist who filled his sprawling mansion with rare types of plants and vegetation. In fact, he had an almost symbiotic relationship with all forms of plant life and even composed special electronic music to commune with them. When an alien species of plant known as a Krynoid, which is hostile to all animal life, was discovered in the Antarctic, Chase ruthlessly obtained one and nurtured it – regardless of the danger it posed to humanity. Thanks to the fourth Doctor the Krynoid was finally destroyed just before it became the size of a house, while Chase

suffered a suitably appropriate end in the machine he used to grind up waste for his garden!

CHEN, MAVIC

Appeared in: 'The Daleks' Masterplan' by Terry Nation & Dennis Spooner (1965/6).
Played by: Kevin Stoney

The sardonic and calculating Guardian of the Solar System in the forty-first century who turned traitor and lent his help to the Daleks in their plan to conquer the Solar Planets. Chen offered them an element of taranium with which they could power their supreme weapon, the Time Destructor, and destroy all resistance on Earth. His callous disregard for the worlds in his care was illustrated in the memorable sentence, 'The solar system is just a *part* of the Galaxy – would you be satisfied with merely a part?' The Daleks, though, true to form, killed him after he had served his purpose.

THE COLLECTOR

Appeared in: 'The Sunmakers' by Robert Holmes (1977).
Played by: Henry Woolf

The Collector was a bald-headed monomaniac official of the Sun Company

The treacherous Guardian of the Solar System, Mavic Chen (Kevin Stoney).

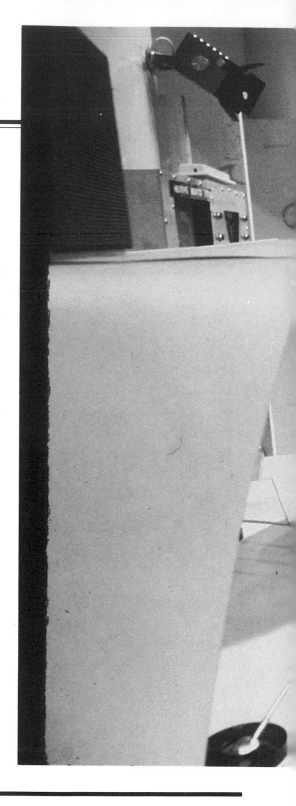

who had enslaved a colony of hapless workers on Pluto by means of an extortionate tax collection. This mean-minded man with his head full of money and profits, was only able to find pleasure in the world of finance and subjecting the colonists to bouts of 'stereo screaming'. He was finally outwitted by the fourth Doctor who, on learning he was actually a member of the Usurian race, fed details of rampant inflation into the company computer. This shock to the system caused the Collector to shrink back to his original form, and he was promptly bottled by the Doctor!

CRANLEIGH, LORD GEORGE

Appeared in: 'Black Orchid' by Terence Dudley.
Played by: Gareth Milne

Lord George Cranleigh was an English gentleman and renowned botanist of the nineteen-twenties who had been captured by savage Indians during an expedition up the Orinoco River and returned home with his mind and body broken. Now a virtual lunatic, Cranleigh was locked away in the closed wing of Cranleigh Hall, but managed to find a way out through a secret passage and carried on his depraved ways. Though the fifth Doctor tried to sympathise with him, the unfortunate madman became obsessed with Nyssa who was the double of his ex-fiancée and while dragging her across the roof of the Hall tripped and fell to his death.

ECKERSLEY

Appeared in: 'The Monster of Peladon' by Brian Hayles (1974).
Played by: Donald Gee

Eckersley was an Earth mining engineer working in the trislicate mines on Peladon whose greed for money caused

him to work in league with some renegade Ice Warriors. It was their plan to seize the mineral wealth of the planet in order to help an invading enemy from Galaxy Five. Fortunately, the third Doctor, who was visiting Peladon, got wind of this and was able to subvert the plan, while the hapless Eckersley met his fate at the hands of Aggedor the Royal Beast of Peladon.

The engineer Eckersley (Donald Gee) with Sarah (Elizabeth Sladen).

EL AKIR

Appeared in: 'The Crusades' by David Whitaker (1965).
Played by: Walter Randall

El Akir was a tyrannical Saracen Emir who delighted in sadistically and cruelly treating his subjects. In the year 1191 he was lying in wait to ambush and kill King Richard the Lionheart who was crusading in the Holy Land – when who should arrive but the first Doctor and his companions. The Emir nearly broke up the little time travelling party when he imprisoned Barbara in his harem – and the Doctor and Vicki only just escaped being burnt at the stake as sorcerers!

FAY, VIVIEN

Appeared in: 'The Stones of Blood' by David Fisher (1978).
Played by: Susan Engel

A notable alien villainess who had hidden on Earth for three thousand years taking on various identities and names. Her real name, though, was Cessair of Diplos, and she had control of the Ogri, stone creatures that fed on the blood of her enemies. Around her neck Vivien Fay wore a precious stone, the Seal of Diplos, which enabled her to change shape and which caught the fourth Doctor's attention while he was in England in 1978 searching for the third segment of the Key to Time – which, in fact, was what the seal was. In attempting to avoid punishment for her crimes, she was turned into a stone megalith.

FEDERICO, COUNT

Appeared in: 'The Masque of Mandragora' by Louis Marks (1976).
Played by: Jon Laurimore

Count Federico was an evil fifteenth-century Italian nobleman, plotting and scheming to steal the dukedom of San Martino from his nephew, Guiliano, the rightful ruler. The Count called on the aid of the court astrologer Hieronymous, unaware that the man had been taken over by a powerful alien energy complex known as the Mandragora Helix, which was planning to plunge Earth back into the Dark Ages. The fourth Doctor had a real battle on his hands to overcome this powerful foe – and in doing so, the Count became one of the victims of the Helix.

FORESTER

Appeared in: 'Planet of the Giants' by Louis Marks (1964).
Played by: Alan Tilvern.

Forester was an unscrupulous and deranged scientist who discovered a new insecticide, DN6, which could be used to increase food production in starving nations. However, he also found that because of its molecular structure it would in time kill every living thing. To protect his invention, though, he was prepared to lie and kill, and it took all the first Doctor's ingenuity to thwart his plans – particularly as the Time Lord happened to be miniaturised at the time!

GARRON

Appeared in: 'The Ribos Operation' by Robert Holmes (1978).
Played by: Iain Cuthbertson

Garron is probably the craftiest and most slippery confidence trickster at loose in the Galaxy, and pulled off one of his most memorable triumphs in 'The Ribos Operation' when he convinced the greedy tyrant Graff Vynda-K that he could sell him the planet Ribos, reputedly the source of one of the most valuable minerals in the galaxy, Jethrik. The fourth Doctor became involved in Garron's 'scam', and even though the

The crafty con-man, Garron (Iain Cuthbertson) on the planet Ribos

Graff eventually realised he had been cheated, his attempt to kill both the con-man and the Time Lord backfired and he himself died in the ensuing explosion. At this, Garron made quietly off with the Graff's spaceship, already laden with spoils. . .

GREEL, MAGNUS

Appeared in: 'The Talons of Weng-Chiang' by Robert Holmes (1977).
Played by: Michael Spice

A war-criminal from the fifty-first century nicknamed 'the Butcher of Brisbane', who developed a faulty time travel machine, powered by Zigma energy, which hurled him, crippled and disfigured, to the year 1889 and thence to London where he masqueraded as Weng-Chiang, the divine leader of the Chinese Tong of the Black Scorpion. In this disguise he was able to prey on young girls and use their life energies in attempts to restore his disfigurement. When he came up against the fourth Doctor, however, his depraved campaign of terror was brought to an appropriate end in his life-absorbing machine!

GRENDEL, COUNT

Appeared in: 'The Andoids of Tara' by David Fisher (1978).
Played by: Peter Jeffrey

An archetypal scheming and villainous nobleman intent on disrupting the peace and tranquillity of his chivalrous world. He planned to usurp the throne of the rightful ruler, Prince Reynart, by marrying Princess Strella whom he had captured and imprisoned. However, when he confused the fourth Doctor's companion, Romana, with the Princess and seized her, too, he found a formidable and ultimately superior opponent on his trail in the shape of the Time Lord from Gallifrey!

GRUGGER, GENERAL

Appeared in : 'Meglos' by John Flanagan and Andrew McCulloch (1980).
Played by: Bill Fraser

General Grugger was the scheming and devious leader of a band of space raiders known as the Gaztaks. He and his men were mercenaries available for hire and were recruited by the cactus-like Meglos to steal the powerful crystal known as the Dodecahedron which powered the underground world of Tigella. When the fourth Doctor became involved in this plot, he impersonated Meglos — and by so doing not only prevented this potentially fatal theft, but caused an explosion which rid the worlds of space and time once and for all of the evil General Grugger.

IRONGRON

Appeared in: 'The Time Warrior' by Robert Holmes (1973/4).
Played by: David Daker

An evil-tempered and loutish Medieval robber chief, Irongron had ambitions way above his own capabilities or those of his ragged army of followers. The bandit's desire for greater strength to his arm seemed to have been answered when a Sontaran, Linx, crashed his starship on Irongron's land and he could offer shelter in return for high technology weapons. Linx, though, found the robber an unreliable accomplice and during a run-in with the third Doctor — who also appeared on the scene — put an end to his career.

JEK, SHARAZ

Appeared in: 'The Caves of Androzani' by Robert Holmes.
Played by: Christopher Gable

A hideously disfigured scientist who concealed his terrible wounds beneath a leather suit and mask. He received the scars when detection equipment provided by his partner, Morgus, failed to warn him of an impending eruption of boiling mud. Driven to live under the surface of Androzani minor, he plotted his revenge against Morgus, now a powerful head of a conglomerate on Androzani Major. The fifth Doctor had to save his companion Peri from Jek's unwelcome attentions, and just escaped with his life when the Jek met Morgus and died in a brutal struggle for supremacy.

KLEIG, ERIC

Appeared in: 'The Tomb of the Cybermen' by Kit Pedler and Gerry Davis (1967).
Played by: George Pastell

Eric Kleig was the ambitious megalomaniac who searched for the tomb of the Cybermen on the planet Telos. He was driven by a belief that by securing the aid of the dormant monsters, human and Cyberman would make an invincible partnership. 'We need your power,' he explained to the Cyber controller after the resurrection had taken place, 'and *you* need our intelligence.' As on other occasions, the Cybermen were not impressed, and Kleig was killed by the very hands that he had brought back to life. The second Doctor, though, quickly refroze the whole group!

LYTTON, COMMANDER

Appeared in: 'The Resurrection of the Daleks' by Eric Saward (1984) and 'Attack of the Cybermen' by Paula Moore (1986).
Played by: Maurice Colbourne

A brutal and unscrupulous alien mercenary soldier who would serve any master if the price was right and became involved with two of the Doctor's greatest enemies, the Daleks and the Cybermen. Originally from the planet Riftan Five, he led an equally tough band of mercenaries and was lucky to escape with his life after exterminating human beings for the Daleks. Fate, though, caught up with Commander Lytton when he journeyed to the Cybermen's planet of Telos for he was turned into a Cyberman himself and died before the process was complete.

MARSHALL OF SOLOS

Appeared in: 'The Mutants' by Bob Baker and Dave Martin (1972).
Played by: Paul Whitsun-Jones

The Marshall was the sadistic and self-important ruler of the Earth Colony, Solos, who was more interested in persecuting the Solonian Mutants and securing himself the position of virtual dictator of the planet than allowing its proposed independence from Earth. In his madness, the Marshall implicated a Solonian, Ky, in the murder of the Earth Administrator – but helped by the third Doctor, despatched by the Time Lords to Solos, this Solonian was able to follow the ancient process of transmogrification into a super-being who put an end to the rule of the evil dictator.

MAXTIBLE, PROFESSOR THEODORE

Appeared in: 'The Evil of the Daleks' by David Whitaker (1967).
Played by: Marius Goring

The ruthless Victorian scientist, Professor Maxtible (Marius Goring).

The Professor was a wealthy Victorian scientist driven by ambition and greed. In the year 1866 he had been working on a theory of time travel based on mirrors and static electricity, but unwittingly it brought him into contact with the Daleks. They promised him the secret of transmuting ordinary lead into gold if he would help them collect human beings to be turned into Dalek-like creatures by injecting them with the 'Dalek Factor'.

Instead, he himself was turned into one of the creatures and was finally fell to his death during the epic civil war on Skaro, engineered by the second Doctor.

PANGOL

Appeared in: 'The Leisure Hive' by David Fisher (1980).
Played by: David Haig

Pangol was a young Argolin obsessed with the ambition to create a cloning system and thereby duplicate himself into an entire army to destroy the reptilian Foamasi who had been warring with his people on Argolis for generations. Pangol was also something of an enigma for no child had been born on the planet for over forty years as a result of a nuclear bombardment by the Foamasi which had made all the Argolin sterile. In fact, Pangol was revealed to have been a baby manufactured by the Tachyon Recreation Generator, and when the fourth Doctor learned of his plans, the Time Lord not only wrecked his grand scheme but returned him to the age of a child again!

PIKE, CAPTAIN

Appeared in: 'The Smugglers' by Brian Hayles (1966).
Played by: Michael Godfrey

Captain Pike was a black-hearted villain and smuggler who earned his name from the sharp spike which he had on his right arm instead of a hand. He and his men terrorised part of the coast of seventeenth-century Cornwall where they were in league with a roguish local squire in taking their pick of contraband and piracy. It was the unexpected arrival of the first Doctor along with the Revenue Men that brought an end to Captain Pike's dirty dealings.

PIRATE CAPTAIN

Appeared in: 'The Pirate Planet' by Douglas Adams (1978).
Played by: Bruce Purchase

The half-man, half-robot, un-named Captain of the most feared pirate spaceship in the galaxy, *The Vantarialis*. He later piloted the parasite planet Zanak around time and space, sucking the energy from other planets. This blood-thirsty villain, complete with a robot parrot, Polyphase Avatron, on his shoulder, met his match in the fourth Doctor, although it was his creator, Queen Xanxia, who ended his life before being shot and killed herself.

ROHM-DUTT

Appeared in: 'The Power of Kroll' by Robert Holmes (1978/9).
Played by: Glyn Owen

Living dangerously as a gun smuggler on the marshy world of Delta Magna's third moon, Rohm-Dutt was a tough and experienced criminal who was secretly employed by the controller of a Refinery to provide non-functioning guns for the down-trodden Swampies. The controller used the fact the Swampies had guns to justify his policy of exterminating them. But Rohm-Dutt's part in this deception was eventually spotted by the fourth Doctor, and the gun runner paid for his treachery with his life when attacked and killed by the enormous, squid-like creature, Kroll.

RORVICK, CAPTAIN

Appeared in: 'Warriors' Gate' by Steve Gallagher (1981).
Played by: Clifford Rose

A sadistic space slave trader, Captain Rorvick inspired fear in, if not much enthusiasm from, the crew of his ship. In the hold, which was made of impervious Dwarf Star Alloy, were a number of luckless time-sensitive Tharils, and their lives along with those of the Captain and his crew were put in peril when the privateer became marooned at the Zero Point. The fourth Doctor was recruited by a Tharil who had earlier escaped from the slave ship to try and free his fellows – but Rorvick sealed his own fate when he tried to blast free of the time trap and only succeeded in releasing the Tharils and killing himself in the ensuing explosion.

The fourth Doctor at the mercy of the slave trader, Captain Rorvick (Clifford Rose).

SALAMANDER

Appeared in: 'The Enemy of the World' by David Whitaker (1967/8).
Played by: Patrick Troughton

A would-be dictator who was hell-bent on enslaving the world from his secret headquarters in Kenowa on the coast of Australia. He created what seemed like natural catastrophes which brought discredit on the various Controllers of the world's national zones and enabled him to replace these men with his own hand-picked followers. However, because Salamander bore a striking resemblance to the second Doctor, he tried to impersonate the Time Lord and steal the TARDIS – only to have the time machine react against him and hurl him out into space to his death.

SCARLIONI, COUNT

Appeared in: 'City of Death' by David Agnew.
Played by: Julian Glover

Ostensibly an obsessive European art collector, Count Scarlioni was actually stealing and selling valuable works of art to finance his time travel experiments. He did not, however, count on the intervention of the fourth Doctor who unmasked him as Scaroth, the last of the Jagaroth race, a hideous creature with one eye. Scaroth intended to travel back in time to prevent the explosion of his spacecraft on primeval Earth. The Doctor realised that the explosion of the Jagaroth spacecraft sparked off the creation of life on Earth, and ensured that the evil Count's plan went no further.

The gruesome-looking Count Scarlioni (Julian Glover).

SHOCKEYE

Appeared in: 'The Two Doctors' by Robert Holmes (1985).
Played by: John Stratton

Shockeye was the revolting Androgum with a voracious appetite whose greatest desire was to eat human flesh. As unpleasant in his habits as he was to look at – with his huge pot-belly, warts and suppurating boils – Shockeye was ever on the look-out for delicacies to cook. He expected to satisfy his craving when he came to present day Seville with his equally evil but more intelligent female accomplice, Chessene, and spotted a number of delicacies including the thighs of the second Doctor's companion, Jamie, and the curvacious figure of Peri, the sixth Doctor's assistant. But greed went before a fall, and all Shockeye got to eat in the end was a fatal dose of cyanide!

The fanatical scientist, Professor Stahlman (Olaf Pooley) on the far left.

SOLON, MEHENDERI

Appeared in: 'The Brain of Morbius' by Robin Bland (1976).
Played by: Philip Madoc

A scheming and thoroughly disreputable man of medicine, Solon was also one of the most talented surgeons in the galaxy and the fourth Doctor found him on the planet Karn busily implanting the still-living brain of the renegade Time Lord Morbius, believed to have been executed, into a monstrous new body. Thus equipped, Morbius planned to conquer the Galaxy, and Solon's reward for his help would have been a high office in his new empire. It took all the Doctor's courage to defeat this evil partnership in what became a battle of wills as much as physical strength.

STAHLMAN, PROFESSOR

Appeared in: 'Inferno' by Don Houghton (1970).
Played by: Olaf Pooley

An arrogant and fanatial scientist obsessed with a dream to penetrate the Earth's core and tap its limitless source of energy which he proposed to call Stahlman's Gas. In fact, the Professor's scheme, 'Project Inferno' actually released a liquid which, when it touched human beings, turned them into ape-like creatures called Primords. Nonetheless, driven on recklessly by his ambition, Stahlman was himself infected by the liquid and only the brave intervention of the third Doctor prevented him from releasing the gases which would have caused a world-wide holocaust.

TEGANA

Appeared in: 'Marco Polo' by John Lucarotti (1964).
Played by: Derren Nesbitt

Tegana was a ruthless and cunning Mongol warlord, ostensibly a peace ambassador to Kublai Khan's Court in Peking, but actually there to assassinate the ageing Chinese ruler. To this end he insinuated himself into the friendship of Marco Polo on his way to the Court, and might well have carried out his plan had not the first Doctor also become a member of the party. In Peking, the Time Lord not only met and played backgammon with the great Khan, but also exposed Tegana's treacherous plan and saw him die by the sword.

TLOTOXL

Appeared in: 'The Aztecs' by John Lucarotti (1964).
Played by: John Ringham

Tlotoxl was the Aztec High Priest of Sacrifice who specialised in the most gruesome tortures and killings. His nasty blood ceremonies were only matched by the nastiness of his mind, both of which horrified the first Doctor and his companions when they arrived in Mexico. Though the first Doctor's companion, Barbara, tried to dissuade him from the terrible ritual sacrifices he carried out, Tlotoxl was not convinced and would rather have liked to have tried his art out on the TARDIS travellers. As it was, the party were very glad to escape unscathed from this bloody period of ancient history . . .

The ruthless tycoon, Tobias Vaughn (Kevin Stoney) with the second Doctor and Jamie (Frazer Hines).

TOYMAKER, THE

Appeared in: 'The Celestial Toymaker' by Brian Hayles (1966).
Played by: Michael Gough

Dressed like a Chinese mandarin and wearing an enigmatic smile, the Toymaker was in fact an evil being who lured people to his mysterious domain and challenged them to play games. The cost of losing was to become the Toymaker's playthings, and the chances of winning were slight because nothing in his Toy Room was ever quite as innocent as it seemed. Fortunately the first Doctor managed to outwit him and escaped unscathed.

VAUGHN, TOBIAS

Appeared in: 'The Invasion' by Derrick Sherwin (1968).
Played by: Kevin Stoney

Another crazed human being who inadvisably threw in his lot with the Cybermen. Tobias Vaughn was a ruthless business tycoon whose company,

International Electromatix, had a monopoly in micro-circuitry, and in return for what he believed would be the position of Earth Ruler, he agreed to install micro-monolithic circuitry in his company's products which could be used to facilitate the Cybermen's invasion. The second Doctor learned of this plan, and managed to convince Vaughn of his stupidity and ultimately wiped out the invading forces.

WINTERS, HILDA

Appeared in: 'Robot' By Terrance Dicks (1974/5).
Played by: Patricia Maynard

A very formidable lady, cool and ruthless, who lead the group of dissident scientists called the Scientific Reform Society. She had plans to start the Third World War with the help of the highly capable Robot, K1, designed by Professor Kettlewell, and a nuclear missile attack. However, her scheme for a new world in which she was to be the supreme ruler was scotched by the newly regenerated fourth Doctor who applied a metal virus to the Robot which destroyed it.

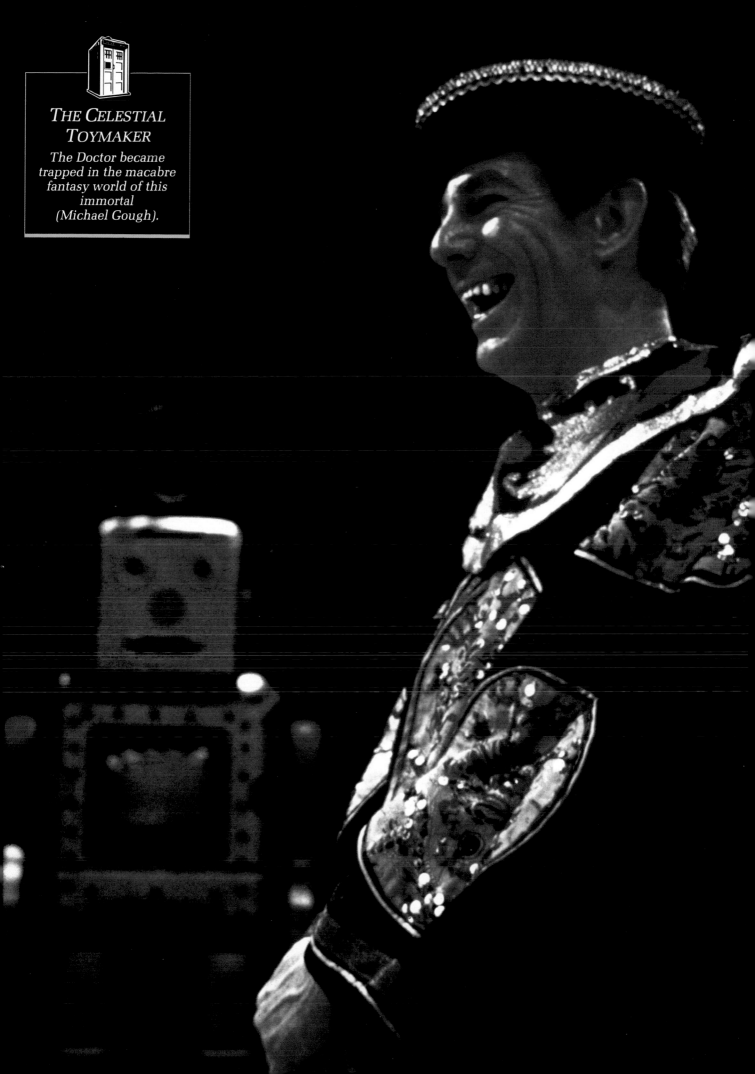

The Celestial Toymaker

The Doctor became trapped in the macabre fantasy world of this immortal (Michael Gough).

LADY ADRASTA

Lady Adrasta (Myra Frances) held the monopoly on metal on her planet of Chloris in 'The Creature from the Pit'.

THE COLLECTOR

The Collector (Henry Woolf) was an evil financial genius and a ruthless employee of the Company in 'The Sunmakers'.

VIVIEN FAY

The beautiful but
deadly Vivien Fay
(Susan Engel) was, in
truth, the master
criminal Cessair of
Diplos.

MAGNUS GREEL

Magnus Greel,
the infamous Butcher of
Brisbane (Michael Spice)
and his cohort Mr Sin
(Deep Roy).

WRACK

Appeared in: 'Enlightenment' by Barbara Clegg (1983).
Played by: Lynda Baron

Wrack was an Eternal, a creature from outside time who could take on any form to beguile the human race which provided her with her link with reality. She appeared as the voluptuous Captain of an eighteenth-century pirate ship, *The Buccaneer* – a tyrannical master of her crew with a callous disregard for life and totally single-minded in her determination never to be beaten or outsmarted. It was the fifth Doctor who discovered she was actually a servant of the Black Guardian.

XANXIA, QUEEN

Appeared in: 'The Pirate Planet' by Douglas Adams (1978).
Played by: Rosalind Lloyd

The evil though ingenious Queen of the mysterious hollow planet Zanak which could travel through space and drain other worlds of their energies. Her right-hand man was the equally villainous Pirate Captain, a half-man, half-machine creature, who piloted the planet. It was the fourth Doctor who discovered that it was the Queen herself who actually needed the energy of other planets to keep her aged and wizened body from dying. The Time Lord cut her off from her sources of energy by organising a rebellion, and it was one of the rebels who finally put an end to Queen Xanxia's existence by shooting her.

ZAROFF, PROFESSOR

Appeared in: 'The Underwater Menace' by Geoffrey Orme (1967).
Played by: Joseph Furst

The archetypal twentieth-century mad scientist who had a plan to raise the lost Continent of Atlantis from the Atlantic floor off the Azores by draining the ocean into the molten core of the Earth. It was the second Doctor who realised such a plan could not work and that the super-heated steam which resulted would cause the planet to break in two. Professor Zaroff met a suitably watery end when his laboratory was deluged by the ocean!

The voluptuous pirate captain, Wrack (Lynda Baron) has the fifth Doctor in a tricky situation.

11 Dangerous Robots

Robots have been a recurring feature in the Doctor's travels, doing their automated best to put a stop to his missions through space and time. Ranging in size from the Giant Robot to the tiny Quarks, they have proved ingenious enemies, though never quite able to match the speed of thought and cleverness of the Time Lord from Gallifrey.

The robots of *Doctor Who* are, in fact, following in a tradition which dates back to the early years of the nineteenth century when the first machines which mimicked the human form appeared. These automata were actually clockwork puppets which carried out a range of functions such as moving their arms and legs; the most advanced could even answer questions and play chess!

The earliest piece of fiction about these inventions was 'Automata' written in 1814 by the German writer, E.T.A. Hoffman (1776–1822) about a machine resembling a Turkish gentleman that could talk. Two years later, Hoffman produced 'The Sandman' about a mysterious and rather evil figure called Dr Coppelius and the beautiful automaton named Olympia which he created. This story is widely considered one of the most important forerunners of the whole genre of robot tales.

Another notable early story was 'Maelzel's Chess Player' (1836) by the tragic American author Edgar Allan Poe (1809–1849) which described a very accomplished automaton created and exhibited by a certain Baron Kempelen.

However, the actual term robot was not coined until 1921 by the Czech playwright Karel Capek (1890–1938), in his drama *R.U.R.* which was first produced in Prague in 1921. The title is an acronym of Rossum's Universal Robots, and in the original Czech the word *robota* means the equivalent of slave labourer. Although in the play the robots were artificial men of organic origin, the term soon came to mean mechanical creatures like those which have featured with such effect during the three decades of *Doctor Who*.

In the twentieth century, the most important writer of fiction on the subject has undoubtedly been the American Isaac Asimov, whose work, as I explained earlier, was a formative influence on Sydney Newman. Asimov's famous collection, *I, Robot* (1950) provided what he called the Three Laws of Robotics: 1. A robot may not injure a human being, or, through inaction, allow a human being to come to harm. 2. A robot must obey the orders given it by human beings except where such orders would conflict with the First Law. 3. A robot must protect its own existence as long as such protection does not conflict with the First or Second Law.

In a nutshell, Asimov saw man and robot not just as allies, but also friends: a factor which has also occasionally occurred in *Doctor Who* in cases such as the Chumblies in 'Galaxy Four' (1965), but most particularly in the case of the robot pet who shared the Doctor's adventures for some years, K9.

Taken as a whole, though, the robots which have crossed the Doctor's path have not had the best of intentions towards him, and the most interesting examples are listed hereunder, with their creators, in order of appearance.

The fourth Doctor with his canine robot friend, K9.

The Yeti-like robot on the rampage in 'The Abominable Snowman'.

ROBOT ERA 1 (WILLIAM HARTNELL)

MECHONOIDS

The Masters of the planet Mechanus who had been sent to colonise that world but instead took it over and used it as a 'zoo' for unwary space travellers. Created by Terry Nation for 'The Chase' (1965).

WAR MACHINES

Hugely powerful, self-contained computers controlled by the supercomputer WOTAN and programmed to take over the Earth. Created by Ian Stuart Black for 'The War Machines' (1966).

ROBOT ERA 2 (PATRICK TROUGHTON)

YETI

Fur-covered robots under the control of the Great Intelligence which terrorised a Tibetan monastry. Created by Mervyn Haisman and Henry Lincoln for 'The Abominable Snowman' (1967) and 'The Web of Fear' (1968).

An awesome group of Mechonoids on the move in 'The Chase'.

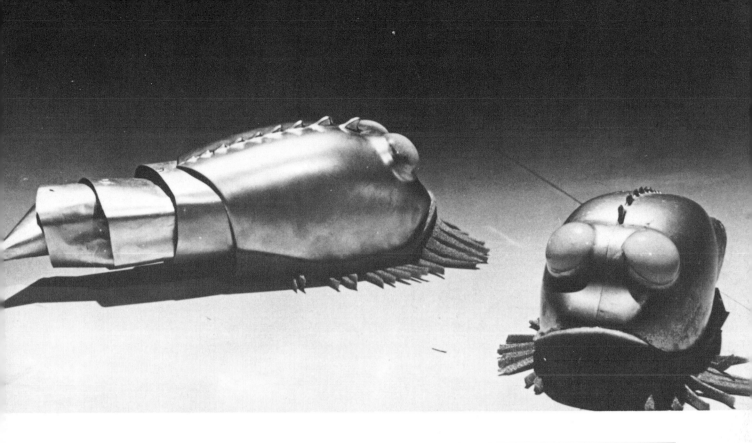

A rather comical-looking Servo Robot who appeared with the Cybermats in the story of 'The Wheel in Space'.

WHITE ROBOTS

Relentless hunters who pursued the second Doctor and his companions across the Land of Fiction. The Time Lord also confronted the dangerous Clockwork Soldiers there. Created by Peter Ling for 'The Mind Robber' (1968).

ROBOT ERA 3 (JON PERTWEE)

SERVO ROBOT

A maintenance robot which operated and protected a space craft, the Silver Carrier. Created by Kit Pedler and written by David Whitaker for 'The Wheel In Space' (1968).

IMC ROBOT

The Interplanetary Mining Corporation's deadly robot servant who terrorised some space colonists until the arrival of the third Doctor in the year 2471. Created by Malcolm Hulke for 'Colony In Space' (1971).

QUARKS

The small but deadly robot servants of the Dominators who threatened the planet Dulkis. Created by Norman Ashby for 'The Dominators' (1968).

ROBOT KNIGHT

An ingenious mechanical soldier built by the Sontaran, Linx, for the robber chief, Irongron. Created by Robert Holmes for 'The Time Warrior' (1973/4).

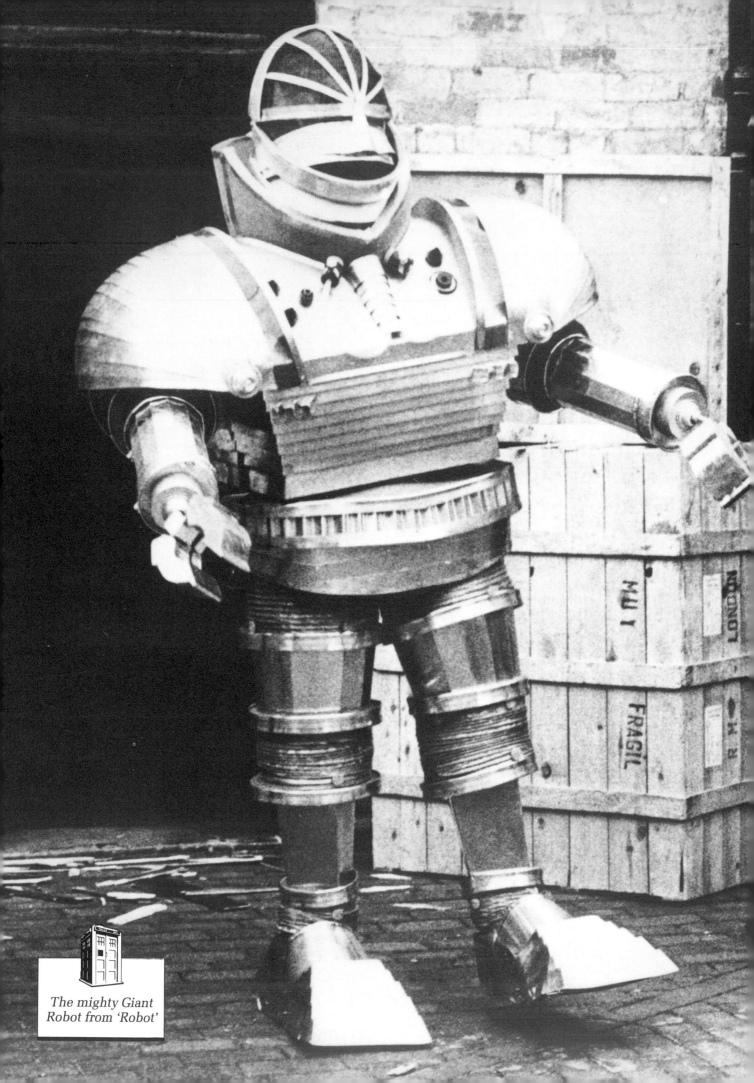

The mighty Giant Robot from 'Robot'

ROBOT ERA 4 (TOM BAKER)

GIANT ROBOT

The awesome creation of the Earth scientist Professor Kettlewell, which went beserk, proved a terrifying first enemy for the fourth Doctor. Created by Terrance Dicks for 'Robot' (1974/5).

STYRE'S ROBOT

Another hostile robot created by a member of the Sontaran race, Field Major Styre, prior to an invasion of the Galaxy. Created by Bob Baker and Dave Martin for 'The Sontaran Experiment' (1975).

MUMMIES

Robots resembling Mummies from Ancient Egypt which were built by the Egyptologist Marcus Scarman who came under the power of the evil god Sutekh. Created by Stephen Harris for 'Pyramids of Mars' (1975).

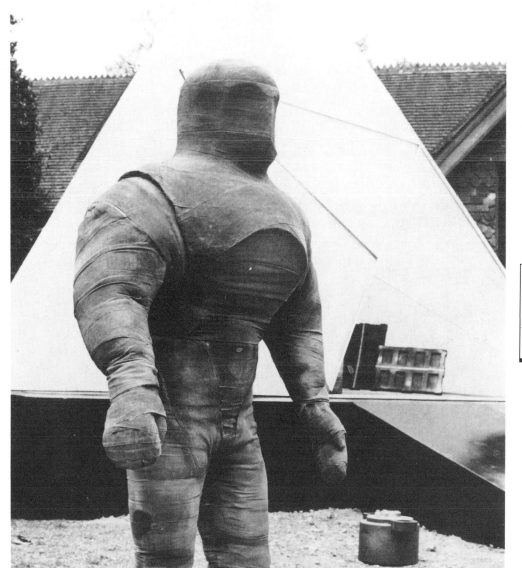

A Mummy-shaped robot from 'Pyramids of Mars'.

ROBOTS OF DEATH

A group of three different types of robots discovered by the fourth Doctor working a mobile factory called the Sandminer: the basic workers were Dums; the Vocs could speak; while the Super Vocs could think for themselves. Created by Chris Boucher for 'The Robots of Death' (1977).

MOVELLANS

Ostensibly a race of beautiful humanoids, the Movellans proved to be a merciless race of robots engaged in a long-standing war with the Daleks. Created by Terry Nation for 'Destiny of the Daleks' (1979).

ROBOT ERA 5 (PETER DAVISON)

TERILEPTIL ANDROID

The robot servant of the Terileptil criminals who planned to wipe out the human race with a deadly bacillus until the fifth Doctor intervened. Created by Eric Saward for 'The Visitation' (1982).

DRONES

The drudge-like robots who worked in the space ship which was transporting suffers from the terrible illness called Lazar's Disease. Created by Steve Gallagher for 'Terminus' (1983).

KAMELION

The remarkable android capable of impersonating any human being, who was created by Terence Dudley for 'The King's Demons' (1983) and reappeared in 'Planet of Fire' (1984).

ROBOT ERA 6 (COLIN BAKER)

DRATHRO

A robot of great intelligence who ruled the humans who lived in the remains of the London Underground on Ravalox (Earth). Created by Robert Holmes for 'The Mysterious Planet' (1986).

L3 ROBOT

A crude robot used by Drathro when the Doctor and Peri visited Ravalox (Earth). Created by Robert Holmes for 'The Mysterious Planet' (1986).

The ingenious Kamelion who twice appeared with the fifth Doctor.

III Evil Monsters

AGGEDOR

'The Curse of Peladon' (1972); 'The Monster of Peladon' (1974)

Location: Peladon
Description: Sacred bear-like monster protecting the planet, capable of spreading terror and death when aroused.
Activated by: Nick Hobbs
Creator: Brian Hayles

ALPHA CENTURI AMBASSADOR

'The Curse of Peladon' (1972); 'The Monster of Peladon' (1974)

Location: Alpha Centuri
Description: Courteous and gentle six-armed creature who represents his planet and is very averse to violence.
Activated by: Stuart Fell, voice by Ysanne Churchman
Creator: Brian Hayles

ANTI-MATTER BEAST

'Planet of Evil' (1975)

Location: Zeta Minor
Description: A creature made up of the anti-matter which originates on the planet – other species, including human beings can be 'infected' with the anti-matter.
Activated by: Frederick Jaeger
Creator: Louis Marks

ARCTURUS AMBASSADOR

'The Curse of Peladon' (1972); 'The Monster of Peladon' (1974)

Location: Arcturus
Description: Unpleasant beast only able to sustain its life in a powerful support container. It is a merciless killer.
Activated by: Murphy Grumbar, voice by Terry Bale
Creator: Brian Hayles

ARIDIANS

'The Chase' (1965)

Location: Aridius
Description: Half-human and half-amphibious creatures who are locked in ceaseless conflict with their enemies, the Mire Beasts.
Activated by: Ian Thompson, Hywel Bennett, Al Raymond, Brian Proudfoot
Creator: Terry Nation

AUTONS

'Spearhead from Space' (1970); 'Terror of the Autons' (1971)

Location: Earth
Description: Deadly humanoid figures made of plastic with ray guns concealed in their wrists – the creation of the Nestene alien collective consciousness.
Activated by: Terry Walsh, Pat Gorman
Creator: Robert Holmes

AXOS

'The Claws of Axos' (1971)

Location: Time Vortex
Description: A dangerous parasite capable of turning itself into attractive, humanoid beings or alternatively a single, tentacled mass.

A parasitical
Axon.

*Two cybermen
on the planet Voga.*

Activated by: Bernard Holley, Roger
Minnis, Geoff Righty, Steve King, David
Aldridge, Patricia Gordino, John Hicks,
Debbie Lee London
Creators: Bob Baker & Dave Martin
Monsters: Marc Boyle, Jack Cooper, Peter
Holmes, Clinton Morris, Steve Smart,
Douglas Roe, Eden Fox, Stuart Myers

BORAD

'Timelash' (1985)

Location: Karfel
Description: Cruel and sadistic ruler of
the planet who imposes his will through
fear of the dreaded Timelash.
Activated by: Robert Ashby
Creator: Glen McCoy

CYBERMEN

'The Tenth Planet' (1966); 'The Moonbase' (1967); 'The Tomb of the Cybermen' (1967); 'The Wheel in Space' (1968); 'Invasion' (1968); 'Revenge of the Cybermen' (1975); 'Earthshock' (1982); 'The Five Doctors' (1983); 'Attack of the Cybermen' (1984)

Location: Originally from Mondas; their tombs are located on Telos
Description: Hugely strong beings whose bodies were once humanoid but, through the replacement of the organs by plastic and metal duplicates, they have become virtual machines bent on the ruthless conquest of weaker species.
Activated by: Harry Brooks, Reg Whitehead, Greg Palmer, John Wills, Peter Greene, Keith Goodman, Michael Kilgarriff, Hans Le Vries, Tony Harwood, John Hogan, Richard Kerley, Ronald Lee, Charles Pemberton, Kenneth Seeger, Jerry Holmes, Gordon Stothard, Pat Gorman, Harry Brooks, Christopher Robbie, Melville Jones, David Banks, Mark Hardy, Jeff Wayne, Graham Cole, Peter Gales-Fleming, Steve Ismay, Norman Bradley, Michael Gordon-Brane, William Kenton, Brian Orrell, John Ainley
Voices by: Peter Hawkins, Roy Skelton
Created by: Gerry Davis and Kit Pedler

DAEMONS

'The Daemons' (1971)

Location: Damos
Description: Nightmare creatures from the far reaches of the galaxy who have awesome powers and an uncanny resemblance to the old Earth concept of the Devil! The Doctor encountered Azal, the last of that race on Earth.
Activated by: Stephen Thorne
Created by: Guy Leopold [Barry Letts]

DALEKS

'The Daleks' (1963/4); 'The Dalek Invasion of Earth' (1964); 'The Chase' (1965); 'Mission to the Unknown' (1965); 'The Daleks' Master Plan' (1965/6); 'Power of the Daleks' (1966); 'Evil of the Daleks' (1967); 'Day of the Daleks' (1972); 'Frontier in Space' (1973); 'Planet of the Daleks' (1973); 'Death to the Daleks'

The second Doctor with a hostile Dalek and friendly Quark.

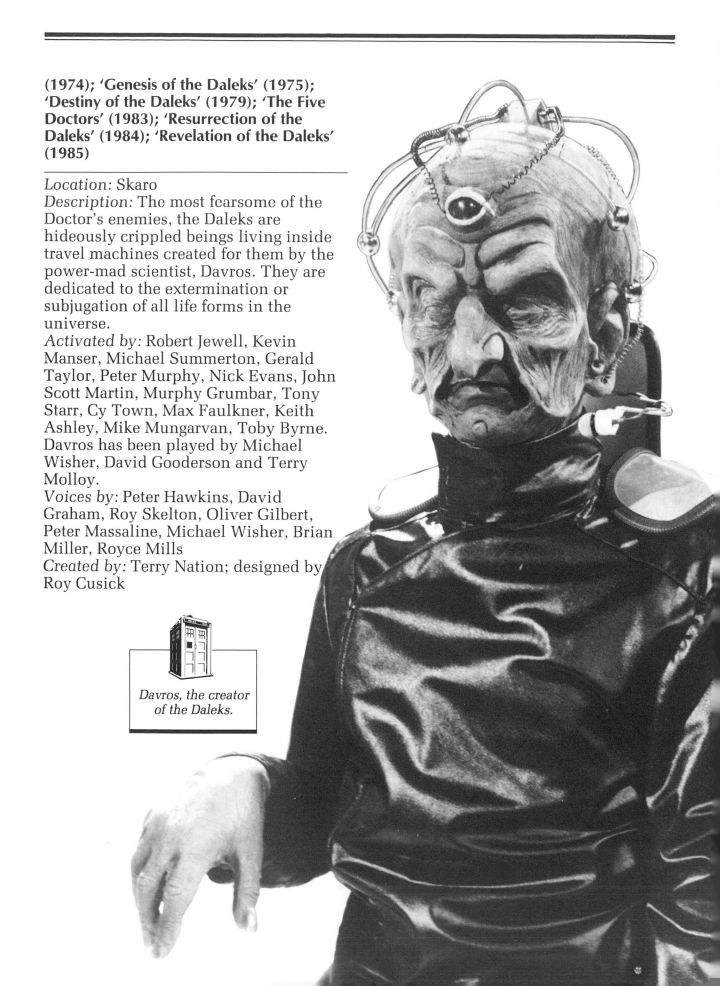

(1974); 'Genesis of the Daleks' (1975); 'Destiny of the Daleks' (1979); 'The Five Doctors' (1983); 'Resurrection of the Daleks' (1984); 'Revelation of the Daleks' (1985)

Location: Skaro

Description: The most fearsome of the Doctor's enemies, the Daleks are hideously crippled beings living inside travel machines created for them by the power-mad scientist, Davros. They are dedicated to the extermination or subjugation of all life forms in the universe.

Activated by: Robert Jewell, Kevin Manser, Michael Summerton, Gerald Taylor, Peter Murphy, Nick Evans, John Scott Martin, Murphy Grumbar, Tony Starr, Cy Town, Max Faulkner, Keith Ashley, Mike Mungarvan, Toby Byrne. Davros has been played by Michael Wisher, David Gooderson and Terry Molloy.

Voices by: Peter Hawkins, David Graham, Roy Skelton, Oliver Gilbert, Peter Massaline, Michael Wisher, Brian Miller, Royce Mills

Created by: Terry Nation; designed by Roy Cusick

Davros, the creator of the Daleks.

DRACONIANS

'Frontier in Space' (1973)

Location: Draconia and its empire
Description: Despite their fearsome dragon-like appearance, these creatures are highly intelligent. They were, however, almost manipulated into a war with Earth by the Master and the Daleks.
Activated by: Roy Pattison, Peter Birrel, Lawrence Davidson, Bill Wilde, and Ian Frost
Created by: Malcolm Hulke

DRASHIGS

'Carnival of Monsters' (1973)

Location: A satellite of Grundle; also found in Vorg's Scope on Inter Minor
Description: Enormous and ugly underwater monsters who live primarily in swamp-land and are particularly vicious when disturbed.
Created by: Robert Holmes

ELDRAD

'The Hand of Fear' (1975)

Location: Kastria
Description: Eldrad was a Kastrian criminal who was completely destroyed except for his hand which remained fossilised until discovered by Sarah Jane Smith. He used the power of a nuclear reactor to regenerate.
Activated by: Stephen Thorne, Judith Paris
Created by: Bob Baker and Dave Martin

ERATO

'The Creature from the Pit' (1979)

Location: Tythonus
Description: Terrifying in appearance, Erato was actually an ambassador from the metal-rich planet of Tythonus who was imprisoned on Chloris until rescued by the fourth Doctor.
Created by: David Fisher

FENDAHL

'Image of the Fendahl' (1977)

Location: Fifth Planet of the Solar System
Description: A mysterious entity which lay dormant in a twelve-million-year-old skull until it fed on human life and materialised on Earth through the body of a medium. Its home planet was put into a time loop by the Time Lords.
Activated by: Wanda Ventham
Created by: Chris Boucher

FOAMASI

'The Leisure Hive' (1980)

Location: Argolis
Description: A reptilian race engaged in constant warfare with the Argolin and capable of the most cunning deception and cruelty.
Activated by: Andrew Lane, David Bulbech, David Korff, James Muir
Created by: David Fisher

THE GARM

'Terminus' (1983)

The reptilian
Foamasi.

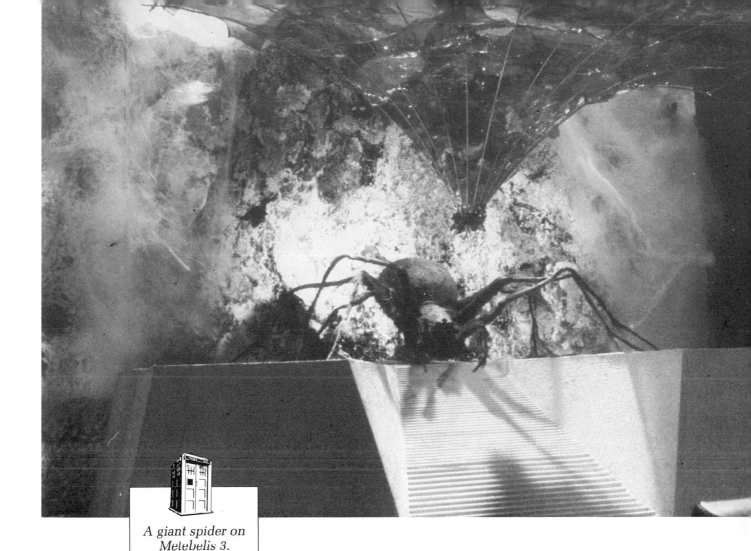

A giant spider on Metebelis 3.

Location: Terminus
Description: A mysterious and essentially benevolent being who attempted to cure the afflicted humans on Terminus.
Activated by: R.J. Bell
Created by: Steve Gallagher

GIANT MAGGOTS

'The Green Death' (1973)

Location: Wales (Earth)
Description: The Giant Maggots were the product of the waste disposed by Global Chemicals into an old disused mine. The third Doctor managed to destroy them, but not before one of them metamorphosed into a deadly flying insect.
Created by: Robert Sloman

GIANT SPIDERS

'Planet of the Spiders' (1974)

Location: Metebelis 3
Description: Enormous spiders led by the Great One which rule the planet Metebelis 3 using human beings as slaves and had plans to invade the Earth until the third Doctor put an end to their schemes, losing his third 'life' in the process.
Spider Voices by: Ysanne Churchman, Kismet Delgado, Maureen Morris
Created by: Robert Sloman

ICE WARRIORS

'The Ice Warriors' (1967); 'The Seeds of Death' (1969); 'The Curse of Peladon' (1972); 'The Monster of Peladon' (1974)

Location: Mars
Description: Lumbering scaly green creatures whose only weakness is their aversion to heat. They have tough, armoured skin and are equipped with sonic guns.
Activated by: Bernard Bresslaw, Roger Jones, Sonny Caldinez, Tony Harwood, Michael Attwell, Alan Bennion and Steve Peters, David Cleeve, Terence Denville, Alan Lenoir, Kevin Moran, Graham Leaman
Created by: Brian Hayles

JOCONDANS

'The Twin Dilemma' (1985)

Location: Joconda
Description: A group of unscrupulous and bold alien kidnappers whose planet has been over-run by the Gastropods of the mutated and slug-like Mestor.
Activated by: Mark Bassenger, Graham Cole, Leslie Conrad, Mike Mungarvan, David Radsley, Robert Smythe, John Wilson, Barry Stanton, Oliver Smith, Seymour Green, Roger Nott
Created by: Anthony Steven (1985)

KRAALS

'The Android Invasion' (1975)

Location: Osidon
Description: An evil and war-like alien race who were planning an invasion of the Earth using the ingenious Androids created by their chief scientist, Styggron.
Activated by: Martin Friend, Roy Skelton
Created by: Terry Nation

KROLL

'The Power of Kroll' (1979)

Location: Delta Magna's third moon
Description: Worshipped as a god by the Swampies of the planet, Kroll was actually a small, squid-like creature which grew to an enormous size through swallowing the fifth segment of the Key to Time.
Created by: Robert Holmes

KRONOS

'The Time Monster' (1972)

Location: Outside the bounds of time and space
Description: An awesome being that lives by feeding on time and was controlled by the Crystal of Konos which was much sought after by the Master.
Activated by: Ingrid Bower, Marc Boyle
Created by: Robert Sloman

KROTONS

'The Krotons' (1968)

Location: Planet of the Gonds
Description: Crystalline beings who look uncannily like robots, the Krotons live on the intelligence of the inhabitants of the planet and lie in wait to be reanimated.
Activated by: Robert La Bassiere and Miles Northover, Robert Grant
Voices by: Roy Skelton and Patrick Tull
Created by: Robert Holmes (1968)

KRYNOIDS

'The Seeds of Doom' (1976)

Location: The Antarctic (Earth)
Description: Pod-like plant life which travelled through space in pairs to bury themselves in the Antarctic wastes, grow rapidly in size and begin a campaign

Two Ice Warriors on Peladon.

A dangerous Kroton hunting the Doctor.

against humanity utilising all plant life as their allies.
Activated by: John Gleeson, Keith Ashley, Ronald Gough
Voice: Mark Jones
Created by: Robert Banks Stewart

The ungainly but deadly Krynoid.

LOCH NESS MONSTER

'Terror of the Zygons' (1975)

Location: Scotland
Description: Initially believed to be the famous Scottish lake monster, the beast is actually a half-animal, half-machine creature, the Skarasen, created by alien Zygons who had crashlanded on the bottom of Loch Ness.
Created by: Robert Banks Stewart

MACRA

'The Macra Terror' (1967)

Location: Earth colony in space
Description: Large and intimidating crab-like creatures who controlled an Earth colony where the luckless inhabitants were forced to quarry the poisonous gas the Macra needed to survive.
Activated by: Robert Jewell
Created by: Ian Stuart Black

One of the aquatic Marshmen.

THE MALUS

'The Awakening' (1984)

Location: Earth
Description: A fearsome-looking alien entity which draws on the psychic energy of human beings to reactivate itself after lying dormant for centuries.
Created by: Eric Pringle (1984)

MANDRELS

'Nightmare of Eden' (1979)

Location: Eden
Description: Monsters that flourish in mud on their native planet, but were released into the space ship *Empress* from a naturalist's samples following an accident. They are also the source of the drug vraxoin.
Activated by: Robert Goodman, David Korff, James Muir, Jan Murzynowski, Derek Suthern
Created by: Bob Baker (1979)

MARA

'Kinda' (1982); 'Snakedance' (1983)

Location: Manussa, Deva Loka
Description: Evil, serpentine-like creature able to control thoughts and use the minds of human beings to pass into the real world.
Created by: Christopher Bailey

MARSHMEN

'Full Circle' (1980)

Location: Alzarius (E-Space)
Description: An alien aquatic race who appear from the swampland of their planet whenever the mysterious period known as Mistfall occurs.
Activated by: Norman Bacon, Barney Lawrence, Stephen Calcutt, Graham Cole, Keith Guest, James Jackson, Steve Kelly, Stephen Watson
Created by: Andrew Smith

The spikey Meglos creature, in the guise of the fourth Doctor.

One of the gentle Menoptera under attack.

MEGLOS

'Meglos' (1980)

Location: Zolfa-Thura
Description: A cactus-like creature who formed an uneasy alliance with the Gaztak space raiders to steal Tigella's vital source of supply, the Dodecahedron.
Activated by: Tom Baker, Christopher Owen
Created by: John Flanagan and Andrew McCulloch

MENOPTERA

'The Web Planet' (1965)

Location: Vortis
Description: Butterfly-like creatures who had been driven from their home planet by the Zarbi and were helped in their objective to return by the first Doctor.
Activated by: Roslyn de Winter, Arne Gordon, Arthur Blake, Jolyon Booth, Jocelyn Birdsall, Martin Jarvis, Ian Thompson, Barbara Joss, Ken McGarvie.
Created by: Bill Strutton

MESTOR

'The Twin Dilemma' (1984)

Location: Jaconda
Description: A mutated, slug-like Gastropod with tremendously powerful telepathic and telekinetic abilities who led an army of insatiable monsters devastating whichever worlds they landed upon.
Activated by: Edwin Richfield
Created by: Anthony Steven

MONOIDS

'The Ark' (1966)

Location: Ark
Description: The former slaves of the human race escaping from an Earth threatened with destruction, who were turned into the masters as a result of contact with the common cold!
Activated by: Edmund Coulter, Frank George, Ralph Corrigan and John Caser, Bernard Barnsley, Eric Blackburn, Denis Marlow, Bill Richards, Chris Webb
Created by: Paul Erickson
Voices: John Halstead, Roy Skelton

MORLOX

'Timelash' (1985)

Location: Karfel
Description: Savage creatures who live in caves on the outskirts of the kingdom ruled over by the ruthless dictator, the Borad, and his terrible weapon of fear, the Timelash.
Created by: Glen McCoy

MUTANTS

'The Mutants' (1972)

Location: Solos
Description: Ugly but oppressed natives of the planet, the Mutants – sometimes known as 'Muts' – were the prey of the sadistic Marshall of Solos who was reluctant to give up the running of the Earth colony.
Activated by: John Scott Martin, Laurie Goode, Bill Gosling, Nick Thompson Hill, Mike Hungarvan, Richy Newby,

The powerful sea creature, the Myrka.

who bear a striking resemblance to the Minotaur of ancient Greek legend, and who swarm through the galaxy leaving devasted planets in their wake.
Activated by: Robin Sherringham, Bob Appleby, Trevor St. John Hacker
Created by: Anthony Read
Voices: Clifford Norgate

OGRI

'The Stones of Blood' (1978)

Location: Ogros
Description: Vicious stone creatures that feed on human blood and can pose as stone statues. Two of them were partners-in-crime with Vivien Fay.
Created by: David Fisher

OGRONS

'Day of the Daleks' (1972); 'Frontier in Space' (1973)

Location: Unnamed Planet
Description: Very primitive and savage creatures who originated on a far-flung planet. They are ape-like in appearance and have twice served the Daleks.
Activated by: Stephen Thorne, Michael Kilgarriff and Rick Lester
Created by: Louis Marks

PRIMORDS

'Inferno' (1970)

Location: Earth
Description: Terrifying ape-like creatures who were created by human contact with Stahlman's Gas, and with their capability for violence threatened the whole of humanity.
Activated by: Dave Carter, Pat Gormon,

Eddie Sommer, Mike Torres
Created by: Bob Baker and Dave Martin

THE MYRKA

'Warriors of the Deep' (1984)

Location: Earth
Description: A savagely powerful deep sea creature which was used by the Sea Devils and the Silurians when they attempted to take control of an underwater base in their scheme to destroy all mankind in the year 2084
Activated by: John Asquith, William Perrie
Created by: Johnny Byrne

NIMON

'The Horns of Nimon' (1979/80)

Location: Skonnos
Description: Cunning and evil aliens

Philip Ryan, Peter Thompson and Walter
Henry
Created by: Don Houghton

ROBOMEN

'The Dalek Invasion of Earth' (1964)

Location: Earth
Description: Former human beings
turned into walking zombies by the
Daleks – who used them as messengers of
death and destruction.
Activated by: Peter Badger, Adrian
Drotsky, Martyn Huntley, Bill Moss, Reg
Tyler
Created by: Terry Nation

RUTANS

'Horror of Fang Rock' (1977)

Location: Earth
Description: The Rutans are a powerful
alien entity usually seen as a blob-like
amphibious species, but able to

transform themselves into human shape
– as one did when taking over a human
during their ongoing war with the
Sontarians.
Activated by: Colin Douglas
Created by: Robert Holmes (in 'The Time
Warrior' 1973)

SEA DEVILS

'The Sea Devils' (1972); 'Warriors of the Deep' (1984)

Location: Earth
Description: Extremely clever
underwater creatures looking rather like
human lizards who have plans to revive
colonies of their kind all over the world.
They are close cousins of the Silvrians.
Activated by: Pat Gorman, Peter
Forbes-Robertson, Marc Boyle, Peter
Brace, Alan Chuntz, Jack Cooper, Stuart
Fell, Bill Horrigan, Mike Horsburgh,
Steve Ismay, Brian Nolan, Frank Seton,
Mike Stevens, Terry Walsh, Derek Ware,
Geoffrey Witberich
Created by: Malcolm Hulke

Two Robomen
pursuing the film
Doctor, Peter
Cushing, and his
companion, Bernard
Cribbins, through a
devastated London.

SENSORITES

'The Sensorites' (1964)

Location: The Sense-Sphere
Description: A remarkable race of telepathic aliens who all look identical with huge, bald heads and bewhiskered chins. They began to fear for their world when Earthmen came to their planet and when a series of mysterious deaths swept the Sensorite Nation.
Activated by: Ken Tyllsen, Joe Greig, Peter Glaze and Arthur Newall, Gerry Martin, Anthony Rogers
Created by: Peter R. Newman

SIL

'Vengeance On Varos' (1985); 'Mindwarp' (1986)

Location: Thoros Beta
Description: A repulsive slug-like creature whose nature is to cheat and lie and who has twice crossed paths with the sixth Doctor.
Activated by: Nabil Shaban
Created by: Philip Martin

SILURIANS

'Doctor Who and the Silurians' (1970); 'Warriors of the Deep' (1984)

Location: Earth
Description: The original inhabitants of the Earth, the Silurians are highly intelligent, man-like reptiles who possess a third eye through which they can focus powerful destructive forces. The Sea Devils are their kin.
Activated by: Pat Gorman, Dave Carter, Nigel John, Paul Barton, Simon Cain, John Churchill and Dave Carter

Voices by: Peter Halliday
Created by: Malcolm Hulke

SONTARANS

'The Time Warrior' (1974); 'The Sontaran Experiment' (1975); 'The Invasion of Time' (1978); 'The Two Doctors' (1985)

Location: Far Space
Description: A race dedicated to war, in particular against their ancient enemies, the Rutans. The Sontarans are extremely strong, live on raw energy, and can only be killed by piercing the probic vent behind their necks.
Activated by: Kevin Lindsay, Stuart Fell, Derek Deadman, Clinton Greyn, Jim Raynham
Created by: Robert Holmes

SUTEKH

'Pyramids of Mars' (1975)

Location: Mars
Description: Mysterious shrouded figure who is the last of the Osiran race and hell-bent on destroying all life in the universe.
Activated by: Gabriel Woolf
Created by: Stephen Harris

TERILEPTILS

'The Visitation' (1982)

Location: Far Space
Description: The four menacing Terileptils who reached Earth in a space capsule were actually escaped criminals from Raaga, and though one died, the other three were soon involved in a plot to develop a bacillus to destroy the Human race.
Activated by: Chris Bradshaw, Michael

Three dangerous Tractators.

Leader, Michael Melia, David Summer
Created by: Eric Saward

THARILS

'Warriors' Gate' (1981)

Location: E-Space
Description: An extraordinary race of time-sensitive aliens who were once slave owners and rulers of an enormous empire in space. Now they themselves are the quarry of unscrupulous men . . .
Activated by: David Weston, Jeremy Gittins, Carl Bohun, Laurie Goode, Michael Gordon-Browne, Andy Harb, James Muir, Joe Santo
Created by: Steve Gallagher

TRACTATORS

'Frantios' (1984)

Location: Frontios
Description: Repulsive, slug-like creatures who lurk in caves creating enormously powerful gravitational fields to catch the unwary and further the evil designs of the mutated Gravis.
Activated by: William Bowen, George Campbell, Hedi Khursandi, Michael Malcolm, Stephen Speed
Created by: Christopher H. Bidmead

URBANKANS

'Four to Doomsday' (1982)

Location: Urbanka
Description: A highly sophisticated group of reptile-like aliens set to steal from Earth the most precious of its mineral resources – so that the ruler, Monarch, can achieve his ultimate ambition of journeying back in time to the creation of the Universe.

The Monarch of the Urbankan race.

Activated by: Stratford Johns, Annie Lambert, Paul Shelley
Created by: Terence Dudley

USURIANS

'The Sunmakers' (1977)

Location: Pluto
Description: Grasping and unfeeling race of aliens who control the colony of human beings working on this artificially-warmed planet by imposing exhorbitant taxes. But resistance to their injustice is engineered through a brilliant fraud.
Activated by: Henry Woolf
Created by: Robert Holmes

JAGAROTH SPACE CRUISER

The explosion of the Jagaroth space cruiser was responsible for the beginning of life on Earth, even though Scaroth (Julian Glover) tried to prevent it.

NIMON TRAVEL CAPSULE

The Nimon were a race of intergalactic parasites who travelled through Black Holes in their travel capsules.

EARTH SHUTTLECRAFT

An Earth shuttlecraft landing at the base on Titan, one of the moons of Saturn, in 'The Invisible Enemy'.

ETERNAL SAILING SHIP

The fifth Dotor on one of the strangest journeys of his many lives - on the bridge of the Eternals' sailing ship!

IMC ROBOT

The mining corporation IMC used this robot to terrorise Earth colonists on Exarius in the year 2471.

TERILEPTIL ADROID

The Terileptil android was just one of the many dangers Nyssa and her friends had to face on Earth in 1666.

MOVELLANS

Sworn enemies of the
Daleks, the beautiful
Movellans were, in fact,
merciless robots.

ROBOTS OF DEATH

One of the terrifying
Voc robots whom the
fourth Doctor and Leela
encountered on board
the Sandminer.

VAMPIRES

'State of Decay' (1980)

Location: Medieval Planet in E-Space
Description: The three servants of the Great Vampire – the last of a powerful race of blood-sucking creatures from the far reaches of space – perpetrated his evil ways on a backward planet and prepared for the day when he will rise again from his tomb.
Activated by: William Lindsay, Rachel Davies and Emrys James
Created by: Terrance Dicks

VARDANS

'The Invasion of Time' (1978)

Location: Far Space
Description: Extraordinarily complex and clever alien race who can travel along any wavelength, and were used by the Sontarans in an attempt to conquer Gallifrey.
Activated by: Stan McGowan, Tom Kelly
Created by: David Agnew

VERVOIDS

'Terror of the Vervoids' (1986)

Location: Space liner *Hyperion III*
Description: Terrifying, vegetable-like creatures who hatch from pods and have an innate instinct to eliminate the human race which made them a dreadful threat to all life on board the space liner, *Hyperion III*.
Activated by: Paul Hillier, Jerry Manley, Bill Perrie, Gess Whitfield, Peppi Borza, Bob Appleby
Created by: Pip and Jane Baker

VIRUS NUCLEUS

'The Invisible Enemy' (1977)

Location: Space
Description: A cosmic virus which attacks and enters any life forms travelling in space, sometimes without them being aware of its presence. It can also take on a life form of its own and possesses awesome power.
Activated by: John Scott Martin
Voice by: John Leeson
Created by: Bob Baker and Dave Martin

VOORD

'The Keys of Marinus' (1964)

Location: Marinus
Description: Dangerous and clever aliens who invaded Marinus under their leader Yartek to take possession of this vulnerable island kingdom.
Activated by: Stephen Dartnell, Martin Cort, Peter Stenson and Gordon Wales
Created by: Terry Nation

WIRRN

'The Ark in Space' (1975)

Location: Andromeda
Description: The Wirrn are large, wasp-like creatures which have been exiled from their own planet and sought to establish themselves on an Earth space station. They utilise the bodies of humans to incubate their eggs.
Activated by: Stuart Fell, Nick Hobbs
Created by: Robert Holmes

ZARBI

'The Web Planet' (1965)

Location: Vortis
Description: Towering, ant-like creatures under the control of the Animus which had taken possession of the planet Vortis from the Menoptera. The first Doctor proved more than a match for the Zarbi and destroyed their evil master.
Activated by: Robert Jewell, Jack Pitt, Gerald Taylor, Hugh Lund, John Scott Martin and Kevin Manser
Created by: Bill Strutton

Two Zarbi harrass the first Doctor.

ZYGONS

'Terror of the Zygons' (1975)

Location: Earth

Description: Following the destruction of their home planet, the Zygons took up residence at the bottom of Loch Ness in Scotland. They are able to change shape at will and have plans to take over the world, utilising what is believed to be the Loch Ness Monster but is actually a half-animal, half-machine creature called a Skarasen.

Activated by: John Woodnutt, Keith Ashley and Ronald Gough

Created by: Robert Banks Stewart

A Zygon inflicting pain on the fourth Doctor.

Creating alien worlds - a Doctor Who film crew on location.

6
A TOURIST'S GUIDE TO ALIEN WORLDS

The Doctor has visited a great many planets in a large number of different galaxies during his travels. Some of these he has merely mentioned in passing, while in the cases of others we have been eye-witnesses to the dramatic adventures in which he has become involved as a visitor. In the pages which follow the reader will find a summary of all these alien worlds the Time Lord from Gallifrey has visited, in addition to information on their terrain, environment and the temperament of their inhabitants! However, care is strongly advised in visiting almost all of them. . .

A Tourist's Guide To

ALZARIUS

Location: **Universe of E-Space**

Alzarius regularly presents a view of shifting grey mists to space. Beneath this curtain lies a world of dense forests and marshland. Every fifty years, a season of mists known as Mistfall occurs which causes the inhabitants of the planet, the scaley Marshmen, to appear. The Marshmen are, in fact, a part of the ecology of this planet, where venomous spiders are hatched from melon-like river-fruits, these spiders somehow evolved into the Marshmen, and the Marshmen into the humanoid occupants of a crashed spacecraft, the Starliner.

The fourth Doctor was unintentionally plunged into Alzarius during one Mistfall in the story 'Full Circle' written by Andrew Smith.

ANDROZANI MAJOR AND MINOR

Location: **The Sirius System**

Two of the five planets which make up the Sirius system. The larger, Androzani Major, is a heavily populated and industrialised world run by the powerful

Marshmen emerging from the mist-shrouded swamps of Alzarius.

Alien Worlds

Federation, who jealously covet the small planet, Androzani Minor, as the two orbit one another in space. The reason for this interest is the drug Spectrox the raw material of which is only found on the bleak little planet beneath its surface of rocky deserts and constantly erupting mud-bursts. Spectrox is said to be the most valuable substance in the universe – in its raw state a deadly poison; but when processed, the elixir of life . . .

The fifth Doctor was catapulted into a desperate struggle for possession of this valuable commodity in 'The Caves of Androzani' written by Robert Holmes.

ARGOLIS

Appropriately known as 'the Leisure Planet' and a magnet drawing tourists from all over the Galaxy, Argolis has been described as a miracle of beauty, lit by a sea of light and colour unlike anything else to be found in space or time. This beauty had, though, been artificially created as a result of warfare between the Argolin and an equally war-like race, the reptilian Foamasi. The war had caused the Foamasi planet to be reduced to a burned husk, and Argolis into a dust-shrouded world, through which the ultra-violet light of its four suns pierced to turn the skies into something resembling a million rainbows. The only tragedy of this beauty is that the atmosphere is wholly poisonous to all but the Foamasi and life forms must never venture beyond the glass enclosures onto the sands of Argolis . . .

Into this unique environment came the fourth Doctor to stop the destructive plans of a group of Foamasi saboteurs in 'The Leisure Hive' by David Fisher.

ARIDIUS

Location: The Cosmos

A world as inhospitable and as barren as its name suggests although it does boast two life forms – the formerly aquatic Aridians and their hideous enemies the Mire Beasts. Consisting of huge tracks of desert, Aridius provided a brief respite for the first Doctor and his companions when they landed there.

The brief visit to Aridius was chronicled in 'The Chase' written by Terry Nation.

ATRIOS

Location: Edge of the helical galaxy

One of twin planets, the other being Zeos. The two planets are locked in a brutal war of attrition, and all life on Atrios is lived underground. This is a result of the bombardment from Zeos which has created such high radiation levels on the surface that all existence there is impossible. Six dynasties of the Royal House of Atrios governed the planet, until the intervention of the evil Shadow – a servant of the Black Guardian. He lived on an artificial planet which was located midway between Atrios and Zeos.

Into this drama stepped the fourth Doctor in his search for the sixth and final segment of the Key to Time in the story of 'The Armageddon Factor' by Bob Baker and Dave Martin.

AXOS

Location: locked in a time loop

The beautiful golden humanoids known as the Axons seem among the most curious inhabitants of the universe. For the spaceship in which they travel is actually their home planet and they are forever searching for the raw energy on which it depends to function. Referred to as 'the scavengers of space', they have developed a unique technology which has enabled them to 'grow' rather than build their space home which somewhat resembles the interior of a human heart! The source of this technology is the substance called Axonite which can absorb, convert, transmit, and programme all other forms of energy in existence.

The third Doctor became involved with the Axons and their 'home' when they visited Earth in the story of 'The Claws of Axos' by Bob Baker and Dave Martin.

The focus of pleasure, 'The Leisure Hive', on Argolis.

BI-AL FOUNDATION

Location: Asteroid Belt near Titan

A centre for Alien Biomorphology, the Bi-Al Foundation is one of the largest and most impressive research hospitals in the galaxy. Established by a number of Earth business conglomerates in the forty-ninth century, it occupies almost the entire centre of a huge, hollowed-out asteroid, designated K4067. The Foundation's position in the asteroid belt is ideal for travellers on their way to the outer planets who may have contacted one of the myriad illnesses or injuries which can be suffered in space. It presents a welcoming sight to space with its thousands of gleaming windows and the huge, glowing red cross symbol.

It was to this haven for all travellers that the fourth Doctor came in the story of 'The Invisible Enemy' by Bob Baker and Dave Martin, seeking help to combat a virus that had struck an Earth shuttlecraft and also the Time Lord himself. Here he met Professor Marius and his dog-shaped computer, K9, who, of course, became the Doctor's companion for quite some time thereafter.

BLACK HOLES

A Black Hole is a phenomenon of space which comes into existence as the result of the death and collapse of a giant star – one that has a mass three or more times that of our Sun. They have featured quite extensively in the Doctor's history, for it was by turning a star into a Black Hole that the Time Lords Rassilon and Omega were able to capture the power necessary to develop Time Travel and create the

first TARDIS – as was explained in 'The Three Doctors' by Bob Baker and Dave Martin.

These worlds of anti-matter can also provide faster-than-light travel by allowing a traveller to pass through the centre and emerge without any loss of time somewhere else in the galaxy, as did the conquest-bent aliens the Nimon, in the fourth Doctor's adventure, 'The Horns of Nimon'.

CALUFRAX

The beautiful but ill-fated planet that became the prey of the predatory time-hopping planet, Zanak, which can cruise the galaxies attaching itself to vulnerable worlds, sucking out their energy and life. It is, in fact, the second segment of the Key to Time which the fourth Doctor pursued across the vast reaches of space – a fact he did not discover until Calufrax had been reduced to a condensed ball of matter the size of an Earth football!

Calufrax was one of the ingenious creations which Douglas Adams provided for Doctor Who. It was featured in the story 'The Pirate Planet'.

CASTROVALVA

An orderly world of cultured people, known as the Castrovalvans, this planet's history is to be found in the series of volumes called *A Condensed Chronicle of Castrovalva*. It is a sunny planet, with its culture reflected in the neat buildings which are constructed in a variety of styles but somehow reminiscent of the Roman civilisation at its highest point. They are described evocatively as the 'Dwellings of Simplicity'.

The fourth Doctor stunned by Mentiads on beautiful Calufrax.

The ornate main hall of the castle on Castrovalva.

It was to this world that the newly regenerated fifth Doctor came to rest and recover from his traumatic experience in the story of 'Castrovalva' by Christopher H. Bidmead – but instead found himself pitched at once into another struggle with the Master! Castrovalva was created by the Master from the Logopolitan Block Transfer Computations and he became trapped in it when it folded in on itself.

CHLORIS

An immensely fertile planet, Chloris suffers from the fact that it is almost totally devoid of ore minerals as the many worked-out mine shafts bear witness. But in circling its sun every 427 Earth days, it has built up a jungle-like terrain rich in chlorophyll as well as

One of the jungle-like forests on Chloris.

generating the carniverous Wolf Weeds. Chloris' desparate need for metal was exploited by the ruthless ruler, Lady Adrasta, who had a monopoly of what supplies of this mineral existed on the planet. She was not pleased when an alien ambassador, Erato, from the metal-rich world of Tythonos, arrived to barter for supplies of much-needed chlorophyll.

The fourth Doctor found himself thrown into alliance with the ambassador in the story of 'The Creature From The Pit' by David Fisher – and was eventually able to satisfy the needs of both planets after the overthrow of Lady Adrasta.

DELTA MAGNA

Delta Magna is a heavily industrialised planet rather like Earth in appearance and first colonised by people from that over-crowded world. In time it, too, became overpopulated and a refinery was set up on the third of its desolate, watery moons, to process methane for the mother world. The moon is a place of overcast grey skies, almost perpetual drizzle, and water everywhere. Its native inhabitants, known colourfully as Swampies, feel deprived and resentful at the presence of the colonists.

The fourth Doctor found himself in this damp and unpleasant world during his search for the fifth segment of the Key to Time in Robert Holmes' story, 'The Power of Kroll', in which the refinery's machinery awakened the ancient god Kroll to wreak vengeance on the intruders.

DESPERUS

Desperus is the planet where convicted murderers from Earth are sent in the year AD 4000, as was explained in the mammoth twelve-part adventure 'The Daleks' Master Plan' written by Terry Nation. Not surprisingly, this world is as dreary and as cheerless as its name suggests, and is even known as the Devil's Planet.

The unpleasant climes of Desperus were just one of the locations through which the Doctor and his companions were relentlessly pursued by the Daleks as they tried to recapture their Time Destructor which the Time Lord had snatched to prevent their evil schemes.

DEVA LOKA

At first sight, Deva Loka looks like the human race's idea of Paradise. The planet has a mild climate, warm blue seas and its land masses are covered by sub-tropical jungles. It is a world of plenty, too, rich in trees bearing exotic and edible fruits – all of which have combined to make its people, the Kinda, a gentle, peace-loving race. But like all perfect and undisturbed localities, the arrival of an expeditionary force from Earth threatened the serenity of Deva Loka.

The fifth Doctor became the catalyst in the story of 'Kinda' by Christopher Bailey, which led him to a dramatic confrontation with the serpentine Mara.

DIDO

A barren, sandy world, devoid of any major geographical features or cities, and peopled by a race of friendly beings known as the Didoi. There are, though, creatures living in the deserts called sand monsters which look vicious but are, in reality, friendly. It is here that the first Doctor arrived to find a crashed spaceship from Earth – and there carried out an investigation into the mysterious deaths of all the crew members save a man named Bennett and a girl, Vicki.

The story of 'The Rescue' on Dido by David Whitaker resulted in the unmasking of Bennett as the murderer of the crew, and a new companion for the Doctor in the form of Vicki.

DOOMED PLANET

Location: Galaxy Four

An unnamed and deserted planet with a black surface and curious plant life, it was just two days away from exploding in the story of 'Galaxy Four' by William Emms. It was also the setting for the struggle between the race of female Drahvins and the Rills, both of whom had become stranded on the inhospitable world. The Drahvins are a race of tough and beautiful humanoid women, while the Rills are hideous alien creatures able to breathe only an atmosphere consisting of ammonia.

The first Doctor discovers that — contrary to appearances — it is the Drahvins who are the aggressors, coming from a society where women dominate and only a select number of men are allowed to survive for reproduction purposes. He therefore helps the wise and peace-loving Rills to escape by using power from his TARDIS.

DULKIS

Location: a remote spiral galaxy

A pale, world covered with immense dusty plateaux and occasional huge grey stretches of ocean. The land masses are

A glimpse of the paradise planet of Deva Loka.

broken by ridges of sandstone cliffs, and journeys have to be undertaken over a difficult terrain consisting of sand and rock splinters. The former site of an atomic testing station known as the 'Island of Death' has become a symbol to the people of the planet about the dangers of warfare, and so when the second Doctor arrives in the TARDIS he does not expect to be thrown into a situation where an alien race is threatening to destroy both the Dulcians and their world.

In the story of 'The Dominators' by Norman Ashby, the Doctor needs to call on all his ingenuity and cunning to defeat the Dominators and their robot slaves, the Quarks, who want to turn Dulkis into a radioactive mass to fuel their space fleet.

EARTH

Location: the Solar System

This blue and green world, the third planet outward from the Sun and possessing its own moon, has featured in a great many of the Doctor's adventures since we first saw him on Earth in 1963 in 'An Unearthly Child'. The planet is an oblate spheroid and circles the Sun at a distance of 93 million miles once every 365 days. It has 57.5 million square miles of land mass while the seas cover over 70 per cent of the rest of the surface. Theories as to the Earth's creation abound: one suggests it was formed by a swarm of meteorities which arose when matter, drawn from the Sun by the attraction of a passing star, condensed. A date for its formation has been advanced as 2,800 million years ago.

In the history of *Doctor Who*, it has

been suggested in 'City of Death' by David Agnew that the explosion of Scaroth's spaceship on Earth about 400 million BC was responsible for the creation of life. Other stories have revealed that the Silurians and Sea Devils were occupying the planet 200 millions years ago at the same time as dinosaurs roamed the various continents. The first Doctor was, of course, credited with giving fire to the cavemen about the year 500,000 BC; and it was the third Doctor who was exiled to Earth by the Time Lords for infringement of their laws.

The fifth Doctor saw Earth in several of its ages in the story 'Earthshock'.

The 'root' defence of the city on Exxilon.

EXARIUS

Exarius was the rather bleak planet which the third Doctor visited on a mission for the Time Lords, although he was not aware of their 'interference'. Rather Earth-like in appearance (although it has two moons), it was immediately declared by the Doctor's companion, Jo, to be 'like somewhere in North Wales'. Despite the similarities, the stretches of rock and scrubland which make up much of Exarius did not seem ideal for the colonists from Earth who settled there in the year 2471. And when there were widespread crop failures and the colonists found themselves menaced by monster lizards, it was clearly a case for the Doctor.

A further element in the story of 'Colony in Space' by Malcolm Hulke was the intervention of the Master searching for the Doomsday Weapon which lay hidden on the planet.

EXXILON

A mysterious world of sand dunes and swirling green fogs, Exxilon was once home to one of the Seven Hundred Wonders of the Universe, the computerised living City which had

expelled its degenerate population who lived on its outskirts, worshipping the edifice as a god. The planet is also the one place in the Galaxy where the rare mineral parinnium can be found. Parinnium is the only known antidote to a plague which was ravaging the Galaxy.

There too the third Doctor fought and defeated his oldest enemies in 'Death to the Daleks' by Terry Nation.

The Gravis and a prisoner on the colony world of Frontios.

FRONTIOS

Location: Veruna System

A forlorn-looking planet for much of the time, Frontios nevertheless has the necessary atmosphere and environment to support a colony of Earth settlers who arrived there after the disintegration of their own world. The planet also has the attraction of a rich supply of precious minerals which may help the colonists secure their future. The fifth Doctor found himself hovering over the planet in 'Frontios' by Christopher H. Bidmead, but was anxious not to become involved in the settling-in process of these colonists.

However, when the hideous-looking

Tractators appeared and threatened to destroy the embryo colony, the youthful Doctor was inexorably drawn into the drama on Frontios.

GALLIFREY

Location: **The Constellation of Kasterborus**

The Doctor's home planet and the far-famed world of the Time Lords. Gallifrey, seen from space, is a sun-lit place covered by high mountain ranges and vast wastelands. It is on these deserts that the Time Lords have built their various domed cities to protect themselves from the deceptively harsh environment of the planet. Foremost among these is Capitol City, the seat of government and learning, where the Doctor was educated and where he has returned either voluntarily or under orders, ever since the place was first glimpsed in 'The War Games' by Malcolm Hulke and Terrance Dicks. It was not actually mentioned by name, though, until 'The Time Warrior' by Robert Holmes.

Beyond the confines of these sophisticated cities live the outcasts of the Gallifreyan race, a group of tough and resourceful men and women who have chosen to exist in the wilderness following their own code of life. The planet has, of course, nearly been destroyed by Omega (in 'The Three Doctors') and the Master (in 'The Deadly Assassin') while invasions by the Vardans and Sontarans (in 'The Invasion of Time') were successfully repelled by the fourth Doctor.

The Society of the Time Lords on Gallifrey is covered in more detail elsewhere in this book, but the other stories which are actually set on the planet include 'The Deadly Assassin', 'Arc of Infinity', 'The Five Doctors', 'War Games', 'Colony in Space' and 'The Three Doctors'.

GOND

The planet of the Gonds has two suns and evil-smelling vapours drift eternally across its bleak terrain. The City of the Gonds is one of the few places where life is concentrated, and all around this is an area known as the Wasteland which has all the appearance of a dead landscape except for the occasional stunted tree or withered plant. The oppressive silence which hangs over much of the planet is only broken by the occasional sighing of gentle winds.

The little world is peopled by the peace-loving Gonds who were held in slavery by the evil Krotons, robot-like creatures with a system based on tellurium who fed on their captives' intelligence. It took all the second Doctor's ingenuity to restore the Gonds' harmonious life-style in 'The Krotons' by Robert Holmes.

HYPERSPACE

Hyperspace is not a planet but a dimension into which the Doctor – and other travellers with powerful enough space craft – can project themselves to achieve very fast speeds. It is a dimension that the fourth Doctor was particularly given to using when escaping from persistent enemies or else while on the tail of some elusive criminal.

Example of his use of Hyperspace can be found in stories like two of the Key to Time segments, 'The Pirate Planet' by

Douglas Adams and 'The Stones of Blood' by David Fisher, and also in Bob Baker's 'Nightmare of Eden' when two space craft actually become fused when one of them was semi-materialised and about to jump into this further dimension.

INTER MINOR

Location: Acteon Galaxy

Described as an extremely xenophobic world, Inter Minor is also a busy, colourful and warm planet enjoying the rays of twin suns. A highly industrialised place, it boasts an excellent spaceport in Capital City, the seat of President Zarb's government. After years of self-imposed isolation following a Space Plague brought to the planet by a visitor, Inter Minor was at last receiving travellers and trade from other worlds when the third Doctor appeared, having expected to find himself on Metebelis 3! Here he comes into contact with the two strata of Minoran society, the Officials and the Functionaries, who are going through a difficult period of readjustment following the President's directive to achieve a more equal society.

JACONDA

For long years, Jaconda had been one of the beautiful planets that the time travellers might come across in the far reaches of the galaxy. With its well-wooded countryside, lush meadows and friendly, easy-going inhabitants, it was an oasis among many barren worlds. That was until the devastation which was wreaked upon it by giant gastropods who devoured every living thing and left the population close to starvation.

When the newly regenerated sixth Doctor, still recovering from the trauma of sacrificing his fifth body to save Peri's life, arrived on Jaconda he was stunned at what had happened and set out to discover the reason in 'The Twin Dilemma' by Anthony Steven. This story also brought him into contact with his old Time Lord mentor, Azmael, who paid for his involvement in solving the problems of the planet with his life.

KARFEL

Twin suns warm the sandy surface of this troubled planet where the heat as much as internal problems make life difficult for the population. To escape the harsh climate, most of the people live inside vast domes where the conditions are controlled and the environment enhanced by plant life and artificial lakes. Their actual homes are built in pyramid shapes, and one giant pyramid, the Central Citadel, houses the council of the Inner Sanctum and the regiment of Karfelon guardoliers. Beyond these domes live the outcasts of Karfel who are forced to seek refuge in underground caves and tunnels.

The planet was terrorised by its tyrannical overlord, the Borad, who had brought his world and its people to the brink of interplanetary war. Indeed, it took all the sixth Doctor's abrasive talent to resolve the problems of Karfel as related by Glen McCoy in 'Timelash' – a story that is also memorable because of the Doctor's remarkable meeting with one of the 'fathers' of Time Travel, Herbert George Wells, whose famous novel, it is claimed, was actually *inspired* by the Doctor rather than the other way around!

KARN

Location: **Constellation of Kasterborus**

A planet that has been likened to a Gothic nightmare on Earth, complete with inhospitable rocky deserts and towering dark mountains. It is a bleak and desolate place at the best of times and the few ruined buildings to be seen hint at a civilisation once powerful but now vanished. This stormy planet is a most suitable home for the witch-like Sisterhood, keepers of the Sacred Flame from which the immortality drug, the Elixir of Life, is prepared. This drug is shared by the Sisters with their neighbours the Time Lords of Gallifrey – one of whose number, the evil renegade Lord Morbius, once unsuccessfully attacked the planet.

It is Morbius's brain which has been kept alive and reinstated in a monstrous body by a mad surgeon, and which provides the central problem for the fourth Doctor during his adventure on Karn in 'The Brain of Morbius' by Robin Bland (Terrance Dicks).

KASTRIA

A terribly ravaged planet, Kastria is lashed by constant snowstorms and scoured by solar winds. Long ago it was the home of a silicon-based life form known as Kastrians who evolved from rocks into roughly human shape. Once, too, it was protected from the depredations of space by a force field but this has gone down, leaving the world to die. Now the lifeless surface and empty corridors of the buildings on the planet bear witness to the vaunting ambitions of Eldrad, a Kastrian criminal executed by his own race – but later regenerated on Earth as a result of the discovery of his fossilised hand.

The revived Eldrad was returned to Kastria by the fourth Doctor, and there he tried unsuccessfully to revive his race which had died out in the millions of years during which he had been away – as is related by Bob Baker and Dave Martin in 'The Hand of Fear'.

KEMBEL

A treacherously lush planet over-run by the Varga plants which infest the surface and which attack any life-forms foolish enough to trespass upon it. Nevertheless, it was chosen by the Daleks as an ideal place from which to launch their plan in the year AD 4000 of uniting several alien races to wipe out the human beings of the Solar System.

Information about Kembel was initially given during the first Doctor's time in 'Mission to the Unknown' by Terry Nation, and then expanded upon in the epic story of 'The Daleks' Masterplan' – on which Dennis Spooner collaborated with Nation. However, during the course of the second story Kembel was terribly ravaged by the Time Destructor so desperately sought by the Daleks.

LOGOPOLIS

A world of symmetry and order where logic is the most powerful force. It is a beautiful planet, too, with pale rose-coloured sands stretching for uncounted miles beneath opalescent skies. The most important place on Logopolis is the City of Logic inhabited by a colony of pure mathematicians whose lives are dedicated to calculating and preserving the structure of the Universe.

It is here that the fourth Doctor arrived in the story of 'Logopolis' by Christopher H. Bidmead and uncovered yet another plot by the Master to blackmail the Cosmos into accepting him as their overlord. The story climaxed in the Doctor falling to his death – followed immediately by his regeneration into the body of the younger fifth Doctor.

MANUSSA

Location: **Scrampus System**

An exotic little world which is the third planet in the Federation System. It has twice been colonised by two mighty Empires, that of the Manussans and the Sumarans, but both have been mysteriously swallowed up in barbarism. Now the inhabitants eke out their existence by a basic system of agriculture and through tourism which, because of its atmosphere and terrain, allows human beings unlimited access to the planet's mixture of small settlements and caverns.

Landing on Manussa, the fifth Doctor became embroiled in the plan of the evil Mara to return to the planet, using Tegan as the unsuspecting medium. The story is told in 'Snakedance' by Christopher Bailey.

Ancient rituals on the exotic world of Manussa.

MARINUS

A world of burnished lands and dazzling green seas, which immediately entrances visitors. But appearances are deceptive for the terrain actually consists of twisted, gleaming rocks sharp as glass and the sea is as deadly as acid. There is an ice-bound wilderness, too, as well as a deserted jungle, and two great cities, Morphoton and Millenius.

The first Doctor arrived on Marinus as it was being invaded by the evil Voord and was persuaded by Arbitan, the leader of the peace-loving inhabitants, to help them in their struggle for survival. The story is told in 'The Keys of Marinus' by Terry Nation.

MARS

Location: **Solar System**

The famous 'Red Planet', fourth in order of distance from the Sun about 141,500,000 miles away. Passes closer to the Earth than any other planet in the Solar System bar Venus. Although it is smaller than the Earth, it has a similar rotation period of just over twenty-four hours and a substantial atmosphere. A Martian year, though, amounts to 687 days. Once thought to be criss-crossed by canals, it has since been shown to contain dusty desert landmasses (which may harbour basic life-forms) and have ice caps at both poles. It also has two small moons, Phobos and Deimos, and has been visited by spacecraft from Earth on several occasions.

The Ice Warriors are believed to have lived on Mars in prehistoric times, and the planet has featured in several of the

At the gates of Morphoton on Marinus - the first Doctor, Ian and Susan.

The spectacular Mechonoid City on the planet of Mechanus.

Doctor's adventures including 'The Ice Warriors' by Brian Hayles, 'Image of the Fendahl' by Chris Boucher, and perhaps most prominently of all in 'Pyramids of Mars' by Stephen Harris.

MECHANUS

A world which gives every indication to passing space travellers of being swathed in dense jungles. One distinctive feature is the gleaming Mechonoid city which stands above the tightly packed foliage and is home to the robots who were originally dispatched to colonise the planet. Instead, though, the Mechanoids have become the rulers of the place and use it as a kind of zoo to catch and study unwary space travellers who fall into their clutches.

The first Doctor arrived on Mechanus while being pursued by the Daleks in Terry Nation's story 'The Chase', and though initially he was made a prisoner by the cumbersome robots, he soon escaped to defeat his old arch-enemies once again.

METEBELIS 3

Location: Acteon Galaxy

A strikingly attractive planet with ranges of blue mountains towering over tawny, desert-like landscapes dotted with fantastically shaped boulders. The surface is, in fact, strewn with a profusion of multi-coloured gem stones, and this material richness is matched by the spicy tang of the dry and hot atmosphere. The beauty of Metebelis 3 is unfortunately not matched by the

inhabitants who are a race of giant spiders who came originally with some human colonists but have since grown to control them.

The third Doctor made two trips to the planet: in 'The Green Death' by Robert Sloman where he collected a blue crystal as a souvenir, and in 'Planet of the Spiders', also by Sloman, in which he managed to defeat the Great Spider in a finale which damaged his body to such an extent that he was forced to regenerate.

MONDAS

Location: Solar System

Mondas is a mysterious twin planet of Earth and is powered by a drive mechanism which enabled it to travel throughout the galaxy. A planet of great continents and seas as well as varying temperatures. Like the earth, a race of inhabitants evolved, but they developed Cybernetics earlier than the humans and when the planet began its long journey back towards the earth, the inhabitants had become Cybermen through years of replacement surgery.

Mondas was running out of energy and the Cybermen planned to take that energy from the Earth converting Earth's population into Cybermen too.

The Cybermen and Mondas were first introduced in the story 'The Tenth Planet' by Kit Pedler and Gerry Davis, and climaxed with the first Doctor's regeneration into his second *persona*. The Cybermen too were destined for more appearances and so far have had encounters with all the Doctors and have proved to be almost as popular enemies as the Daleks themselves!

The barren surface of the Moon taken over by Cybermen.

MOON

Location: The Solar System

The Earth's only natural satellite at a distance of 238,857 miles with a revolution period of just over twenty-seven days. The Moon has a diameter of 2,160 miles and its mass is just over one eightieth of that of Earth. It is a barren world of plains and lunar mountains, with a whole variety of craters which range from small pits to vast expanses as much as 150 miles across. The body has virtually no atmosphere and no light, merely reflecting the rays of the sun.

The Moon has, of course, been visited by astronauts from Earth, and the Doctor, too, has been there on several occasions, in such adventures as 'The Moonbase' by Kit Pedler (where it has been invaded by Cybermen), 'The Seeds of Death' by Brian Hayles (where Ice Warriors are in occupation), and in 'Frontier In Space' by Malcolm Hulke (where it is a penitentiary).

NECROS

A world as macabre as its deathly sounding name and obsession with dying indicates. Dark landmasses and turbulent weather make it a morbid place where one might well expect to find the evil Daleks feeling at home. Certainly because of its industries – in particular cryogenic suspension known as 'Tranquil Repose' – it proved an ideal place for Davros, the crippled Kaled scientist and creator of the inhuman machines, to get up to his usual machinations against the human race in general and the sixth Doctor in particular.

The colourful and erratic regeneration of the Time Lord found himself chilled by Necros in the story 'Revelation of the Daleks' written by Eric Saward. It was a suitably gloomy exit for the Doctor before his enforced absence of eighteen months from the screen.

The monster Aggedor which lurked on the world of Peladon.

OSEIDON

Oseidon is a once attractive planet which has been devastated and brutalised by its ugly, short-tempered inhabitants, the Kraals. Their ferocious temperament led to many savage atomic wars in the past which left the world's mountain ranges horribly disfigured and its plains scarred and pit-holed. Even the terrible casualties these wars caused and which reduced their numbers to a mere handful, did not curb the Kraals' war-like instincts. And with the help of their chief scientist, Styggron, they developed Androids to enable them to seek out fresh prey elsewhere.

It was the fourth Doctor who stumbled upon the Kraals' plan to invade Earth and exterminate the human race with a lethal virus in the story of 'The Android Invasion' by Terry Nation.

PELADON

Rightly called a barbaric planet, Peladon is a mixture of wild desert terrain and cruel-looking mountain ranges, like that of Mount Megeshra, forever torn by howling winds and claps of thunder. It is circled by three moons, and according to the old text books is guarded by Aggedor, the Royal Beast of Peladon, who tradition maintains is the defender of both the planet and its king. The world is also rich in the important mineral trisilicate, much coveted by certain alien races and only found elsewhere on Mars.

The third Doctor visited Peladon twice, firstly in 'The Curse of Peladon' by Brian Hayles when the planet was seeking membership of the Galactic Federation, and then fifty years later in 'The Monster of Peladon', also by Hayles, when some renegade Ice Warriors were discovered to be behind a plot to steal trisilicate to help an invading enemy from Galaxy Five.

The fourth Doctor in a difficult situation on the Planet of Evil.

PLANET OF EVIL

Location: **Edge of the helical galaxy**

A huge, black asteroid floating midway between the warring planets of Atrios and Zeos. The asteroid is honeycombed with tunnels and passageways leading to a whole variety of caves, some as tiny as cells and others like great mansion halls: all lit by a pale, green light. The place is, in fact, the headquarters of the wraith-like Shadow and his hooded minions who are carrying out the destructive master plan of the terrible Black Guardian.

It is the fourth Doctor who penetrates this bizarre hideaway in the sixth story of the Key to Time sequence entitled 'The Armageddon Factor' by Bob Baker and Dave Martin.

PLUTO

Location: **The Solar System**

Pluto was considered to be the outermost planet of the system which includes the Earth, Pluto circles the Sun in a decidedly eccentric orbit at least 3,600,000,000 miles away. It is a small world with a diameter of less than 4,000 miles and is intensely cold with temperatures plunging to below −200 degrees centigrade!

It was therefore something of a surprise when the fourth Doctor landed on Pluto some millions of years in the future and found several artificial orbiting suns had been launched around the planet and were warming and sustaining a human colony toiling away on the surface. Aided by Leela and K9 in the story of 'The Sunmakers' by Robert Holmes, the Doctor uncovered a plot by the alien Usurians to enslave and exploit these people.

REFUSIS

The Earth-like planet that had been picked by the authorities on Earth as the new home for a selected group of people in a huge space ship who escaped just before their world was about to plunge into the Sun. Refusis is a place of temperate climates, richly-wooded landscapes and warm blue seas where a new life can be built after the 700 year journey across the vast reaches of space.

Having seen the epic voyage begin, the first Doctor sped forward 700 years in the TARDIS and was there on Refusis and able to help the human beings make peace with the Monoids and all live together on the new world in the story of 'The Ark' by Paul Erickson.

The Medieval world
of Ribos.

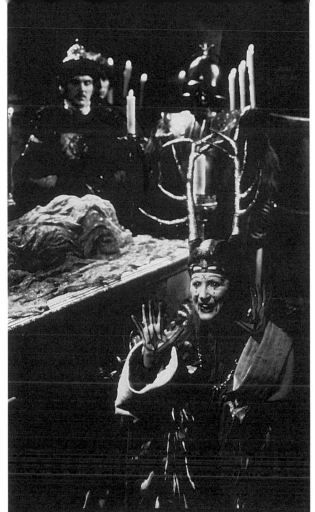

Refusis: the planet
picked for an Earth
colony and visited by
the first Doctor,
Steven and Vicki.

RIBOS

Location: Constellation of Skythra

A world of almost perpetual winter
where the light of the planet's sun
manages only to reach the surface as a
pale green glow. Because this world has
an unequal ellipse it enters a particularly
harsh winterphase every so often when it
is completely covered by ice. The
harshness of this Ice time is particularly
cruel on the inhabitants whose
technology has yet to reach that of Earth
in the Middle Ages. Only in the main
city of Shurr is there any kind of relief
from the biting cold . . .

The fourth Doctor visited this chilly
spot and was also forced to risk his life in
the monster-infested catacombs below
the surface when searching for the first
segment of the Key to Time in the story
of 'The Ribos Operation' by Robert
Holmes.

SARN

Sarn is a terrifyingly beautiful world of fire, regularly subjected to volcanic eruptions which cause magnetic eruptions in the atmosphere and make life difficult for all forms of life. It is, in fact, a colony of the planet Trion. Fire Mountain dominates the Sarn landscape, and in its shadow is the finest building on the planet, the Hall of Fire with its pillars and high ceiling, which has somehow survived all the eruptions.

On visiting the planet, the fifth Doctor confessed it reminded him of Pompeii, but the biggest problem he had to confront in the story of the 'Planet of Fire' by Peter Grimwade was the reappearance once again of his old foe, the Master.

SENSE-SPHERE

The Sense-Sphere is the home of the Sensorites. These telepathic aliens have a genuine fear for their safety and that of their wonderfully simplistic but entirely functional world. Their planet is also the source of an extremely rare mineral, molybdenum, and when the Sensorites learnt that a space ship from twenty-eighth century Earth had discovered this fact they felt compelled to hold the crew captive to prevent exploitation of their resources.

When the first Doctor landed inside the Earth space ship in the story 'The Sensorites' by Peter R. Newman, he found himself sympathising with these gentle people and helped them to resolve their problems.

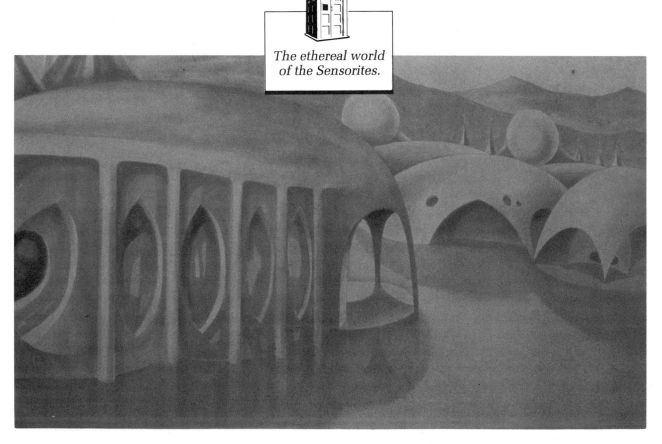

The ethereal world of the Sensorites.

LOGOPOLIS

A view of the cells of Logopolis and its impressive radar dish.

GALLIFREY

Even the legendary world of the Time Lords became victim of the aggressive might of the Sontarans.

SPIRIDON

One of the greatest Dalek armies ever assembled was found on Spiridon.

VOGA

The opulent planet of gold played a crucial role in the great Cyberwars.

METEBELIS 3

High rise blocks on the planet of the giant spiders.

SHADA

Location: Constellation of Kasterborus

Perhaps the most mysterious of all the worlds featured in the Doctor's adventures – became no one has yet seen it on the screen! It is actually a small, rock-covered planet used as a prison world by the High Council of the Time Lords: though they officially deny its existence. The prisoners who have transgressed the laws of Gallifrey are held in secure but not uncomfortable cell blocks with views across a featureless landscape which has been deliberately chosen to make any attempted escapes easier to spot.

The fourth Doctor was plunged into this world in Douglas Adams' story, 'Shada' while pursuing the megalomaniac scientist, Skagra, and was finally drawn into a spectacular battle of wills which involved other convicts on the prison planet.

SKARO

The famous home planet of the Doctor's most persistent and deadly adversaries, the Daleks. The craters and ravaged terrain of the dark world bear eloquent witness to the civil wars which have been fought across it for so many years. Originally it was inhabited by two races: the peaceful and unassuming Dals who only wished to be left in peace to farm, and the war-like Thals. Unhappily, skirmishes between the two groups turned into open warfare and for almost a thousand years the world was never free from the roar of battle. Later, the Thals evolved into perfect human beings, while the Dals became known as the Kaleds, and from their ranks arose a clever but demented scientist called Davros who betrayed them in order to create the Daleks!

The first Doctor encountered the Daleks when he found himself in the forbidding Dalek city on Skaro in Terry Nation's story 'The Daleks' (also known as 'The Dead Planet'). Since then they have unsuccessfuly tried to put an end to each and every one of his incarnations!

A panoramic view of the Dalek's home planet of Skaro.

SKONNOS

Once one of the great planets of the Universe and in control of a vast space empire, today much of Skonnos lies in ruins. The Skonnons had discovered high technology and space flight long before their neighbours, but instead of using their undoubted talents to develop their pleasant, green world, they chose to conquer the galaxy instead. But like the ancient Roman Empire on Earth, dissension broke out among the leaders, and there followed a whole succession of Emperors, none of whom could do anything to stop the rot. And as the Skonnons declined, so their Empire disintegrated.

The fourth Doctor became involved in the affairs of Skonnos in the story of 'The Horns of Nimon' by Anthony Read when the Nimon tried unsuccessfully to help the planet regain its past glories.

SOLOS

Another very curious world with arguably the longest winter and summer spans to be found anywhere in the universe – for both last five hundred years each! This naturally brings about enormous changes in the environment of Solos, with warmth and tropical foliage giving way to cold and icy desolation. The transition of the seasons also brings about a most dramatic change in the Solons themselves – for they are transformed from huge insectoid creatures into super-human beings in much the same way that a butterfly emerges from its chrysalis.

The third Doctor and his companion Jo were eye-witnesses to this moment of transition when the planet was also being given its freedom from Earth domination in the story of 'The Mutants' by Bob Baker and Dave Martin.

SPIRIDON

A truly amazing planet, swathed in dense jungle foliage of sinister fleshy vines and creepers, but also possessing an intensely cold environment. In fact, Spiridon has a central core of ice and this gives rise every so often to ice volcanos, known locally as icecanos! Another danger comes from the venom-spitting plants that can give the unwary visitor a nasty fungus disease. And as if these factors are not enough for one planet, the people of Spiridon also possess the secret of invisibility!

It was this capability that actually first drew the Daleks to the planet in the hope that they might discover the secret for themselves. But thanks to the arrival of the third Doctor and the help he received from some Thals also on the track of the Daleks, their plans were again defeated in the story of 'The Planet of the Daleks' by Terry Nation.

TARA

To step onto the planet Tara is rather like being transported back to Elizabethan England – complete with its attractive green landscape, neatly-fenced fields and wooded hills. Even the castles could have fallen through a time warp, and the people enjoy a society based on honour and chivalry. The fourth Doctor and his companion certainly enjoyed their time in this fairy-tale world – until Romana was marked down as the future wife of the Taran monarch-to-be and the Time Lord had to call on all his ingenuity and

The changing world of Solos which the third Doctor visited at a crucial moment in its history.

The pageantry of the Throne Room on the planet of Tara.

his swordsmanship to overcome the evil Count Grendel.

Another interesting revelation in the story of 'The Androids of Tara' by David Fisher is, as the title suggests, that along with their devotion to traditional ways, the Tarans also possess the science to create advanced androids of deadly efficiency!

TELOS

Telos is a deceptively empty-looking and even uninteresting planet until a visitor gets closer – vast stretches of arid, dusty terrain with great crater mountains jutting up against a blank sky. But behind this blandness lies the fact that this is where a group of the destructive Cybermen were cryogenically stored in underground shelters. A party of archaeologists later stumbled upon their Tombs and unleashed yet another threat to the peace of the galaxy.

The second Doctor was dropped into the middle of this drama in the story of 'The Tomb of the Cybermen' by Kit Pedler and Gerry Davis, and not only had to re-freeze the evil monsters but also neutralise their dangerous little metallic 'pets', the Cybermats. The sixth Doctor also returned to Telos in 'Attack of the Cybermen'.

THOROS-BETA

Literally one of the most colourful planets the Doctor has ever visited – a world with a green sky and pink seas. It is also a planet where science and medicine have been developed to a high degree, though an obsession with transplant surgery still has some way to go to achieving complete success. The sixth Doctor landed here in the twenty-fourth century, and apart from meeting the flamboyant King Yrcanos who fancied Peri as his future Queen, came up against the conniving Sil bent on another evil scheme, this time involving brain transference.

Thoros-Beta, in fact, became the setting for one of the Doctor's most unhappy adventures, 'Mindwarp', the second segment of 'The Trial of a Time Lord' sequence, when he found himself accused of criminal folly, neglect and wilful interference – not to mention the 'death' of Peri. But the truth, of course, was eventually to emerge . . .

TIGELLA

Location: **The Priam Planetary System**

Tigella, the sister planet of Zolfa-Thura, is an inhospitable place where the aggressive vegetation on the surface has forced the two races of people, the Savants and the Deons, to live below the surface in a honeycomb of caves and the tunnels which spread all around the globe. What has made this extraordinary civilisation possible is the Dodecahedron, a giant crystal which arrived from the skies aeons ago and has been utilised in the Power Room as the source for the underground world's heating, lighting and air conditioning, as well as for hydroponic farms and food storage.

The whole of Tigella is dependent upon it, in fact, and when it begins to fail, Zastor, the leader, calls in the help of his old friend, the Doctor, who appears in his fourth regeneration in 'Meglos' by John Flanagan and Andrew McCulloch, to save the subterranean people from disaster.

TIGUS

An ugly and barren-looking world, shrouded in dust swarms, with its surface pock-marked by volcanoes which erupt unpredictably and make life on its surface very dangerous for any life forms. It was here while fleeing from the Daleks that the first Doctor unexpectedly landed and came across another Time Lord, the Meddling Monk. But it was not only the environment that proved treacherous for him, for the Monk promptly betrayed him to the monsters from Skaro.

The details of this confrontation and visit to the world of Tigus were given by Terry Nation in collaboration with Dennis Spooner for the epic-length story of 'The Daleks' Masterplan'.

TITAN

Location: **The Solar System**

Titan, which is perpetually shrouded in a reddish-brown haze, is the largest of the ten moons circling the planet Saturn in an orbit 759,500 miles away. It is also the largest moon in the Solar System as well as being bigger even than the planet Mercury! It has an atmosphere about 1.6 times denser than that on Earth, and as this contains nitrogen there have been suggestions the planet might just be a primordial Earth!

The fourth Doctor came into contact with Titan in the story of 'The Invisible Enemy' by Bob Baker and Dave Martin when a space virus, the Nucleus, attacked both a base on the planet and the Time Lord himself in what proved a vain attempt to conquer the far-flung moon.

TITAN THREE

According to space lore, Titan Three has the reputation of being the most desolate and unvisited planet in the Universe. And certainly when viewed from the surface this is not hard to understand, for the sunlight is watery at best, and cold winds continually blow across the terrain throwing up clouds of the powdery, grey dust that covers everything. Perhaps, though, the greatest drawback is its thin atmosphere which contains a very rare gas, which although it is not poisonous can bring about extreme depression when breathed in by humanoid life-forms.

This was just another one of the perils that the sixth Doctor and his companion Peri had to be careful of when they went there for the Time Lord to recuperate in the strange story of 'The Twin Dilemma' by Anthony Steven.

TRAKEN

Location: **Mettula Orionsis**

This is actually a cluster of worlds called the Traken Union which have become famous for the harmony in which they all exist together. A major factor in this excellent relationship is a bioelectrical power known as the Source and controlled by the Keeper of Traken. However, when the present holder of this office begins to sense an all-pervading evil threatening to invade the Union he calls on the help of the Doctor.

The fourth Doctor is happy enough to oblige in the story of 'The Keeper of Traken' by Johnny Byrne, until he discovers that the cause of the trouble, the terrifying Melkur, is actually his old

Danger lurks everywhere on the Vampire Planet for the fourth Doctor and Romana.

enemy, the Master. Although the fellow renegade Time Lord is finally defeated by the Doctor, he takes advantage of the Source to provide himself with a new body – that of Tremas, Nyssa's father.

VAMPIRE PLANET

Location: E-Space

A curious, dark world that resembles the Earth of the Middle Ages. Indeed, the similarities do not end there for a day on the Vampire Planet is equivalent to 23.3 Earth hours, and a year to 350 days. The atmosphere and gravity are similar, too, and the landscape of dense forests, ploughed fields and simple villages could equally have been torn from the pages of an Earth history book. Only the great Tower pointing into the sky like an arrow seems out of place.

And when the fourth Doctor investigated this strange edifice in 'State of Decay' by Terrance Dicks he discovered that it was, in fact, a space ship housing the servants of the Great Vampire. The Time Lord was only able to end their reign of terror through his knowledge of the ancient ritual of staking vampires.

VAROS

Few more evil and cynical worlds exist in the length and breadth of the Universe than Varos, where torture and death are the staple ingredients of video entertainment. The population, who live in a cheerless environment dominated by the video screen, are kept contented and docile by an endless stream of gratuitous violence and most seem quite indifferent to any thoughts of change in their society.

The sixth Doctor was naturally appalled when he and Peri found themselves on the planet in 'Vengeance On Varos' by Philip Martin, and though the Time Lord might have been successful in curtailing the trade in video torture, he met an evil foe in the form of the slippery Sil – who would soon cross his path again.

VOGA

Location: The Solar System

The fabled planet of gold that attracted fortune hunters and aliens of all descriptions for thousands of years. The excavations of these people are evident everywhere in the dank and cavelike environment of the world, and no doubt further mining would have continued had not the little world been largely destroyed by the Cybermen – to whom gold is deadly. However, a number of Vogans managed to survive the terrible Cyberwars and lay in the ruins of their planetoid awaiting the moment to exact revenge.

The fourth Doctor came among the Vogans in 'Revenge of the Cybermen' by Gerry Davis when he was able to defeat the Cybermen as well as preventing the destruction of what remains of Voga.

VORTIS

Location: Isop

A cold and bleak world closely resembling the Earth's Moon. Vortis was originally a moonless world until the force of the Animus attracted several satellites into the planet's orbit. On the surface strange pointed crags rise up in irregular patterns. There are mist-shrouded acid pools too, although nothing moves in the almost totally windless environment. Among the crags and gullies of the place live the huge Zarbi creatures with their hard metallic bodies and pincer claws. Enslaved by the alien Animus, they waged a fierce war with the butterfly-like Menoptera, the original masters of Vortis.

This world was one of the earliest to be explored by the first Doctor in the story of 'The Web Planet' by Bill Strutton, in which he was finally able to restore the Menoptera to their rightful position.

VULCAN

Location: **The Solar System**

Vulcan is a lush, almost tropical world which presents an inviting face to space travellers. Indeed, in the far future it has been turned into an Earth colony, although much of it is totally hostile terrain to the colonists as it consists of vast stretches of treacherous swamp land. One such is the Mercury Swamp which has claimed several crashed spaceships and their crews.

The second Doctor undertook his first adventure on Vulcan in 'The Power of the Daleks' by David Whitaker and Dennis Spooner, and discovered that his old enemies had secretly infiltrated the planet and set up a reproduction plant. It took all of his powers of detection to locate the evil monsters' power source

and turn it against them in order to save the colony from destruction.

WAR PLANET

It is, as its name suggests, a world given over to warfare, and has been divided into several zones by a race of belligerent aliens who have 'collected' Earth soldiers from many periods of history and are training them into a fighting force to conquer the universe. Controlling this vast battleground are the War Lord and his assistant, the War Chief, who is actually a renegade Time Lord like the Doctor.

The second Doctor put an end to his machinations after his adventure on the planet in 'The War Games' by Malcolm Hulke and Terrance Dicks when, aided by his fellow Time Lords, he was able to restore the hapless soldiers to their rightful place in time.

XEROS

Xeros is another very unusual planet in that it has been turned into a vast Space Museum with samples of alien life and cultures from all over the known galaxies. The museum is the handiwork of the Moroks, a war-like race who have taken their 'exhibits' by conquest and now settled on the previously pleasant and cultured world of the Xerons. But unrest is already growing among these downtrodden people when the first Doctor arrives unexpectedly.

In the story of 'The Space Museum' by Glyn Jones, the Doctor helps the Xerons to break the Moroks' evil rule and reclaim their planet.

A Zarbi on the bleak surface of the planet Vortis.

XOANON

This planet is named after the computer that is its ruler, for otherwise it appears to have no name! It is a primitive, jungle world full of dense foliage and many traps for the unwary. It is also the home world of two tribes, the Sevateem, who are the descendents of an Earth survey team, and their mortal enemies, the Tesh, who also originated from the same team, but in the interim have developed destructive psychic powers.

The fourth Doctor found himself captured by the Sevateem when he arrived on the planet in 'The Face of Evil' by Chris Boucher, but was able to manipulate the computer, Xoanon, into putting a stop to the war between the tribes – at the same time finding himself with a new companion from the Sevateem, the beautiful warrior named Leela.

ZANAK

Location: Free flying

Zanak is a planet with the ability to move about in space and attach itself like a parasite to other worlds and bleed them of their energy and power. On the surface, though, it appears to be a pleasant and prosperous placed ruled by an enigmatic figure, half-man and half-machine, called the Captain. In fact, it is a hollow planet equipped with huge transmat engines which enable it to jump through the space vortex in search of victims.

The fourth Doctor encounters Zanak in the story of 'The Pirate Planet' by Douglas Adams when it has already

reduced the world of Calufrax to the size of a football. Since Earth is its next intended victim, the Time Lord is called upon to act quickly and with considerable cunning.

ZEOS

Location: Edge of the helical galaxy

Zeos is the twin planet of Atrios, with whom it is involved in a terrible nuclear war. The endless orange corridors below the surface of the planet bear every sign of being deserted, except for a giant pyramid-shaped computer called Mentalis which the fourth Doctor proves to be the source of the bombardment on Atrios.

This computer has also been programmed to destroy itself and both Atrios and Zeos should the plans of the evil Shadow who lives on a third planet, the Planet of Evil, be thwarted. This mysterious figure is finally revealed by the Doctor to be a servant of the terrible Black Guardian in the sixth story of the Key to Time sequence, 'The Armageddon Factor' by Bob Baker and Dave Martin.

ZETA MINOR

Location: Edge of the Morestrans' known Universe

Zeta Minor is a world covered with lush vegetation and which is unique as it is a portal into an anti-matter Universe. This portal is 'guarded' by an anti-matter force which prevents material from one universe being taken by the other.

The fourth Doctor landed on Zeta

Minor as a result of an appeal for help from a geological expedition, and in 'The Planet of Evil' by Louis Marks had to capture the anti-matter monster and return it to the universe from whence it came in order to return Zeta Minor to normal.

ZOLFA-THURA

Location: The Priam Planetary System

This is the sister planet of Tigella, now a wasteland of sand and ashes, and distinguished only by five enormous metal screens standing silently and unmoving on the surface. It was once the home of a great technological civilisation, the Zolfa-Thurans, who were supposed to have made incredible breakthroughs in energy-matrix technology – but all perished in a huge planetary war.

The fourth Doctor visited the planet during the story of 'Meglos' by John Flanagan and Andrew McCulloch, when he was called to Tigella to prevent the Dodecahedron crystal – which is its source of power – from failing, and there discovered a plot actually to steal the precious gem. Behind this scheme is the cactus-like Meglos, who is based on Zolfa-Thura, where the Doctor finally puts a stop to his plans.

The primitive jungle world of Xoanon where the fourth Doctor met Leela.

Model of the Dalek Flying Saucer
(Courtesy: Julian Vince).

Spaceship Astra crashed on the planet Dido.

7
SPACE CRAFT CHECKLIST

During the TARDIS's many journeys it has come across a whole variety

of other space craft ranging from Mavic Chen's squat-looking 'Spar'

encountered by the first Doctor to the pencil-slim explorer ship which

so surprised the fourth Doctor when he found it was the home of

vampires!

These machines, which are a tribute to the inventiveness of the

Special Effects Department at the BBC over the past three decades, have

given an added dimension to the Doctor's adventures, and hereunder

are listed some of the best of them.

Space Craft Checklist

Part of the huge Dalek Flying Saucer built for the film, 'Daleks - Invasion Earth 2150'.

DALEK FLYING SAUCERS

First sighted: 1964

The Dalek Saucers, which look exactly like archetypal Unidentified Flying Objects (UFOs), appeared over London in Terry Nation's story, 'The Dalek Invasion of Earth'. In this adventure the first Doctor was taken aboard a Saucer hovering over Trafalgar Square during the Daleks' attempted take-over of the Earth.

When this story was later made into a full-length film entitled *The Daleks: Invasion Earth 2150 AD* (1966), a 120-foot model of one of these saucers was built at Shepperton Studios, straddling a devastated section of London. Though it looked very impressive in the film, the craft was, in fact, only the underneath section. On the other hand, the saucers which were seen flying were just three-foot long models, though the crash of one of them caught in a magnetic whirlpool at the end of the picture made a spectacular finale!

SPACESHIP ASTRA

First sighted: 1965

The hapless Earth spaceship number 201 with its back broken, but still patriotically displaying the British flag on one shattered fin, was found on the surface of the planet Dido by the first Doctor in 'The Rescue' by David Whitaker. Inside, he met Vicki, destined to replace Susan in the TARDIS, and the supposedly paralysed crew-member, Bennett, who was to be unmasked as the villain of the piece, Koquillion.

THE 'SPAR' SHIP

First sighted: 1966

The squat and rather grandiose space vehicle belonging to Mavic Chen, the Guardian of the Solar System, whose treachery when he betrayed Earth and gave a taranium element to the Daleks to power their Time Destructor was exposed by the first Doctor in 'The Daleks' Masterplan' by Terry Nation and Dennis Spooner.

THE ARK

First sighted: 1966

A huge spacecraft, as its name suggests, which was flying away from the Earth bearing miniaturised samples of human and animal life. The reason for this exodus was that the Earth was about to plunge into the Sun, and the craft was on a 700-year voyage to an Earth-like planet named Refusis. The first Doctor was called upon to prevent the human race being wiped out when the common cold virus threatened the craft and its dormant passengers in the story, 'The Ark' by Paul Erickson.

Mavic Chen's space craft, The Spar.

THE WHEEL

First sighted: 1968

The Wheel is a giant space station of the kind conceived on Earth by the NASA Space Agency in America. The second Doctor found the Wheel under threat from both the Cybermen and a meteorite storm in the story called 'The Wheel In Space' by David Whitaker, in which the author drew on Kit Pedler's knowledge of up-to-the-minue science for his creation of the Wheel.

AXOS

First sighted: 1971

Called the 'living spaceship', this extraordinary organic vehicle brought the beautiful and apparently friendly Axons to Earth in 'The Claws of Axos' by Bob Baker and Dave Martin. Inside, the ship resembled a human heart – but there was no love or compassion in the Axons who planned to drain the planet of its energy and were, in fact, part of a plot engineered by the Master and only thwarted by the courage of the third Doctor.

THE MASTER'S PRISON SHIP

First sighted: 1973

This Earth vessel had been built in the twenty-fifth century to ferry convicted criminals to imprisonment in its steel cells blocks – that is, until it was hijacked by the Master from the colony on Sirius IV. Although somewhat squat

The Master's Prison Ship.

designs of conquest through space and time. Like their occupants who are incredibly strong and feed on energy, these space ships have immense power and are extremely difficult to destroy. The third Doctor first encountered one in 'The Time Warrior' by Robert Holmes, and they reappeared in 'The Sontaran Experiment' by Bob Baker and Dave Martin (1975), 'The Invasion of Time' by David Agnew (1978) and 'The Two Doctors' again by Robert Holmes (1985).

in appearance and lacking any defensive or offensive equipment, it was still capable of moving swiftly between star systems. The Prison Ship was the most notable of several spacecraft that the third Doctor encountered in what was to prove his last duel with the first Master in the story 'Frontier in Space' by Malcolm Hulke.

SONTARAN SHIPS

First sighted: **1973**

The curious ball-like ships in which the Sontarans have pursued their militaristic

One of the curious ball-shaped Sontaran space machines.

NERVA BEACON

First sighted: 1975

Nerva Beacon was a satellite orbiting near Jupiter before the 30th Century, warning space travellers of the presence of the newly discovered '13th moon', named Voga. The fourth Doctor managed to prevent the Cybermen from crashing the Beacon into Voga in an attempt to destroy the 'planet of gold' in the Gerry Davis story 'Revenge of the Cybermen'.

Many years after this, when earth was ravaged by solar flares, the Beacon was re-equipped as a Space Ark, carrying the collected specimens of all forms of life, including humans, so that Earth could be re-inhabited once it was safe to do so. The fourth Doctor again saved the cryogenically stored humans from

becoming the hosts of the parasitic Wirrn in the Robert Holmes story 'The Ark in Space'.

EARTH SHUTTLECRAFT

First sighted: 1977

Not dissimilar in appearance to the American NASA Space Shuttle, these tough little craft with their storage holds amidships can carry a number of interchangeable pods. They are without weapons, but can raise a force shield to protect themselves against meteor storms. The fourth Doctor encountered one – complete with an unsuspected space virus aboard – en route for Titan, and thereafter found himself with a battle on his hands for his own life in the story of 'The Invisible Enemy' by Bob Baker and Dave Martin.

The Earth shuttle craft landing on Titan.

MOVELLAN SHIP

First sighted: 1979

A curious, spinning-top shaped space vehicle – but capable of immense speeds and powerfully equipped to defend itself against attack. It belongs to the Movellans, a strikingly attractive humanoid race, but who – the fourth Doctor discovers – are actually a merciless race of robots who have been engaged in warfare with the Daleks for centuries. They had reached a stalemate when the Time Lord encountered them in 'Destiny of the Daleks' by Terry Nation, where he was once again triumphant over his oldest foes.

NIMON TRAVEL CAPSULE

First sighted: 1979

One of the most flexible forms of transport to be found anywhere in the galaxy, this Space Capsule makes use of Black Holes to transmit its occupants wherever they wish to go. The Nimon utilise gravitational whirlpools linked to two power sources at the start and conclusion of the required journey for the propulsion of the Capsules. The fourth Doctor came across the Nimon in the middle of yet another of their ruthless jumps across space draining energy from planets in the story 'The Horns of Nimon' by Anthony Read.

JAGAROTH STAR CRUISER

First sighted: 1979

The Jagaroth are a race of warmongering aliens with the most advanced technology and equipment. A striking example of this talent is the Jagaroth Star Cruiser, an extremely versatile globular space machine, capable of hyper-speed and bristling with armaments, as well as the ability to land on any terrain its crew choose – thanks to the fully-retractable legs and gyroscopic stabilising ring. The fourth Doctor literally dropped at the feet of this fearsome fighting machine in the story of 'The City of Death' by David Agnew when he found himself battling for the freedom of the galaxy with the awesome Count Scarlioni alias Scaroth, last of the Jagaroth.

THE HYDRAX

First sighted: 1980

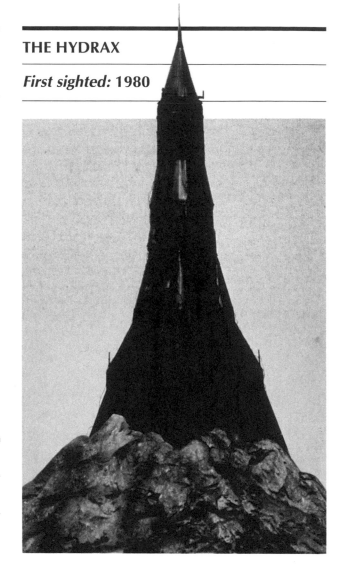

When the fourth Doctor first saw the extraordinary pencil-slim Tower which served as the castle of King Zargo and Queen Camilla, he could be forgiven for not recognising it as a spaceship. But that is precisely what it is – having originally been an Earth exploration ship, the *Hydrax*, which landed on the planet a thousand years earlier. The Time Lord was in for an even bigger surprise, though, when he discovered that the King and Queen were actually vampires in the story 'State of Decay' by Terrance Dicks.

PRIVATEER SHIP

First sighted: 1981

A hyper-speed space vehicle made of impervious dwarf star alloy used by Captain Rorvik in his nefarious activities about the galaxy decribed in 'Warriors' Gate' by Steve Gallagher. However, when the Captain takes into his hold a group of time-sensitive Tharils for transportation, he soon finds his craft trapped in a misty void – as does the fourth Doctor, who is also unwittingly drawn into the same place.

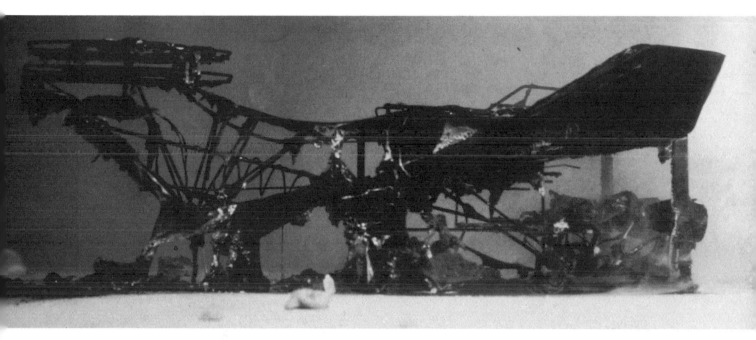

The remnants of Captain Rorvik's Privateer Ship.

TERMINUS

First sighted: 1983

Another giant space station much used by travellers in space and time, and to which the fifth Doctor and his companions headed in the stricken space transport vessel full of sufferers of the terrible leprosy-like illness, Lazar's Disease. Aside from the ingenious space vehicles, the story of 'Terminus' by Steve Gallagher contained the dramatic attempt on the doctor's life by Turlough, and Nyssa's decision to stay and help the pitiful Lazar sufferers.

The Eternals' fleet of
old sailing vessels.

THE ETERNALS' SHIPS

First sighted: 1983

A clutch of spacecraft in the form of old sailing ships. These vessels fly in space much as they might do on the Oceans of the World, using the planets as buoys! They are actually the proud possessions of the Eternals, a group of all-powerful immortals who though they appear to be just like humans in the story 'Enlightenment' by Barbara Clegg, are actually engaged in a bitter race for supremacy. The ships provided a stylish and unusual backdrop to the other part of the story concerning the fifth Doctor's battle with another of his old adversaries, The Black Guardian.

SPACE STATION J7

First sighted: 1984

Station J7 is an orbiting Space Research Centre where work has been going on for some years into the possibility of time travel. Indeed, the Professors Kartz and Reimer conducting the experiment are virtually on the point of launching a time capsule, when the Time Lords intevene by sending the Doctor, in the shape of his second incarnation, to investigate in the story of 'The Two Doctors' by Robert Holmes. The hierarchy of Gallifrey feel time travel should only be the preserve of a select few – and in resolving this issue, as well as putting a stop to the blood-thirsty activities of two Androgums and a Sontaran strike force, the Doctor needs the combined skills of both his second and sixth incarnations.

TIME LORDS' TRIAL SHIP

First sighted: 1986

The most spectacular and impressive space station ever seen on *Doctor Who*, this was the vehicle to which the Time Lords drew the sixth Doctor by a tractor beam to face his trial, accused of interference in the affairs of others and directly occasioning crime. It was the invention of script-writer Robert Holmes, the author of the first segment of 'The Trial of a Time Lord', and if ever a machine displayed just how far the space ship technology of the programme had come in its three decades, it was undoubtedly the Time Lords' Trial Ship . . .

HYPERION III

First sighted: 1986

The *Hyperion III* was a deep space liner voyaging between Earth and the far reaches of the Galaxy, on which the sixth Doctor and his latest companion, Melanie Bush, found themselves during the third segment of his Trial by Pip and Jane Baker. In the luxuriously appointed living quarters and public rooms of this superb liner, the Time Lord found himself inexorably drawn into the mystery of a series of murders which had been committed on board, as well as the escape from its hold of some flesh-eating creatures called the Vervoids. Not to mention a plot to hijack the liner which threatened to send it plunging into a Black Hole. It was undoubtedly one of the Time Lord's most dramatic and memorable space voyages of recent years!

8

TIME TRAVEL UPDATE

Stories and Developments
in the continuing saga of
Doctor Who, 1983–1987.

Since the publication of my twenty-first anniversary volume, *Doctor Who: A Celebration*, there have been a number of important developments in the continuing story of the Time Lord from Gallifrey, including the dramatic events of the eighteen-month cancellation of the series and unexpected arrival of a seventh Doctor. Also included here are the plots of all the screened stories from 'The Five Doctors' to 'The Trial of a Time Lord', as well as the radio serial, 'Slipback', which are described with fascinating background information by *Doctor Who* expert, Jeremy Bentham.

I New Lives For The Doctor

Wednesday, February 27, 1985, was the day the unthinkable *almost* happened. The day when *Doctor Who* was cancelled and there were real fears the good Time Lord might never be seen again.

It was a day that I – like millions of the Doctor's fans around the world – will never forget. Just as those of us old enough can remember what we were doing the day President Kennedy was assassinated in America (which was also, of course, the day the first Doctor made his debut on television), so we can also vividly recall the impact the news of the BBC's decision to shelve the programme for eighteen months had upon us.

I had just been out for a quiet lunch with my wife and returned home to find the phone almost jumping off the hook. It was a reporter from the Press Association who, immediately I answered, asked: 'The BBC are dropping *Doctor Who*. As you've been called the programme's official historian would you like to comment?'

As you might imagine I was quite taken aback by the news. Lost for words might be nearer the truth.

'Why, that's amazing,' I said as I let what the reporter had said sink in. 'Appalling, in fact.'

Cartoon from SUNDAY MIRROR, March 3 1985.

"Doctor, we're prescribing a rest."

I paused then, and my old training as a journalist reasserted itself. Just *what* had the BBC decided? Were they actually killing off the show or was this just another controversy about to envelop the programme as it had done so often before during its twenty-two year history? I didn't want to feel I was making unjustified headlines for anyone.

'What exactly has happened?' I asked the voice at the other end of the phone. 'Are you telling me the BBC is ending the show after all these years?'

'Not quite,' the reporter replied after a momentary pause. 'Michael Grade has just announced that it is being taken off the air for eighteen months. He wants to save £2 million to use on other drama projects.'

I heaved a sigh of relief. It wasn't *quite* as bad as I had at first feared. The Doctor was going into a time lock rather than oblivion. But I could still imagine what the world-wide reaction was going to be once the news became public.

'There will be a tremendous outcry to save the programme,' I said. 'There are 110 million viewers in fifty-four countries and they won't like this. *Doctor Who* is unique, you see – what other programme could change the central actor and still hold a magical grip over each new generation?'

I also reminded the man from the PA that Michael Grade's earlier decision to interrupt the run of the soap opera, *Dallas*, in order to combat the plans of ITV who had secured the series from the BBC, had been reversed by a public outcry and I expected the same to happen again. (After much wrangling, of course, *Dallas* continued to be shown by the BBC.)

'You can't tamper with a national institution without expecting a furore,' I added.

I had scarcely put the phone down from this call, when it rang again. This time it was Paul Donovan of the *Daily Mail* who was ahead of many of his colleagues. He repeated the facts I had already heard and I gave him my now measured response.

Then Paul dropped another bombshell into what I had earlier believed would be a pleasant and relaxing day. Had I heard that the BBC were planning *another* science fiction serial, called *Star Cops*, which might ultimately replace *Doctor Who*, he asked.

I had to admit that I had only heard about it in the vaguest terms – that there were rumours the Corporation fancied doing another 'straight' sf series not unlike the late and much lamented *Blake's 7*.

'But there is no way the fans of *Doctor Who* would accept any kind of substitute,' I insisted. (Later, a BBC spokesman was to reveal that plans for such a series *did* exist, but it would in no way be a replacement. 'The two shows could be run cheerfully in the same week just as *Doctor Who* was with *Blake's 7*,' he added.)

Before the phone could ring again I tried to get through to John Nathan-Turner at the *Doctor Who* Production Office for some more information. As I half-expected, the lines were already blocked with callers, but by persistence, I did finally manage. And there I found myself talking to a familiar but totally unexpected voice.

It was that of the second Doctor, Patrick Troughton, who had stopped by the office as soon as he heard the news to see if he could be of any help. He had already fielded a great many questions from reporters and fans, assuring them all that this was not the end of the programme to which he had contributed so much and which still had a place of affection in his heart.

Patrick was as angry at the decision as anyone, and told me he thought there was more to it than just being a question of saving money on a show that cost an average of £180,000 per series. He was sure it was part of the Corporation's campaign then under way to obtain a higher licence fee of £65 instead of the existing £46.

'It is possible the BBC is hoping there will be a public outcry about the series being too expensive for their resources,' he said. 'I would have thought most people will put two and two together and realise what is in the minds of the BBC executives.'

This claim was, though, later denied by a BBC spokesman, who said, 'Doctor Who almost certainly does earn far more through sales than it costs to make, but it has to come out of the drama budget, and sales go into the BBC's general coffers. The drama budget this year was just not big enough for everything,' he added.

Colin Baker, then the current Doctor, was also quick on the attack. 'I'm astounded that the BBC sees fit to axe its most popular product,' he said, 'If I were an ordinary member of the public I would express my rage. The programme is part of the British way of life.'

Which is precisely what people *did* do – over 80,000 of them either telephoning or writing to the BBC to protest at the decision during the next few days and weeks.

The British *Doctor Who* Appreciation Society were very much at the forefront of these protests, the co-ordinator, David Saunders, pointing out that the four thousand members were worried about the long term future of the show. They feared that shelving it might just be the first step towards cancelling *Doctor Who* altogether.

DWAS speedily mounted a campaign in the press and on local TV stations to protest at the BBC's decision, and some fans even got together and produced a record, *Doctor In Distress*, which featured several well-known pop personalities as well as some of the stars of the show, in order to raise money in a kind of 'Band Aid' operation!

In Europe, where the show has some 150,000 fans in various clubs, the outrage was just as marked – while across the Atlantic, Ron Katz of the *Doctor Who* Fan Club of America announced that his organisation would 'raise the $5 million to save the show if needed!'

The *Save Doctor Who* campaign even generated letters to the national press, including several to that most august of British papers, *The*

The Doctor on trial in new television series

By Angella Johnson

Doctor Who, one of television's longest running science-fiction programmes, returns to the BBC on September 6 after an 18-month absence.

Colin Baker plays the 900-year-old time traveller for the second time in the show's 23-year history.

The new series consists of a 14-part epic, "The Trial of a Time Lord", which sees the Doctor on trial before the Time Lords of Gallifrey on his own super-advanced planet.

He is accused of constantly meddling in the affairs of others. The penalty, if found guilty, is death.

Throughout the trial adventures from the past, present and future are used as evidence of the Doctor's interfering by Valeyard, the prosecutor, played by Michael Jayston.

The series has minimum violence and the script is peppered with humour.

Mr John Nathan-Turner, the producer, said: "Some people wrote in to the BBC complaining that the programme was too dependent on violent clashes between characters. So we toned down the action and substituted the violence with humorous intercourse between the actors."

A lineup of stars, including Honor Blackman, Joan Sims, Tony Selby and Lynda Bellingham, will appear in the series. The Doctor's assistant, Peri, is played by Nicola Bryant who is followed by Melanie, played by Bonnie Langford.

Some 110 million viewers worldwide watch Doctor Who as he projects himself from one intergalactic problem to another in his police telephone box. There are several hundred fan clubs in more than 60 countries:

The Doctor on Trial - in more ways than one! From THE TIMES, August 30, 1986.

Times. A Mr Peter Anghelides of Sale in Cheshire spoke for a great many others when he called the BBC's decision 'deplorable' and continued:

'The programme is innovative in terms of scripting, direction and organisation, a testing ground for many production techniques and a carefully budgeted drama series . . . If the BBC can tamper with their own institutions in such an off-hand way, can they really complain about threats to the institution of the BBC itself, for example by broadcast advertising?'

The sister paper, *The Sunday Times*, also took up the theme in its comment column, 'Buzz':

'Why did the BBC pick on *Doctor Who* when they probably could have saved just as much cash by cancelling a couple of worthy but little-watched adult education series or even a few manufactured darts and snooker tournaments?' it asked.

'Insiders are quick to deny that *Doctor Who* is the victim of a licence fee stunt, but there is a view that its shelving was a misjudgement on the part of BBC1's controller, Michael Grade, the man behind the *Dallas* fracas. Certainly nobody could claim that the veteran sci-fi series is in ailing health – with Saturday night audiences running at 8 million it has rarely been more popular. Nor is the BBC's overseas sales team delirious at the thought of losing one of its most consistent money-spinners . . .'

The columns of the *Radio Times* were predictably deluged with comments. M.S. Ball from Merseyside underlined what the two newspapers had said, but in more personal terms.

'Cash may indeed be short,' the letter said, 'but where is the BBC's loyalty to the audience that has been so faithful to the series for over twenty-one years?

'*Doctor Who* is a unique show and it commands a massive following at home plus a huge overseas audience; in some ways it is the flagship of the BBC. If this decision is an attempt by stealth to abandon the series altogether, then it is a quite reprehensible betrayal of audience loyalty . . .'

Another reader, S. Reeves of Birmingham, asked which other show for the past twenty-two years had 'been consistently innovative, amusing, frightening and entertaining for adults and children alike' and said it was 'as much a part of life as cups of tea or cricket.' And the viewer added, 'If the BBC does not know the answers it should ask some of the millions of people who tune in every week to watch the adventures of the world's most popular and loved hero.'

Theresa Croshaw was absolutely adamant about what she felt. 'I am not prepared to pay a higher licence fee if the Doctor is to be suspended – perhaps permanently. If he goes, my TV goes. Alternatively, Michael Grade could go. Perhaps we should slap him into a TARDIS – the Master's, of course!'

Adrian Cale of Northamptonshire had the last word on this theme. 'Can it be true?' he asked. 'The Master has regenerated and is calling himself Michael Grade!'

There was, though, one voice raised in dissent among all these attacks. Chris Howarth of Manchester felt some good might come of the decision.

'Having had time to think it over,' he wrote, 'I am not sure it's such a bad idea after all, if the break will be used to improve the series. The current crop of *Doctor Who* episodes has been some of the most mind-numbingly dull I have ever witnessed . . . I feel that *Doctor Who*'s producers are too complacent if they think we can be fobbed off with old monsters and companions instead of decent scripts.'

Seen with hindsight, this was to prove a very prophetic comment . . .

In the immediate aftermath of all this comment, Bill Cotton, the Managing Director of BBC Television, assured the fans and public alike that *Doctor Who* was not being killed off and that he was confident the programme had 'a great future on BBC1'.

His comments were then re-emphasised by Michael Grade – who had actually been on a ski-ing holiday when the furore broke out – in a statement to the *Radio Times* on March 23. His reply was blunt and to the point.

'The response of *Doctor Who* enthusiasts is bordering on the hysterical given the exact nature of the BBC's decision,' he said. '*Doctor Who* has not been cancelled, just delayed for a year. The ratings for the current series have been disappointing and we need time to consider the reasons for this.

'The current series is an experimental forty-five minutes length and this has not proved as popular as we had hoped. We were looking to make some financial savings in the coming year and it seems that after twenty-one years a short rest would do the Doctor no harm at all. Long-running television series do get tired and it is because we want another twenty-one years of *Doctor Who* that we have prescribed a good rest.'

And a good rest was what the show got – although producer John Nathan-Turner and script editor Eric Saward were busy devising the crucial next season throughout the rest of 1985. In April 1986, the world's press were summoned to a Stone Age Village in Hampshire to learn that the Doctor was once again back before the cameras making a new season of fourteen episodes which were to go under the evocative umbrella title of 'The Trial of a Time Lord'. It was somehow appropriate that the sixth Doctor should reappear at such a venue, for hadn't the very first Doctor back in his earliest story, 'An Unearthly Child' begun his adventures among Stone Age people?

The reporters found an enthusiastic Colin Baker at work in the replica of the ancient village at Butser Hill near Petersfield.

'It's great to be back,' he said. 'The last year has gone very slowly. Objectively I suppose the programme is in the dock – but I'm pleased to find that I don't feel that way. I wondered if I would feel hunted every second in front of the cameras because you don't do you best work that way. I'm glad that I don't.

'I was frustrated more than angry about all the upsets last year because you are being put at the mercy of other people's decisions. I believe the part of the Doctor was made for me, and vice-versa, and if I could have my way I would play him all year round with just Christmas and two week's holiday.'

Colin also explained that there would be less violence and more humour in the new series in which the Doctor was on trial for alleged crimes of his own. 'From now on I shall use wit instead of *Dirty Harry* tactics to solve my confrontations,' he added.

John Nathan-Turner also took up this point on the location. 'The humour is something I definitely want to heighten,' he explained. 'It won't be slapstick but witty. And like every other programme we are watching the violence.

'Some people have complained to the BBC that the programme was too dependent on clashes between characters, so we have toned down the action and substituted the violence with humorous intercourse between the actors.'

It was also announced that the Doctor was to have a new companion – Nicola Bryant as Peri making way half-way through the new series for the song-and-dance star, Bonnie Langford, as Melanie, a computer expert and keep fit fanatic.

Only the *Daily Express* of the newspapers which covered this story added a word of caution. 'The message is clear,' said writer John Millar, 'that much loved time traveller, the Doctor, is on trial for his life – both off and on the TV screen. And if Michael Grade isn't happy with the series, *Doctor Who* could be returning just to be exterminated!'

On September 6 1986, after an 18-month absence, *Doctor Who* returned to the television screen for its latest season – but within days another bombshell had fallen on the programme. For in its issue of September 11, the newspaper of the acting profession, *The Stage*, reported that Script Editor Eric Saward had 'abruptly departed' from the programme because of dissent between himself and the producer, John Nathan-Turner.

Saward, it was said, claimed that he had found it increasingly difficult to work on *Doctor Who* because of 'budget restrictions and the quality of the scripts not being of the calibre to attract rising young talent.'

Whatever the ins or outs of this situation – and the BBC has steadfastly refused to comment – plus the threat hanging over 'The Trial of Time Lord' that it might be the Doctor's last adventure, the reactions the series drew soon afterwards were undoubtedly favourable from both critics and fans.

The Stage's Alan P. Stewart, for instance, wrote, 'On Saturday, December 6, several million people held their breath as they watched what might possibly have been the very last episode of *Doctor Who*. Would the BBC, in accordance with speculation, dare to put an end to the greatest science fiction hero of all time, and a series which had lasted a successful twenty-three years?

'Thankfully, however, the good Doctor triumphed once again, and lives on to fight another day. The BBC did not repeat the mistake made in the – still much talked about – final episode of *Blake's 7* in which all the heroes were seen to be massacred and the victory went to the 'bad guys'. In fact, a tremendous sigh of relief rose from the nation as the

Doctor emerged the victor in what must have been the most satisfying ending to a series for many a year.

'The fourteen-part adventure tended to drag in the odd place, but the improved special effects and make-up more than compensated. It was refreshing to see a bit more effort put into the series than normal. All told, the series was a step in the right direction and I hope that the BBC will continue to make more. In the words of the Master, "The Cosmos without the Doctor scarcely bears thinking about!" '

Alan Stewart also raised an interesting point about the actual storyline. 'Amazingly enough,' he said, 'nowhere during the story, especially when the Doctor was being tried for genocide, did anybody recall the episode when, during Tom Baker's era, the Time Lords ordered the Doctor to destroy the entire Dalek race. Would they *really* try somebody for a crime of which they themselves had approved?'

The fans wrote in great numbers to *Radio Times*, the large majority voicing their approval of 'The Trial of a Time Lord'. Tim Collins of Epping in Essex said it had been 'great fun and a joy to watch', while Susan Flower of Chesham in Buckinghamshire wrote that the whole series had been 'very enjoyable – the extra humour adding to the stories without any loss to the adventure feeling.'

Miss Flower also raised an interesting point about the fascinating and enigmatic figure of the Valeyard whose presence had so dominated the story.

'If one had to find fault, my biggest quarrel would be with the time paradoxes,' she said, 'especially those brought up at the end. If the Valeyard really is a latter-day incarnation of the Doctor, why did he want to kill the Doctor? It's like going back in time and killing yourself as a child. And, anyway, what were the Doctor and the Valeyard doing in the same time stream?

'But one always has to take the scientific aspects of *Doctor Who* with a pinch of salt – it's still great,' she added.

It was quite evident from such letters and comments, that the epic trial had left unanswered as many interesting points as it had solved. It had, in fact, also reactivated the love of controversy that has been the life-blood of the programme over the years.

However, the controversy which was to engulf the programme within a week was quite unlike any other that had occurred before. Because on December 18, Colin Baker – the man who had said his objective was to be the longest-serving Doctor and would 'play the part all year round' – dramatically announced he was giving up the role forthwith.

A report in *The Times* of December 19 stated bluntly that Colin Baker's decision 'was made after a BBC decision not to ask him to play the Doctor in all of the next series, which starts filming in March.'

The item continued, 'The BBC wanted to replace Mr Baker, 41, with a new actor – or actress – after four of the fourteen episodes. Yesterday, he said he would not accept an offer to play only four episodes.

'The BBC denied there had been any disagreement,' *The Times* added.

However, shortly after Christmas, on January 6, 1987, Colin Baker told his version of the events which had led to his departure in an exclusive two-part interview with Sue Carroll of *The Sun* newspaper.

In this, he claimed that it was Michael Grade who had axed him because 'he never liked me'.

Said Colin, 'When I was told I couldn't quite take it in, it was such a shock. I'd fought so hard for the show, I was stunned. If I knew why I was sacked then I would feel better about it all. But I got fobbed off with excuses about Michael Grade thinking that three years as *Doctor Who* was long enough.

'The worst thing of all was that they actually wanted me to come back and do four more episodes just so that I could be killed off and fit in with their plans!' he added.

Despite believing that he had been made a 'scapegoat', Colin said he would always remember his time as the Doctor with great affection.

'I can honestly say that working on *Doctor Who* was one of the

Cartoon from THE SUN, *January 6, 1987.*

Dr Who changes

Colin Baker has left his role as Doctor Who after three years.

His decision was made after a BBC decision not to ask him to play the doctor in all of the next series, which starts filming in March.

The BBC wanted to replace Mr Baker, aged 41, with a new actor — or actress — after four of the 14 episodes.

Yesterday he said he would not accept an offer to play only four episodes.

The BBC denied there had been any disagreement.

The sixth Doctor leaves - a typical newspaper report from December 19, 1986.

FRANKLIN

"SORRY, THERE ARE NO VACANCIES ON MERCURY . . . SHALL I TRY MARS?"

happiest working experiences of my life. It was a fantastic team and there were always plenty of pranks.

'Once when the production team discovered I was terrified of spiders, they set me up. I arrived in my dressing room to find they'd festooned the place with massive plastic spiders even to the extent of filling the loo with them!

'On another occasion I was supposed to have my face caked in mud. The prop man pointed out the pile of dirt I was supposed to spread on my face, but he failed to tell me a dog had passed by. They all thought it was very amusing that I had dog muck all over my face!'

Colin said the subject of his weight was also a topic that was regularly raised. 'A lot of things have been said about that, and I would be the first to admit that on *Doctor Who* we would often indulge in pudding eating competitions. I won fair and square one night by eating three in a row!'

On a sadder note, Colin told *The Sun* that he was particularly sorry not to be carrying on the role of the Doctor because of the tremendous help it had been in his work raising money for the Foundation For The Study of Infant Deaths – a cause which is close to his heart, and that of his wife, because of the baby son they lost in a cot death in 1985.

Naturally enough, the news of Colin Baker's departure from the programme immediately prompted widespread headlines about his successor. And once again there was renewed speculation that the part might be played by a woman – a suggestion that had been first advanced – though not all that seriously – by Tom Baker on his departure. It was proposed very seriously this time, though, by a group of women's rights campaigners – as *The Daily Mail* reported on December 20, 1986.

'A group of Labour Euro-MP's want the next *Doctor Who* to be female,' the reported stated, 'they claim that the change would help break down barriers to women. Yesterday, members of the EEC women's rights committee, meeting in London, wrote to the BBC Director General, Alastair Milne, saying: "It is high time a woman played the part. Children have for years seen a man as the high-tech wizard, with women as mere assistants." The statement was signed by London Euro-MPs Carole Tongue and Mike Elliot, Christine Crawley of Birmingham and Eddy Newman of Manchester.'

The Sunday newspaper, *The News of the World*, took up this idea, asking for suggestions from readers, and on January 11 announced the two favourites: Cilla Black and Su Pollard. Cilla was put forward because 'she could use her *Blind Date* skills to arrange matings among the space aliens', while Su Pollard would be ideal 'because children would love to see chalet maid Peggy from *Hi-De-Hi!* take the part in her outrageous clothes'.

The Seventh Doctor - Sylvester McCoy
Copyright © Rex Features Ltd.

As always, the Doctor Who Production Office had their own ideas, and impatient fans had to wait until only a few days before filming of the new series was due to begin in March 1987 before the announcement of the name of the seventh Doctor Who was given to the world.

Once again the name of the new Doctor proved a big surprise because there had been much speculation that the role was going to be taken by a well-known personality, and names like Simon Cadell, David Warner and even Jeremy Brett, then playing Sherlock Holmes for Granada TV, were bandied about!

But when the versatile Scottish actor Sylvester McCoy was confirmed on Monday, March 2 – after having been earlier predicted in *The Sun* on February 28 – the interest was just as widespread as if it had been one of those famous actors. For here was an avowedly unusual and eccentric performer, one of whose claims to fame was for holding the world record for stuffing a ferret down his trousers!

It was just the kind of detail ready-made for headline writers when carrying news of the casting of the seventh Doctor – and at a stroke the programme seemed to be returning to a Time Lord in the same kind of mould as Patrick Troughton and Tom Baker, arguably the most influential Doctors in the series.

However, fans of the show were immediately split in their opinions about the appointment of 43-year-old Sylvester. Some were disappointed after having hoped for a big name, while others thought

the gamble of picking McCoy from the enormous number of possibilities – the *Daily Mirror* claimed there had been '5,000 applicants for the role including some famous names' – was a bold and imaginative one. For his part, the new Doctor was delighted at the challenge the role offered.

'I want to turn him into a combination of David Bellamy and Magnus Pike,' Sylvester told the press conference in London, referring to the well-known natural history and scientific television personalities. 'I love people like that who are so madly interested in everything they do.'

Though McCoy's name might not have been immediately familiar to the general public, he did have years of varied acting work behind him. And a curious similarity in his background to one of his predecessors, Tom Baker – for he had also once trained for three years to be a priest!

Sylvester, who is 5ft 6ins tall, began his acting career as a performer in public houses with a bizarre act hammering a six-inch nail up his nose as well as the aforementioned ferret trick. When asked by one journalist how dangerous this trick was, he replied: 'You can't train ferrets and they do bite, but I've been lucky. I've only been bitten once – on the finger!'

Work in television followed, and Sylvester came to public notice on the popular children's show *Tiswas* and also in the comedy series *Big Jim and the Figaro Club*. Comedy is not his only forte, though, and he can also list appearances in the dramatic series *The Last Place On Earth* about Scott of the Antarctic, and in a number of Shakespearean productions.

While appearing in *Antony and Cleopatra*, for instance, he was even compared by one critic to the famous American star, Robert De Niro. 'That is one review I *did* keep – when I'd recovered from the shock!' he says.

In 1986, though, Sylvester was cast in a role which foreshadowed his becoming the seventh Doctor. For he played the magical and mysterious Pied Piper in a National Theatre production.

Another omen of things to come was his appearance with Bonnie Langford in the Gilbert and Sullivan light opera, *The Pirates of Penzance*. Now the couple are together once more as the Doctor and Melanie.

'I'm looking forward to working with Bonnie again,' Sylvester told the press conference. 'And to tussling with Kate O'Mara, who plays the Rani, and who will be one of my first adversaries.'

McCoy has an undoubted ability at playing clowns who have both heart and intelligence, and with the series again shifting the emphasis towards stories mixing space technology with comedy, the Doctor has an exciting new life-span ahead of him.

And the dramas which sprang from that traumatic day in February 1985 are now hopefully very much a thing of the past . . .

II Programme Log

1983–1986

By Jeremy Bentham

THE FIVE DOCTORS (Serial 6K) by Terrance Dick. Director: Peter Moffatt

---

It had to happen. In November 1983, after two decades as Britain's most celebrated science fiction time travel series, *Doctor Who* took a little time out of its own to do some celebrating – a glorious ninety minute specially made TV movie to mark the show's attainment of its twentieth anniversary.

The first half of the story finds the present Doctor (Peter Davison) and his earlier selves (Richard Hurndall, Patrick Troughton, Jon Pertwee and Tom Baker) lifted out of their time streams and returned to Gallifrey, the Time Lords' own planet. But the area into which they are deposited hides many dark secrets; secrets that stretch back to the very dawn of the Time Lords' history, when the nobles of Gallifrey were anything but noble in purpose. For this is the Death Zone, a forbidden area of the planet once used by the old Time Lords as a kind of arena, where representatives of distant worlds would battle each other for the amusement of Gallifreyan aristocracy. Long ago abandoned by more civilised dynasties, the Death Zone is now empty, save for the presence of the Dark Tower, the burial mausoleum of the most famous Time Lord of all, Rassilon.

Striving to reach the Dark Tower, wherein the Doctors feel lies the answer to their kidnapping, the various expeditionary groups encounter a host of opponents: Yeti, Daleks, Cybermen, a Raston Warrior robot and, perhaps most dangerous of all, the Doctors' arch enemy, the Master – all anxious to know why the Tower has once again become an active symbol of evil.

The answer comes swiftly, but to the Doctors it is a moment of tragedy. For their enemy is none other than Lord President Borusa, leader of the Time Lord High Council and one-time tutor and adviser to the Doctor(s). Now in his final regeneration and desperate to avert the ending of his existence, Borusa seeks the secret of immortality which he knows was discovered by Rassilon.

But the Dark Tower has many mysteries, and to his eternal horror Borusa learns that while Rassilon's body may be long dead, his spirit and lifeforce are eternal, commanding powers beyond the understanding of the assembled Doctors.

Borusa gets his wish, and is granted eternal life – but life as a fully conscious entity, trapped forever beneath the tomb of Rassilon, there to

The Five Doctors - including Richard Hurndall as the first Doctor and a waxwork model as the fourth Doctor!

learn the wisdom great age alone can bring. Gallifrey has lost a tyrant, but gained a stone . . .

The task of putting together a production that would do justice to so many years of travelling was a mammoth feat for the show's Producer, John Nathan-Turner. His aim was nothing less than a bringing together of all five Doctors, a host of their former companions and assistants, plus a gallery of old foes and villains, all mixed into a plot that would go some way towards extending the history of the Time Lords, and thus the inherent mythology of the programme itself.

An early casualty in this mammoth enterprise was Robert Holmes, to whom Script Editor Eric Saward gave first refusal on the writing front. Arguably the show's most adept author, Holmes nonetheless found the job of fashioning a good story out of knitting together so many pre-established elements beyond him, and left Saward no option but to seek a replacement somewhat late in the day. So, after Holmes' resignation, only one other name in the annals of 'Who-dom' was felt could possibly do justice to so great an endeavour: the programme's former, and longest-running, Script Editor, Terrance Dicks.

Abandoning, out of necessity, any ambitions to write a 'clever' story, Dicks instead weaved his tale around one of the oldest and most proven *Who* plot devices – the quest. Lifted out of their respective time zones each Doctor, plus at least one companion, would forge a path, like an updated Child Roland, to the Dark Tower of the Time Lords, there to meet . . . what?

Sadly William Hartnell had died some years earlier, but in searching for another senior actor to play the first Doctor, John Nathan-Turner was incredibly lucky in casting Richard Hurndall. Once in full costume and wearing the unmistakable wig of long, silver hair, Hurndall's resemblance to Hartnell was so acute that even Carole Ann Ford, who had worked with Hartnell, had to stop and convince herself she was not dreaming during their first day together on location.

Richard Hurndall gave an uncannily accurate performance as the first Doctor with Susan (Carole Ann Ford).

There was still a place for Hartnell himself though; a short, pre-credits introduction to the special used an extract of him from the 1964 story, 'The Dalek Invasion of Earth', promising that at some future date he would return. And how . . .

With the fourth Doctor, John Nathan-Turner was less lucky. Not having long since left the title role, Tom Baker was unhappy at the thought of returning so soon to a show that was no longer 'his'. After much deliberating he elected to withdraw, occasioning a headache for those trying to justify the title, 'The Five Doctors'.

In a bold move, Nathan-Turner decided to make use of film footage of Tom Baker and Lalla Ward (Romana) from the unseen Douglas Adams story 'Shada', which had been scrapped after a prolonged studio strike in 1979. The ploy worked, with just enough clip footage found to slake the thirsts of the millions of Tom Baker fans worldwide.

'The Five Doctors' premiered on the night of the actual anniversary,

November 23, but oddly enough not on BBC1 in Great Britain, but on Channel 11 in the acknowledged capital of US fandom, Chicago, Illinois. The Doctor's homeland had to wait two more days till the 25th, where it was scheduled as the highlight to an evening-long charity 'Telethon' in aid of 'Children in Need'. British fans did get some reward for patience however; the UK print carried an extra scene cut from the American edition, as the Master comes across the corpses of two Time Lords killed earlier by the forces of the Death Zone.

WARRIORS OF THE DEEP (Serial 6L) by Johnny Byrne.
Director: Pennant Roberts

From the bleak wastes of the Death Zone the Doctor, Tegan and Turlough travel in the TARDIS back to an even more inhospitable environment – a military sea base isolated at the bottom of the ocean in the Earth year 2084.

At this time in the planet's history two power blocs have become dominant, policing the world with a range of space-born weapons capable of ending all life on the surface. Each side lives in constant fear of attack by the other; attacks which they know will be launched from hidden underwater stations like Sea Base Four.

Shortly before the Doctor's arrival, powerful scanners pick up traces of an unidentified submarine and immediately the base is on full alert. Could this vessel have been any bearing on the mysterious death of the colony's Synch Operator? And what of garrison officers Nilson and Solow who, via a medical implant, hold a mastery over his successor, Maddox?

The mystery submarine is revealed to contain three Silurians, the leader of whom, Icthar, is a survivor from the Derbyshire shelter destroyed by UNIT in 'Doctor Who and the Silurians'. Icthar is plotting the extermination of humankind by triggering a war between the super-powers: a war which will leave these reptiles once more the masters of Earth. To do this Icthar knows he must attack and take control of the Sea Base, and has planned a two-pronged attack using a nest of re-awakened Sea Devils (the Silurians' marine cousins) and a savagely powerful beast, the Myrka.

Into the middle of this situation steps the crew of the TARDIS, immediately finding themselves prime suspects as saboteurs in the employ of the rival super-power. In the ensuing chase the Doctor almost drowns in a large tank of water before he, Tegan and Turlough are captured and brought before Vorshak, Commander of the Sea Base.

Explanations are forgotten, though, as the Silurian attack commences. The base defences crumble rapidly beneath this determined assault, the situation worsening as Solow and Nilson succeed in forcing Maddox to disable the main computer. Having succeeded in their task, Solow intends to escape, but in the attempt she falls victim to the power of the Myrka. In desperation Vorshak releases the Doctor who, in turn, constructs an ultra-violet gun which kills the monster. But he is too late. The Silurians secure the bridge, taking prisoner the time travellers and the surviving base officers. Nilson's escape attempt is also foiled and he is killed by the Sea Devils.

Icthar and the Doctor meet, but despite the latter's plea for a civilised resolution to this conflict, the Silurian leader will not be swayed. Using their own technical equipment, linked to the base's computer system, the creatures intend to launch a missile attack on Earth. Each bloc will blame the other and the final war will be triggered.

The survivors are imprisoned but Tegan and Turlough are able to escape and release the Doctor. Among the station's store rooms he discovers cannisters of a gas lethal to the reptiles. At first reluctant to use it, the Doctor eventually realises he has no choice. The creatures perish in time for the missile countdown to be stopped, but as he surveys the massed corpses of Humans, Silurians and Sea Devils alike the Doctor murmurs, 'There has to be a better way . . .'

Although by a different author, 'Warriors of the Deep' looks very carefully over its shoulder at the two Malcolm Hulke Silurian/Sea Devil stories that went before. It retained elements of the moral parable about who by right owns the Earth – humans, or their reptile predecessors and seniors – and it cast the Doctor in the middle as an unwilling arbiter, caught between two civilised but warlike people, and forced in the end to commit murder against the once great and noble reptile species; just as he had done twelve years earlier.

Creating the Silurian and Sea Devil masks became the responsibility of the Visual Effects Department. Sufficient pieces were salvaged of a 1972 Sea Devil head to permit mouldings to be taken for the five or so costumes required in this serial. But in order to fit Samurai-style battle helmets over the masks, it was decided to omit the webbed fins that had so characterised the seventies versions. Of the original Silurians, however, nothing whatsoever survived, and so newcomer Stan Mitchell, a one-time sculptor at Madame Tussauds Waxworks in London, created a whole new appearance for these land-based creatures – the only flaw in their construction arising because nobody at the Workshop could recall what the illuminated third eye in each Silurian's crest was used for. Wrongly they assumed it to be a means of identifying which Silurian was speaking (i.e. flashing in synch with the voice, Dalek-style). In the first versions, the eye was both a source of vision and a weapon. Identification of speech was effected by the simple technique of the actor inside the mask prodding an internally-fitted peg with his tongue, causing the oval rubber mouth to twitch in time with the dubbed voice.

Peter Davison's Doctor also underwent something of a transformation for this story too. Between shooting 'The Five Doctors' and 'Warriors of the Deep', Davison had been engaged to resurrect his portrayal of Tristan Farnon for a Christmas special production of *All Creatures Great and Small*. This entailed losing his flowing locks of long hair that are almost expected of any actor playing the Doctor.

Essentially a studio-bound story, episode one did feature a number of location filmed inserts, primarily at a swimming bath down on the south coast where the Doctor-drowning climax was shot. An accomplished swimmer, Peter Davison did the submerged sequences himself for this, the programme's first use of an underwater camera.

Another link to the show's past was provided by the location of the Sea Devil's hibernation shelter. Shot on the 'Facilities' stage at Shepperton Studios, these scenes marked the end of almost a twenty year absence of *Doctor Who* from Shepperton. The two Peter Cushing Dalek films had been shot there in the sixties.

THE AWAKENING (Serial 6M) by Eric Pringle.
Director: Michael Owen Morris

Unquestionably one of the most successful *Doctor Who* stories of all had been Barry Letts and Robert Sloman's 1971 masterpiece 'The Daemons', which had used as the basis of its plot an outbreak of psychic phenomena in a cut-off, rural English village. Harnessing the psionic energy of the villagers' fear and terror, the Master evoked the daemon Azal, in truth a creature from another world, dormant for thousands of years in a Bronze Age burial mound. The final confrontation between the Doctor and Azal took place in the crypt of a local church, where a '. . . foolish act of self-sacrifice' on companion Jo Grant's behalf ended the daemon's reign with an explosion large enough to demolish the entire building.

In 1971, that story had brought *Doctor Who* firmly back into the public eye, establishing the seventies trend for *Who* audiences comprised mainly of adults. And as 1984 dawned, the current incumbents of the Production Office looked optimistically towards a case of history repeating itself as they unleashed 'The Awakening'; another tale of the psychic and the supernatural, once again set in the heart of the English countryside.

This time the focus of unworldly powers is Little Hodcombe, a village fiercely proud of its place in the history books. Several centuries ago, in the midst of the English Civil War, Royalists and Roundheads clashed at Little Hodcombe in a battle renowned for its butchery and slaughter. Since that date, each year on the anniversary, the villagers close off the hamlet and, organised by descendants of the Royalist family who settled there, re-enact the events of 1643. Supposedly it is a harmless game; an opportunity for people to indulge their energies and enthusiasm in a display of zestful high spirits. But in recent years, encouraged by current landowner Sir George Hutchinson, the games have taken on a more savage tone. People have been hurt, property has been damaged, the reckless youths are running amok, encouraged by their elders. The sole voice of sanity appears to be school teacher Jane Hampden, but she is just one woman against an entire village.

The TARDIS arrives. The Doctor has brought Tegan to Little Hodcombe to visit her grandfather, local amateur historian Andrew Verney. But Verney has disappeared without trace, and Tegan is told by

Sir George that attention is far too focused on the war game for a search to be mounted. In the meantime, Hutchinson 'suggests' the travellers join in with their celebrations, and since Jane Hampden refuses the part, he proposes Tegan as Queen of the May: an unpopular role in the village as, by pagan tradition, the Queen dies at the height of the revels. Not surprisingly Tegan is unimpressed and runs off to search alone for her grandfather.

The Doctor too senses something amiss and at the earliest opportunity makes a break for freedom. Hutchinson is furious and instructs his troopers to hunt down the fugitives.

As Jane, Tegan, Turlough and the Doctor seek to evade their pursuers, more evidence comes to light that strange forces are at work in the village. In the disused crypt of the church the Doctor finds Will Chandler battering his way out of a Priest's Hole. Chandler's mode of dress and conviction that it is 1643, and not 1984, tells the Doctor that a time warp is somehow linking the two years together. But what is causing this to happen?

Gradually the truth is revealed. Long, long ago, it transpires, an alien spacecraft brought to Earth a deadly cargo, the Malus. The Malus' role is to generate, by psychic energy, a state of fear into its environment. As the victims' fear rises, so the Malus will feed and grow stronger, extending its influence and the terror it brings until the whole planet is swamped by anarchy and confusion. At that point the world will be weak, an easy target for a full scale invasion by these alien conquerors.

The battle at Little Hodcombe was the trigger that activated the Malus. Slowly, very slowly, it has gathered power over the centuries, manifesting its evil through the Hutchinson family. Now it stands poised for the quantum leap that will spread its influence out across the world – the psionic forces unleashed if the war games end in killing will free the Malus from its semi-dormant state beneath the church.

Fearing that Sir George has become deranged, his deputy, Colonel Wolsey, throws in his lot with the time travellers and helps to free Tegan from a fiery fate that would have caused the psionic surge of horror and revulsion needed fully to revive the Malus.

A last battle is fought in the church crypt. As the Doctor isolates his enemy from the emotions of the villagers, the Malus launches an all out attack by psychic projection through the medium of Sir George. But in the ensuing terror Hutchinson is pushed by Will Chandler into the maw of the Malus, thereby killing the creature's medium. The last act of the defeated monster is to vent its rage, and its existence, on the building housing it. The Doctor's group escapes just in time to watch the fiery destruction of the church and its crypt.

'The Awakening' was penned by Lake District writer Eric Pringle, a long-time admirer of *Doctor Who*, brought to the attention of Eric Saward through a Dalek script he had submitted freelance. Deciding that a psychic powers/English village story was wanted for *Doctor*

Who's twenty-first season, Saward encouraged Pringle to write the characters and the situation from local knowledge of the Lakeland area. In the end, however, budget limitations saw the finished serial location filmed in the village of Shapwick, Dorset.

Pringle's original storyline ran to four twenty-five minute scripts, and dwelt much more on the insidious shift of the games and the people from innocent pageantry to savage recklessness. Unfortunately, in a season of twenty-six episodes, one story had to become a two-parter, and 'The Awakening' lost the toss. But Pringle still holds his original scripts and is proud of the local newspaper feature done about him when it became known he had written for one of Britain's greatest TV institutions.

FRONTIOS (Serial 6N) by Christopher H. Bidmead. Director: Ron Jones

A new breed of monsters, the Tractators, reared their heads in this story, maintaining *Doctor Who*'s high reputation for creature design, matched only by the early sixties American series, *The Outer Limits*. Overall inspiration for the Tractators, unlikely though comparison seems, came from Ridley Scott's classic horror film *Alien*. The original concept in that film was for an all bone and membrane monster that could uncurl itself from a tightly knotted ball into the powerful, looming shape which menaced the astronauts. Visually this idea was not too apparent in the finished version of Scott's movie, but the idea intrigued former *Doctor Who* Script Editor Christopher Bidmead sufficiently for him to suggest it to the Director and the Designers on 'Frontios' for the Tractators.

What Bidmead envisaged were scenes of people stumbling through darkened caves, climbing past innocuous-looking rocks, those rocks then uncurling behind them to reveal the monstrous form of the Tractators. Similarly, as the creature attacked, it would wrap itself around its prey rather like a woodlouse, ultimately engulfing the hapless stray.

The Doctor and Teegan confront the Gravis in 'Frontios'.

Sadly Bidmead's hopes were not to be. Budget need for not just one Tractator but some half dozen of the beasts meant that spending on each had to be kept for absolute essentials only, with no room whatsoever for experimentation – a common regret voiced by anyone who has ever worked in the Visual Effects medium.

The Tractator bodies were made up of jointed panels, and Director Ron Jones did go to great lengths in hiring professional dancers to operate them; in the knowledge that dancers can achieve greater poise and balance than conventional actors. But the cumbersome nature of the delivered costumes prevented all but very simple movements. The casings were so heavy and suffocating to wear that the dancers had to be fed oxygen through hoses in between takes.

The venue for Bidmead's gruesome tale of parasitism is a planet right on the edge of the known Universe, beyond even the Time Lords' official sphere of influence. The TARDIS is drawn there after it temporarily materialises in the path of a swarm of meteorites. Landing to effect repairs the Doctor and company find a small colony of Earth people, marooned here since their spacecraft crashed, and ruled over by the young and inexperienced Plantagenet and his very severe first officer, Brazen. Although their community is still based around the wreck, the ship is a useless hulk, forcing the survivors to re-invent their technology virtually from scratch.

The colony is also under attack by unseen enemies who bombard them periodically with meteorites (such as the one which damaged the TARDIS), and who are believed responsible for a series of mysterious disappearances, among them the former leader of the group, Captain Revere.

As ever, the Doctor's party is treated at first with hostility by Brazen and Plantagenet. Even when the travellers come to the aid of Chief Science Officer Range, and his daughter Norna, helping them tend the wounds of those injured by the meteor storms, they are threatened with execution as spies. As another storm begins the Doctor decides it is time to go. He leads his party back to the ship, only to find a smoking crater where once it stood. Nothing is left of the TARDIS, save the hat-stand from the control room . . .

Determined to find the cause of their plight, the Doctor gains access to the spaceship's sealed off research laboratory. Setting Turlough and Norna the task of analysing the meteor storms, he is interrupted in his studies by a medical emergency. Unable to cope with the pressures of leading this beleagured colony, Plantaganet has suffered a heart attack. Only the Doctor's skills and his gift for improvisation save the life of the young monarch.

Left to their own devices, Turlough and Norna make a startling discovery. Beneath the ship is a vast hive of inter-connecting cave passages. And lurking in these caves are the Tractators; slug-like creatures able to generate enormously powerful gravitational fields. It is they, led by the mutated Gravis, who dragged the Earthmen and the TARDIS here. It is they who cause the meteor storms. And, most horrific of all, it is they who are responsible for the Colony disappearances. The Tractators's technology, such as it is, is based around harnessing the mental and physical energies of the humans they ensnare. Proof of this comes when the Doctor, seeking to rescue his friends, comes upon an excavating machine, powered by the remnants of Captain Revere.

The Doctor also finds the remains of the TARDIS, pulled apart and drawn underground by the power of the Tractators. Once they have harvested sufficient humans, the Gravis intends to pilot the planet into habited solar systems, there to commence its plan of colonisation and expansion, built on the energies of the prey they will absorb.

However, while the Gravis is powerful, it is also guileless. By offering it access to time as well as space the Doctor persuades the creature to re-assemble the TARDIS. Once this is done the Gravis is cut off from its fellows, and without leadership the others quickly revert to harmless, Earth-burrowing creatures. The Colony is saved and is free now to continue its growth unfettered by the parasitism of the Tractators. As for the Gravis, the Doctor intends removing it to a remote and barren planet whence it can do no harm. All he asks of Brazen and Plantaganet is that they don't report his interference to the Time Lords.

In this, the last of his stories for Peter Davison, Christopher Bidmead came closest to showing the plans he would have laid for the sixth Doctor had he continued as series Script Editor. As with 'Castrovalva' he insisted upon giving the Doctor a pair of narrow-rimmed spectacles and a strong air of lateral thoughtfulness, enforcing his belief that the sixth Doctor should be an old man trapped in a young man's body.

One event which marred this otherwise straightforward but effective story was the tragic murder, during production, of actor Peter Arne who had been cast as Science Officer Range. With the show well into rehearsals his part was taken at short notice by veteran actor William Lucas.

RESURRECTION OF THE DALEKS (Serial 6P) by Eric Saward.
Director: Matthew Robinson

Every Doctor has faced them. From the shining domes of their metal city on Skaro to the towering majesty of the Great Pyramids of Egypt he has found and opposed their machinations. Many times he has won battles against them, but still victory in the final war eludes him.

They are evil beyond belief, consumed with a hatred and a contempt of all other sentient life forms. Unwaveringly they are dedicated to a creed of universal supremacy, of conquering all the planets in the heavens and exterminating any for whom they have no use. They are the Daleks.

When last the Doctor encountered them (still in his fourth incarnation) the Daleks were fighting a space war against the robot Movellans. Unable to break the stalemate of both sides employing absolute logic in their military strategy, the Daleks had returned to Skaro and regenerated the body of Davros, their creator. But intervention by the Doctor blocked their plans. The Dalek task force was destroyed and Davros taken prisoner by the Earth Government.

Now, ninety years later, he lies in suspended animation, the lone prisoner in a space station orbiting the Earth.

Suddenly, without warning, a heavily-armed space cruiser attacks the station, immobilising its defences and quickly out-manoeuvring the puny resistance efforts of the bored and disconsolate crew. Aided by a squad of mercenary troopers under the leadership of the mysterious Commander Lytton, the Daleks capture the prison-dock and set about freeing Davros from his tomb of ice.

For the Doctor, involvement in this latest Dalek plan starts when the TARDIS becomes trapped in a time corridor and is forced to materialise in a disused warehouse in dockland London, 1984. Searching for the actual link point to the corridor, Tegan, Turlough and the Doctor find several alien artefacts, and are themselves found by an army Bomb Disposal team.

Explanations are cut short firstly when it is noticed that Turlough has vanished, and more alarmingly by the materialisation of a Dalek in the warehouse. A fierce struggle ensues but the Doctor's long knowledge of these creatures enables the group to destroy the machine.

Aboard the space station (the other end of the time corridor) a somewhat lost Turlough is found by a group of survivors from the crew, led by Styles and Mercer. With no escape route, their intention is to detonate the self-destruct mechanism which was always their fail-safe procedure if ever it looked as though Davros would be taken. Turlough, not keen to die, tries to persuade Mercer to use the Time Corridor as an escape means. But while they are away, Lytton's troopers find and kill Styles and her team.

Back in the warehouse the Doctor gradually becomes aware of changes in the personalities of the army colonel and his soldiers, coupled with a dawning suspicion that they have become captives. He formulates an escape plan with Stein, a refugee prisoner from the Dalek cruiser, and with him as a guide the Doctor takes the TARDIS along the time corridor to find his old foes. But once there, Stein turns on him, revealing himself as a Dalek agent.

The complexity of the Supreme Dalek's plan unfolds. Android replicas, like Stein and recently the bomb disposal team, will be placed in key positions on Earth, their job being to cause chaos and undermine resistance prior to the Dalek invasion. The Doctor too will undergo replication and be sent back to Gallifrey to destroy the High Council of Time Lords. But before any of this can happen, the Daleks need from Davros the antidote to a virus, lethal to Daleks, with which the Movellans won their war.

The flaws in this scheme are the Replicas. They are too humanly programmed and, left to supervise the Doctor's duplication, Stein revolts and releases him. They return to the TARDIS where the Doctor finds Mercer, Tegan and Turlough. Grimly he decides he must kill Davros, distasteful though such an act is to him. Accompanied by Mercer and Stein he sets off to accomplish his task, but when faced with the chance to pull the trigger, his inability to murder in cold blood restrains him.

In the meantime fighting has broken out in the station. Suspecting treachery, the Dalek Supreme has ordered the extermination of Davros and Lytton; a move causing retaliation from both parties. Davros releases a quantity of the Movellan virus, discovering too late he is subject to its effects as well. Lytton, the Doctor and his friends only just escape to Earth before Stein succeeds in setting off the auto-destruct, destroying the cruiser as well as the space station.

In the Wapping warehouse the Doctor finds a pitched battle in progress between Lytton's troopers, the Dalek Supreme's executioners, and Daleks reprogrammed by Davros. In desperation the Doctor releases more of the Movellan virus (from the cylinder artefacts he discovered earlier) which kills the half-robots, but not before virtually everyone else is left dead or dying. Sickened by this carnage, which always seems to follow in the wake of the Doctor, Tegan makes her decision to leave him. It is an emotional farewell, a sad and tearful parting that forces the Doctor to wonder if it is not time he mended his ways . . .

Although shot in four parts, British viewers saw this serial in two forty-five minute segments, the first time any premier-run *Doctor Who* had been shown in anything other than its established twenty-five minute format. Ever since the start of Peter Davison's era the show had been out of its Saturday slot, sent hunting for ratings in the potentially more profitable weekday evening schedules. The experimental notion of screening *Doctor Who* twice-weekly had been only marginally successful, so when 'Resurrection of the Daleks' clocked up nearly a million more viewers in its once-weekly, forty-five minute form, BBC chiefs studied their calculators and took a decision to plan the next season as a block of thirteen forty-five minute episodes, instead of the usual twenty-six half hours. It was a decision that was to have grave consequences for the future of the series.

PLANET OF FIRE (Serial 6Q) by Peter Grimwade. Director: Fiona Cumming

Unbeknown to the Doctor, Kamelion has again come under the influence of the Master, who is directing him by remote control from his own TARDIS. The Doctor and Turlough are initially too busy to worry about the robot's strange behaviour pattern: they are picking up a distress signal from Earth, a signal disturbingly familiar to Turlough.

Landing on the holiday island of Lanzarote, they trace the source of the signal when Turlough rescues Peri, a young American woman, from drowning. Among her possessions she is carrying an artefact originally salvaged from the sea bed by her archaeologist step-father, Professor Howard Foster. The symbol on the object is identical to a mark branded on Turlough's arm.

While they are occupied with Peri, Kamelion resets the controls of the TARDIS, abruptly transporting its occupants to the mountainous terrain of the planet Sarn. Recent severe volcanic activity has led to civil unrest among the small population. Timanov, the High Priest, tells the people to put their faith in Logar, God of the Fire Mountain, but a group of heretics, spearheaded by Amyand, Roskal and Sorasta, maintains that Logar does not exist. The views of the unbelievers have gathered much support, causing doubt in the mind of Malkon, the Sarn's young but indecisive ruler.

At first the Doctor's arrival is welcomed. He is hailed by Timanov as an emissary from Logar; that is, until a second figure appears, the Master. In truth, it is not the Master, but the changeling Kamelion. Speaking the Master's words, Kamelion denounces the Doctor and insists he be sacrificed to appease the Mountain God. His words are given even more credence when the robot's control slips for a while, allowing his silver facia to appear. The Sarns recall Logar as a silver clad God, and Timanov especially believes this to be a sign of his anger against the heretics.

Taken prisoner earlier by Kamelion, it is Peri who ultimately locates the true whereabouts of the Master when she opens a small box aboard his TARDIS. Inside is the Master, reduced to less than a tenth of his normal size through an accident with his Tissue Compression Eliminator. Restoration to his proper height is only possible by tapping the restorative gases native to Sarn and harnessed by its people to cure sickness and injuries. But in his present state he cannot accomplish this alone, hence his need for Kamelion's aid. And if the Doctor is killed along the way, then so much the better.

Partly swayed by the arguments of the unbelievers, Malkon tries to forbid the sacrifices, but he is shot and wounded by the Master/Kamelion. Turlough, though, is able to release the Doctor and it is now that he reveals some details of his background. Sarn, it transpires, is a prison world to which enemies of his own people, the Trions, were sent. Logar is nothing more than a race memory of the Trion astronauts who brought their exiles to Trion. Earth too was a world to which prisoners were sent, hence Vislor Turlough's 'sentencing' to an English public school by the Trion agent there. As proof, Turlough shows the Doctor the mark on his arm. Malkon bears an identical symbol, the brand of criminals in the eyes of the Trion government.

The Master succeeds in gaining entry to the chamber through which the volcanic gases are channelled, just as the Doctor breaks his link with Kamelion. But the robot is badly damaged. The Doctor promises repairs, but Kamelion declines, knowing his loyalty can so easily be swayed. He asks only one favour of the Doctor – destruction. It is a wish the Doctor regretfully grants.

Angrily the Doctor rounds on the Master, who has just about restored himself to normal size. He opens the valves to full, subjecting the Master to a massive dose of gas and apparently destroying him.

Meantime Turlough has summoned a ship from Trion to rescue the Sarns from their crumbling world. Expecting punishment for escaping exile on Earth, he is relieved when the Captain tells him of a new government in power on Trion. All political criminals have been pardoned, so Turlough can now return home a free man. This he elects to do, leaving the Doctor just one companion for his future travels, a loquacious American who will be quite happy if she never sees her overbearing step-father again. With a smile the Doctor bids Peri welcome.

A story of comings and goings as far as the line-up of *Doctor Who* regular artists was concerned. Having lost Tegan in the previous story, 'Planet of Fire' heralded the introduction of Perpugillian Brown (Peri for short), the re-appearance of the Master, as well as the departures of Turlough and the Doctor's most unusual companion, Kamelion.

Kamelion had been the creation of 'Imagineering', a freelance Effects company, who were asked to supply an android for Terence Dudley's two-parter 'The King's Demons'. Like K9, Kamelion was a functioning robot, but whereas the former derived its servo-driven movements from a radio control unit, Kamelion was fully programmed and controlled through a computer. Theoretically this gave Kamelion enormous potential. Given the right programming it would be able simultaneously to talk, gesture, move its head and body and even, given development, walk. Recognising this potential, John Nathan-Turner instructed the ending of 'The King's Demons' to be changed, allowing Kamelion to become a member of the TARDIS crew.

Sadly, the computer specialist responsible for all Kamelion's internal software died shortly afterwards in a tragic accident. Having left little or nothing in the way of documentation, no-one was able to pick up from where he had left off. At the same time, breakdowns in Kamelion's mechanics were presenting headaches for its designer, Richard Gregory, the upshot of both problems being a difficulty writing Kamelion into any further *Doctor Who* serials. Since it was impossible to guarantee the robot's performance, its planned appearances in post 'King's Demons' stories were curtailed one after the other, leading inevitably to John Nathan-Turner's decision to drop him from the show.

Hence a predominantly static Kamelion appearing finally, and for the final time, in 'Planet of Fire'.

THE CAVES OF ANDROZANI (Serial 6R) by Robert Holmes.
Director: Graeme Harper

Two worlds circle an alien Sun. Androzani Major is a heavily populated, industrialised planet where those who have scaled the ladder of power live in extreme opulence and wealth, their youth maintained and extended by regular doses of the wonder drug, Spectrox. Holding a monopoly on the supply and distribution of Spectrox has made Morgus the planet's biggest tycoon, a position he guards with ruthless determination.

The only source of raw Spectrox is the planet's twin, Androzani

Minor, a barren dustbowl world pitted with caves and vents through which bursts of white-hot mud periodically erupt. The 'mud-bursts' are the principal hazard faced by the three parties currently engaged in hostilities on Minor. On the one hand there is the army, commanded by General Chellak and his first officer, Salateen. They are there to re-open the Spectrox supply lines cut by an occupying force of armed androids. Then there are the gun runners, under Stotz, who in return for processed Spectrox, supply weapons and munitions to the leader of the androids, Sharaz Jek.

Once a scientist and Morgus' partner, Jek was betrayed by the tycoon and left for dead when a mud-burst caught him unawares. In a supreme exercise of self-preservation Jek managed to survive by crawling into a baking chamber. That saved his life, but the heat in the chamber seared the flesh from his face. Now lonely and bitter, he dwells alone in the caves of Androzani Minor, his scarred features hidden beneath a grotesque mask as he plots the downfall of Morgus and his empire.

Jek's skill is in the creation of androids; androids so perfect even Chellack does not realise that a member of his own staff, Salateen, is a replica. Jek substitutes androids for the Doctor and Peri when they are sentenced to face a firing squad, having unwittingly stumbled upon a camp used by Stotz and been accused of gun-running by the General.

The real Salateen, now Jek's prisoner-cum-servant, tells the pair they were rescued because Jek wants companionship in his solitary existence. He is therefore somewhat amused when he learns that both of them recently touched a nest of raw Spectrox. Both Peri and the Doctor are now infected with Spectrox Toxaemia, a poison that will kill both of them within hours and for which there is just one known, and very rare, cure – the milk from the Queen Bats found only in the deepest levels of the cave system. But no human can survive down there. There is no oxygen in those depths and a savage monster lurks down there that lives on flesh.

Undeterred, the Doctor is able to free them all, but while Salateen and Peri head back to Chellak, his own quest leads him to fall foul of the gun runners. Stotz decides to take the Doctor back to Major where he will face interrogation by their employer, Morgus, who has sought to profit even from a war against his former colleague, by supplying the unknowing Jek with his arms.

Determined to save Peri, the Doctor manages to gain control of the gun-runner's ship and he deliberately crashlands it back on Minor. Fighting a war against time and the increasingly debilitating effects of Spectrox Toxaemia, he heads back to the caves.

In the meantime, all has not been well with Morgus. Suspecting the Doctor to be a spy in the pay of the Androzani President, Morgus, in a moment of panic, kills the President and then flees to Minor in his own private space shuttle. With the fate of his business empire hanging by a thread, Morgus enlists Stotz in a sortie to find and kill Sharaz Jek – a venture that will gain them a fortune from the Spectrox Jek has been hoarding.

As a new wave of mud-bursts threatens to flood the cave system, Chellak reaches Jek's laboratory first, and in a struggle pulls the mask from his face. The horror of what lies beneath momentarily stuns the General, long enough for Jek to thrust him from the sealed laboratory, right into the path of a mud-burst.

Stotz and Morgus are next to arrive, but in the ensuing battle all three perish: Sharaz Jek has his revenge, and Morgus and Stotz retribution for their many crimes.

His strength rapidly diminishing, the Doctor manages to carry Peri back to the TARDIS, where he feeds her the small quantity of milk he drew from a Queen Bat. As she recovers, he slumps to the floor, convinced he is dying. He seems to hear the voices of his recent companions, Tegan, Nyssa, Adric, Turlough and Kamelion, encouraging him to fight on. But, drowning out all their pleas, comes the cackling voice of the Master, urging the Doctor to succumb to death.

There is a crash, and before Peri's startled eyes, a new figure is lying before her in the Doctor's clothes. He sits up, arrogantly dismissing her amazed stutters. 'Change, my dear' he explains, 'and not a moment too soon . . .'

'The Caves of Androzani' is the jewel in John Nathan-Turner's crown, a masterpiece of mood, atmosphere and powerful storytelling, littered with dramatic peaks sufficient to keep even the most casual of viewers glued to their seats. The Director on this story was Graeme Harper, a new name in directing, but an old hand Doctor Who-wise. Interviewed about 'Caves', Harper states he did it as a tribute to Douglas Camfield, the definitive action/adventure director whose sudden death just a few months earlier had caused universal sadness among his many protégés in the television industry. Harper had been Camfield's Production Assistant on 'The Seeds of Doom' and had cast Maurice Roeves as Stotz hoping to emulate the hard-hitting image John Challis had given the role of ex-Mercenary Scorby in 'Seeds'.

Breaking with tradition, John Nathan-Turner not only chose to introduce the new Doctor, Colin Baker, in the penultimate story of the season, but also insisted he be given a few lines at the end of Davison's exit episode. For Baker, the benefits of working an extra episode were tempered by the excruciating penalty of having to squeeze his expansive frame into Peter Davison's trim-fitting costume.

**THE TWIN DILEMMA (Serial 6S) by Anthony Steven.
Director: Peter Moffatt**

The new Doctor is in the throes of post-regenerative instability.

Watched by an increasingly anxious Peri, this sixth incarnation displays moods ranging from arrogant self-opinion to mad paranoia as he struts up and down the TARDIS. Venturing into the wardrobe room, he discards his dapper cricketing clothes in favour of an outlandish hotch-potch of coloured, patterned materials; a costume to suit his new, whirlpool personality.

But this rapid mood shifting has a dangerous streak to it. Terrified, Peri suddenly finds she must fight for her life as the Doctor's stability temporarily teeters over the edge and he attempts to strangle her. Fortunately he regains control in time. Shocked by his own behaviour, the Doctor intends to become a hermit. He will seek a bleak, empty world whereupon to live a frugal life of contemplation for as many years (or hundreds of years) as it will take to purge his mind of its latent wickedness. Peri, he insists, will become his disciple, a prospect she dreads as the TARDIS comes to rest on Titan 3, a desolate moon far from the spaceways of the future.

Titan 3, however, is far from empty. First the Doctor and Peri rescue Hugo Lang from the wreckage of his fighter craft and bring him to the TARDIS to recuperate. Then they set off on a rescue mission to a distant structure glimpsed on the TARDIS scanner. From what they can gather talking to Lang, alien raiders have kidnapped two identical twin children, Romulus and Remus Sylvest, from Earth. What makes these children so special is their prodigious mathematical ability, talents of enormous benefit to any enemy. Hence the pursuit of the kidnappers by Hugo' squadron. But just as they were closing on the ship, which had landed on Titan 3, a powerful energy field appeared, wiping out the entire rescue force bar Hugo's craft.

Captured by the Jacondan kidnappers, the Doctor and Peri are brought before their mission leader, the aged Professor Edgeworth. To the Doctor's amazement, Edgeworth is a Time Lord, one of those who taught him many centuries ago. Edgeworth, whose real name is Azmael, has come under the power of Mestor; a mutated slug-like Gastropod with tremendously powerful telepathic and telekinetic abilities.

Azmael leaves the Doctor and Peri sealed in the dome as the raiders lift off on the final leg of the journey back to Jaconda. Unknown to the old Time Lord, his assistant, Drak, has set a self-destruct mechanism in motion. Unable to stop the countdown, the Doctor works furiously to modify the Trans-mat station Azmael and his associates used to beam from their ship. Just in time the two transport back to the TARDIS, and with a much-recovered Hugo Lang they set off for Jaconda.

The Doctor is horrified when he steps outside. The planet that he knew as a verdant paradise has been over-run and devastated by Mestor's Gastropods. Virtually the entire world's food-stock has been devoured by these insatiable monsters.

Bursting in on Azmael, the Doctor learns that Mestor has put the twins to work on a project to move two small planets into the same orbit as Jaconda. This, Mestor has told Azmael, will bring an abundant harvest of food within range of the planet, and hence will alleviate the starvation conditions facing the Jacondans since the Gastropods over-ran their world. This is the one reason why Azmael is helping the Gastropods, that he might feed the people he once ruled before their coming.

When he finds out that Peri has been captured by Mestor's guards, the Doctor agrees to assist the twins, hoping to buy time while he devises a rescue plan. But on checking Romulus and Remus's calculations, the Doctor deduces a major flaw in the project. If Mestor brings the two planets into orbit with Jaconda, the fine balance of gravitational forces will be disrupted, sending Jaconda plunging into its sun. The resulting explosion will destroy everything except a vast hive of Gastropod eggs Mestor has been storing. These will be scattered throughout a large section of the Universe, enabling Mestor to colonise it.

Determined to prevent this, Azmael and the Doctor choose direct confrontation as a means of diverting Mestor's attention, while Peri gets the twins back to the TARDIS.

Mestor finds the protestations of the two Time Lords amusing, and further reveals that when the time is right he will put his consciousness into the Doctor's body, thereby greatly extending his life span. He demonstrates by transferring into the body of Azmael. Seizing an opportunity, the Doctor destroys Mestor's discarded slug body, giving him no means of retreat. Azmael is nearing the end of his thirteenth and final incarnation, and allows the strain of accommodating Mestor to kill him. As Azmael dies, so too does Mestor, thus saving the Universe from devastation by the Gastropods.

Hugo Lang tells the Doctor he will stay behind to help the Jacondans restore their world, so the twins will have to return to Earth in the TARDIS. Back aboard the ship the Doctor tells Peri his regeneration has now stabilised. Whatever her feelings for his former incarnation, she must accept the fact that *he* is now the Doctor – like it or not!

Although credited to Anthony Steven, a considerable amount of work on the script for 'The Twin Dilemma' was shared with Eric Saward, whose main responsibility was retailoring it into a vehicle for introducing the new Doctor.

Colin Baker was chosen for the title role after John Nathan-Turner had been impressed by his wit and flair for repartee at a wedding reception both men had attended. Wanting to inject a sparkle of mercurial humour into the series, Nathan-Turner felt Baker perfect for the role, and also suggested the costume, which would reflect a person whose mind races from one subject to another with no regard for formality or convention.

An unplanned extra was the multi-coloured umbrella, hastily provided to protect the outfit from rain during the press photo-call. Using these photographs as reference, merchandisers and illustrators alike included it with the costume, though in truth, not until Colin Baker's final season in 1986 did it make an official appearance in the series.

ATTACK OF THE CYBERMEN (Serial 6T) by Paula Moore.
Director: Matthew Robinson

In 1986, during the last adventure of his first incarnation, the Doctor witnessed the destruction of the planet Mondas, home world of the Cybermen, as it invaded the orbit of the Earth. In that fiery conflagration most of the Cybermen died, but sufficient numbers escaped to make a second home on planet Telos, where they ruthlessly subjugated the native Cryon population. Since then the Cybermen have sought to increase their dwindled numbers by converting other humans into mechanised beings like themselves.

However, victories for the Cybermen have been few (some due to the direct intervention of the Doctor in his various bodies), and thus, at this point in the future, they are all but driven back to their underground cities on Telos.

But now, the acquisition of a captured time machine has given rise to a bold plan to change the whole course of history. Under the direct command of the Cyber-Controller, a task force of Cybermen has travelled back in time to Earth, 1985, and established a base in the one area already known to them: the sewers of London. Their intention is to divert the path of the approaching Halley's Comet, so that it collides with the Earth. That will so weaken the planet and its population that when Mondas arrives a year later and launches its 'historic' attack, the Cybermen will win. The planet Telos will then be abandoned and destroyed.

The plan is flawless in its logic, but as in all logical equations there are random elements to consider – the X factors. One element the Cybermen could not have foreseen is Commander Lytton, the alien mercenary stranded on Earth by the Doctor (see 'Resurrection of the Daleks').

Lytton has apparently turned to crime for survival, and presently his intention is to rob the vault of a big diamond merchant, with the help of Griffiths, Payne and an undercover policeman, Russell.

The Doctor and Peri pick up a distress call in the TARDIS and trace it to London, 1985. After some running about, they eventually follow the trail to the sewers where they meet Russell. He has been left for dead by the robbers once they had guessed his identity, but the man is sufficiently conscious to blurt out Lytton's name.

Up ahead, Lytton's gang are ambushed and captured by the

bridgehead party of Cybermen. To Griffiths' amazement, Lytton shows no surprise at their encounter. Indeed he tells the Cyber Leader his intention all along was to establish contact with a view to becoming an ally. As proof of his words, Lytton helps the Cybermen capture first the Doctor then his TARDIS, the latter a device which will be of great benefit in their plan to change history.

The Doctor is forced to pilot the TARDIS back to Telos where he learns firsthand of the Cyber-Controller's scheme. It seems as though the Controller's plan is unstoppable, until more random elements enter the calculation.

Escaping her captors Peri falls in with a party of Cryons engaged on sabotaging the tombs of the main Cyber-army who are in a state of suspended animation. Their work is causing Cybermen to awaken prematurely in a deranged state, although they realise this is only an irritant to the Controller, and they are fast running out of time.

Another element is Bates and Stratton. These two are slave workers, labouring on the surface sinking explosives into the planet's crust. These are the bombs that will blow the Telos apart once the main plan has succeeded, and naturally neither man is relishing the prospect of digging his own grave. Bates has a plan of escape, but to make it work will require a suit of Cyberman armour, and access to the captured time machine . . .

Finally there is Lytton. Ostensibly willing to help the Cybermen, his true allegiance is to the Cryons and their cause. At first his efforts to thwart their plans look like failing; the Cyber-Controller rejects his offered help and instead instructs he be cybernised – the process by which humanoids are turned mentally and physically into Cybermen. But the tide turns as the Cryons attack, Bates and Stratton mount their raid, and the Doctor breaks free. The Cybermen fight back but as the crucial moment approaches their fate is in the hands of Lytton, and his willingness to make the ultimate sacrifice . . .

Maurice Colbourne, now star of the glossy BBC sailing series *Howard's Way*, was more than pleased to be offered the chance of re-creating and redeeming the character of Lytton, whose fate had been left undecided at the end of 'Resurrection of the Daleks'.

This open ending had been intentional on writer Eric Saward's behalf. Liking very much the role of Lytton as an enigmatic mercenary, whom the Doctor is later forced to admit he misjudged, Saward always planned that he would return. And if that rematch could be achieved alongside Saward's favourite *Doctor Who* monster, the Cybermen, so much the better.

Hence the contracting of Paula Wolsey to write the story under the preferred name of Paula Moore. Agreements between the BBC and the various Authors' and Writers' unions discourage series Script Editors from penning too many scripts themselves. So getting his Cyberman/ Lytton storyline off the ground meant turning to another writer and offering her the opportunity to pen a full script using Saward's sleeve notes.

One extra touch put into the story, which had been originally suggested for 'The Five Doctors' was a revisit to the 76 Totters Lane junkyard where the series had begun back in 1963. The junkyard set in 'An Unearthly Child' had been a studio mock-up, but for 'Attack of the Cybermen' the production team were able to find a suitable location venue in the backstreets of Acton.

'Attack of the Cybermen' saw *Doctor Who* returning to its regular Saturday evening slot for the first time since Tom Baker's departure, but in the promised forty-five minute episode format. The omens, however, seemed good with part one of the story netting almost nine million viewers, one million more than had watched the 'Resurrection of the Daleks' pilot study.

VENGEANCE ON VAROS (Serial 6V) by Philip Martin. Director: Ron Jones

'TV, the opium of the masses.' Rarely has this oft misquoted reference been so aptly coined than as the underlying theme for this, Philip Martin's debut story for *Doctor Who*.

Philip Martin's big claim to television fame before *Doctor Who* was the highly lauded series, *Gangsters*, an unconventional crime thriller which itself challenged the rules of programme making. The second series in particular featured sequences more in tune with a pop video than a straightforward drama production. It was this oblique style of thinking that warmed the *Doctor Who* Production Office towards Martin's ideas, and with *Gangsters* as a credible starting point, Martin was given permission to try a somewhat experimental, not to mention controversial, story.

The first theme Martin explores in 'Vengeance on Varos' is video gaming. By the summer of 1984, when this serial entered production, the fad for video games was at its height in Britain. Night after night millions of youngsters forsook the traditional pastimes of youth to wage war on seemingly endless varieties of screen-bound alien attackers. From the amusement arcades of London's West End to household TV sets linked to home computers, fanged monsters and flying saucers alike were mercilessly blasted to extinction in addictive orgies of channelled aggression.

What then, Philip Martin thought, of a planet where TV exists to cater for such bloodlust; where the images on the screens, of torture, maiming and death, are not animated graphics but live 'entertainment'? Might it be feasible, he suggested, that the government of a poor and hungry world might seek to divert its people from their un-ending hardship with daily presentations of catharsis-inducing violence?

The second theme Martin extrapolates is the development of television itself. In this future society on Varos, viewers are not just passive spectators. Using their 'voting' buttons, members of the audience can participate in matters as trivial as game shows or as crucial as the election of the Varos Governor. And as a gruesome linking of the two concepts, should a democratic vote show a majority not in favour of a Governor's decision, viewers at home can watch, live, his agonised death as each vote against boosts the power of deadly beams focussed on the chair in which he sits.

Hence the characters of Etta and Arak in the story. They play no part whatsoever in the main plot. They are slaves given the illusion of democratic power. Their role is simply to watch the televised events of the story unfold, adding subjective comments on the entertainment value offered by each such video nasty or Government Broadcast.

The Doctor finds this state of affairs in progress when he lands on Varos, desperate to find a source of the ultra-rare mineral, Zeiton 7, with which to effect a vital repair to the TARDIS. Varos is one of the few worlds in the entire Universe where Zeiton 7 can be mined, a fact of which the local government of Varos is totally ignorant.

Varos sells its Zeiton 7 exclusively to a large, intergalactic combine whose representatives on Varos, currently a maggot-like creature called Sil, deliberately mislead the Varosians about its true value. As far as the Varosians are concerned, their mineral is common, hence the annual struggle by the elected Governor to maintain a market price that will just about feed his people. This year especially, negotiations are not going well. Far from raising the price of Zeiton 7, Sil is proclaiming a market depression and insisting on a price cut. Pressure to accept this offer is mounting, supported by some of the Chiefs of Staff, secretly recipients of bribery payments from Sil's corporation.

The new Governor, however, is proving obstinate. A just and fair man, he knows he is battling insuperable odds, supported only by the courage of his conviction that there must be a better life for his people. He has endured and survived many democratic votes and is now a tired man, constantly balancing his beliefs against his expected duties, desperate to find an ally, but wary of trusting any newcomer.

The TARDIS drops the Doctor and Peri right in the middle of the Punishment Dome, a huge public 'entertainment' complex where every horror imaginable can be brought to bear on its hapless inmates, their cries and sufferings then relayed by cameras and sound mikes to every home on the planet. The travellers' first act is to release from the path of a laser a young rebel leader named Jondar, whose crime was voicing protest at the system governing them.

With the help of Areta, Jondar's friend, the group manages to escape from the complex, only to be pursued and captured by Chief Guard Maldak and his men.

For his actions in spoiling an 'entertainment', the Doctor is promised a taste of television fame. He will be the star of the next 'nasty', helping the balance of payments on Varos by lucrative sales of the edited video release. Peri too will feature in a video export. Along with Areta, she will be handed over to Scientist Quillam for participation in his biological transmutation experiments. Audiences love a good transformation scene, so Peri's evolution from animal to bird should be worth a considerable sum to interested buyers.

Fortunately for all of them, help is at hand. Not only does the Doctor survive his star role, but with help from the Governor, he defeats the plan by Sil and the Chief Officer to seize power and put the planet under direct control by Sil's corporation. Furthermore, fearing a scandal if news of the attempted coup got out, the Corporation instructs Sil to accept whatever price for Zeiton 7 the Governor considers reasonable.

Prosperity for Varos is within the Governor's grasp, but the price, insists the Doctor, must be total abandoning of video nasties. As TV screens go blank all over the planet, Etta and Arak wait patiently for 'normal service to be resumed as soon as possible'.

THE MARK OF THE RANI (Serial 6X) by Pip & Jane Baker. Director: Sarah Hellings

Of the many legends told at *Doctor Who* conventions around the world, one of the most curious concerns the producer of the mega-dollar earning soap series *Dynasty*. Seeking to cast another British actress in the mould of Joan Collins for his series, Aaron Spelling's search had purportedly been fruitless until, one evening, he sat down and caught a late-night showing of *Doctor Who* on his local TV station. The programme he saw was 'The Mark of the Rani' which, as with most *Doctor Whos* shown in America, was transmitted complete, i.e. both episodes shown together.

The next morning, so the story goes, Spelling assigned his casting team to the task of tracking down and making approaches to the actress playing the cool villainess in 'The Mark of the Rani', Kate O'Mara.

During the sixties and early seventies Kate O'Mara had been one of the 'Scream Queens' of the highly popular Hammer Horror Films. However, the demise of the British Horror film industry, in the wake of the *Star Wars* boom, had heralded a similar decline in Kate O'Mara's screen appearances. Up until her accepting the role in *Doctor Who*, she was most remembered for the sea-faring series *Triangle*. *Dynasty* changed all that, leaving Kate O'Mara today a highly sought-after actress for film and television roles on both sides of the Atlantic.

The only loser from this abrupt transition was *Doctor Who*. O'Mara's move from Wood Lane to Hollywood re-opened a gap in the forward planning of the series Producer John Nathan-Turner hoped he had filled.

A female foe for the Doctor was in reply to many letters received by the Production Office bemoaning why all the Doctor's enemies tended towards the masculine gender: from Cybermen to his arch-foe, the Master. The Rani, a Hindu word meaning Queen or Princess, would redress this imbalance. Like the Master, she would be a renegade Time Lord and an expert scientist. Unlike the Master, her motives, which the Doctor would oppose, were amoral rather than deliberately evil.

Her debut story saw the Rani masquerading as an elderly bath house proprietress in a small mining community during the early years of the nineteenth-century. With her TARDIS and her laboratory both hidden behind a false wall, she uses the bath house as a trap to ensnare unwary miners. Rendering them unconscious, the Rani draws from their brains the chemical which induces natural sleep. She does this because there is a desperate need for the drug on the planet she rules, without which her people will die.

Extracting this fluid does not physically damage the victims, save for leaving a red mark on their necks. But it does stop them ever again being able to sleep. Without sleep the miners become hyper-active, aggressive and ultimately violent, attacking even their colleagues and kinfolk.

Lord Ravensworth, the owner of the mine, has no knowledge of all this, and sees the anger vented against the mine and its equipment as an outbreak of Luddism. This saddens him because he is anxious to improve working conditions by encouraging the development of industrial technology. His young Chief Engineer, George Stephenson, is already showing much promise in the area of steam locomotion, and shortly Ravensworth will host a meeting of all the inventors prominent at this time, including Faraday and Davy.

This meeting is one of the reasons why the Master has landed nearby. If he can assassinate these men, then the Industrial Revolution will falter and perhaps fail. The angry and restless victims of the Rani's experiments will make excellent subjects for domination, lending the Master a mob workforce with which to achieve one of his prime ambitions, to become ruler of the Earth.

But his prime objective is, as ever, the defeat and death of the Doctor. Unreliable as always, the TARDIS has dropped its passengers here in this north-east corner of England, instead of Kew Gardens as the Doctor had hoped. Shadowing his old adversary from a distance, the Master's first attempt to despatch the Doctor almost succeeds. Persuading a group of processed miners that the Doctor is an inventor here to implement machinery that will put them out of work, the Master watches gleefully as the gang attacks the colourful Time Lord. They bind him to a pit wagon and set it rolling along a railway leading to a vertical vent-shaft down to the mine.

Just in time the Doctor is rescued by Peri, with a little help from Lord Ravensworth.

Accepting his Lordship's hospitality, the Doctor begins learning of the strange events which have turned peaceful family men into rampaging brutes. He follows a series of clues to the bath house where he too is rendered unconscious, and almost falls victim to the Rani's machinations.

Recognising him as a fellow Time Lord, and then meeting the Master, irritates the Rani. Why can't they both go and squabble somewhere else, she complains, instead of interrupting her vital work here? Reluctantly, she is drawn into the conflict between the two adversaries when the Master steals the precious vial of fluid she has collected from her victims.

After that, all the Doctor's ingenuity is needed to oppose his twin protagonists, even to a point where he is threatened with transmutation into a tree . . .

Finally he locates the Rani's TARDIS, and after a few modifications, sets it on an irreversible journey to the furthermost corners of the Universe with the Rani and the Master as reluctant passengers.

The extensive location filming for this story was done at Blists Hill Open-air Museum at Ironbridge in Shropshire, where there is a perfectly preserved example of a small mining town during the Industrial Revolution. Director Sarah Hellings and her team found there was little they needed to do in achieving the look of the early nineteenth century. About the only problem they encountered was masking off the electric street lamps from the camera's eye.

Although filmed after 'The Two Doctors', it was decided for dramatic reasons to screen this story first, as the following serial 'Timelash' also had the Doctor meeting a character from history.

THE TWO DOCTORS (Serial 6W) by Robert Holmes. Director: Peter Moffatt

The power of time travel is a closely guarded secret, possessed only by a few races throughout the entire cosmos, and policed by the self-proclaimed Lords of Time on Gallifrey. They realise the potential for cataclysm any undisciplined ventures into the past or future can cause, and presently are concerned at the recent discoveries of Professors Kartz and Reimer aboard the orbiting Space Research Centre. Encouraged and funded by the Head of Projects, Dastari, the two men have built a prototype time travel capsule and are close to commencing test flights.

Feeling intervention is warranted, the Time Lords choose the Doctor as their intermediary. Their summons is received by the Doctor in his second incarnation who, with Jamie, foregoes his errant wanderings for a while and travels to the space station to discuss matters with Dastari. But a heated debate between the two men is halted when a Sontaran task force launches a surprise attack. Aided by their collaborators aboard the station, two Androgums named Chessene and Shockeye, Marshal Stike's warriors enter the base unopposed, slaughtering all they find. Jamie is only just able to flee into the air ducts, but the Doctor is cut down by a blast from a Sontaran gun.

The effects of this shot are felt across the years by the Doctor in his sixth body. He knows something terrible has happened, but reasons that whichever of his earlier selves has been attacked cannot be dead, or he too would be similarly demised. Hastily re-setting the controls of the TARDIS, he and Peri depart for the space station.

The scene greeting their arrival is a grim one. The raiders have gone, but a legion of corpses testifies to their acts of aggression. Exploring the empty research centre the Doctor finds some evidence suggesting that his former self has been taken out of time somewhere. But where?

Just outside present day Seville in Spain, a moth-collecting expatriate Briton, Oscar Botcherby, glimpses with mystification the landing descent of a Sontaran space pod.

Having used the limited time travel resources currently available to them, the Sontarans intend taking over a 'safe house' to continue their experiments in secret. Although this operation is nominally headed by Dastari, clearly Chessene is the driving force. Once a flesh-obsessed cannibal like her partner Shockeye, Chessene's intellect was raised to a superior level by Dastari's experiments in Technological Augmentation. But with intelligence came burning ambition and a thirst for power. It was Chessene who contacted and arranged the agreement with Marshal Stike. It was she who selected this run-down villa for use as a 'safe house'. And now it is she who is bringing pressure to bear on the second Doctor, only stunned in the raid, to help in the time travel experiments.

Amid the ducts and tunnels of the space station, Jamie meets up with the sixth Doctor and Peri, and together they make their way to Spain. There they encounter Oscar Botcherby and his friend Anita who alert them to the strange new arrivals at the villa.

Unable to force their captive into working for them, Chessene instructs Dastari to carry out the same Technological Augmentation operation on the second Doctor as he performed on her. Not only will this give her an intellectual equal, she estimates, but if the Doctor also receives a quantity of genetic material from a suitable donor, such as Shockeye, he too will become an Androgum and thus loyal to their cause.

Dastari's initial misgivings about such a transfer prove justified. The

Doctor becomes an Androgum in mind and body, but the mental augmentation does not take, and to Shockeye's delight, the Doctor becomes a flesh-obsessed creature like himself.

Such is the driving instinct for food that the ravenous Time Lord decides to take Shockeye on a tour of Seville to find the best restaurant in town, which just happens to be the one run by Oscar Botcherby. They gorge themselves to excess but when the bill arrives, neither has funds suitable to pay it. As a fight breaks out Shockeye resolves the problem, using his butcher's knife to fillet Oscar alive.

While they are away, the sixth Doctor puts paid to the Sontarans' plan to master time. He sabotages the Kartz/Reimer prototype module, in the process killing Stike, his subordinate Varl and Chessene, but not before the latter has killed Dastari in a fit of rage. But the Doctor's final problem is the powerful Shockeye who, on returning to the villa, flies into a rage, chasing him out into the countryside intent on rending him limb from limb. Luckily the Doctor finds a bottle of cyanide left by Oscar on one of his butterfly hunts. Grimly fighting to hold a handkerchief full of cyanide over the Androgum's face, he is able at last to kill the alien cannibal.

Tissue rejection reverts the second Doctor back to his old self, although in typical fashion, there is no love lost between the two Doctors as they exchange their unfond farewells, and depart for their respective time streams.

Far from being the 'forgotten' Doctor, Patrick Troughton found, after appearances first at the 1983 NFT *Doctor Who* Anniversary Weekend and then at the Ultimate Celebration in Chicago, that he was one of the most remembered in the title role. Mentioning to John Nathan-Turner an idea he had proposed to Barry Letts in 1972 for re-uniting the second Doctor and Jamie with the current regulars, Troughton was predictably pleased at finding a similar concept adopted twelve years later for this twenty-first anniversary show.

Ironically, 'The Two Doctors' became more of a *cause célèbre* than any of its cast or production team could have predicted. Totally by coincidence, it was on air during the dramatic fortnight when the Controller of BBC1, Michael Grade, announced the suspension (mooted as 'cancellation') of *Doctor Who* due to poor ratings and excessive violence.

'The Two Doctors' marked one peak in the criticisms about gratuitous horror, voiced against the current series. The mangling of Lytton's hands in 'Attack of the Cybermen,' followed by the acid bath 'video nasties' in 'Vengeance on Varos' seemed culminated by sequences of Shockeye biting the neck out of a rat, and the present Doctor gassing an opponent to death in this serial. Coupled with strangely low ratings for such an epoch-making serial, these protests added ominous weight to Grade's objections about *Doctor Who*, objections which were to have a fundamental effect on the show's history in the next two years.

TIMELASH (Serial 6Y) by Glen McCoy. Director: Pennant Roberts

Many critics in their observation of *Doctor Who* have remarked on the debt owed by the series to the writings of H.G. Wells, 'the Father of Science-fiction'. Even Sydney Newman, the show's creator, acknowledges 'The Time Machine' as the hub around which he weaved his concept of a visitor lost in the fourth and fifth dimensions. And not a few literary commentators have likened the Daleks to the death-ray armed, 'glittering leviathans' of 'War of the Worlds'.

So it was perhaps appropriate that in 'Timelash' a little of the debt was recognised and, somewhat cheekily, turned on its head. Far from H.G. Wells inspiring *Doctor Who*, writer Glen McCoy dared suggest that *Doctor Who* might, after all, have inspired H.G. Wells . . .

The setting is the planet Karfel, a planet on the brink of war with its neighbours, the Bandrills. The people of Karfel are ruled by the Borad, an aged and ruthless dictator who demands total submission to his will, under pain of death or, even worse, sentencing to the Timelash.

Development of the Timelash has given the Borad and his puppet council a weapon to quell all but the strongest of rebellious hearts. Once thrust into the Timelash cabinet's maw, a sentenced prisoner accepts there is no return. His one-way trip down a time corridor can land him anywhere, from a molten pool at the dawn of creation, to an airless world in the far-flung future.

Regular public broadcasts of screaming victims hurled mercilessly into the gaping abyss keep the Karfelons loyal to the Borad, even though a rising majority realises there is no way Karfel can win the forthcoming interplanetary conflict. Certain free-thinking citizens inside the underground city, and a small band of rebels in the cave tunnels beyond, have attempted acts of insurrection, but the Borad's sophisticated monitoring system warns him of all opposition, and his android guardoliers are ruthless in their policing.

Even members of the so-called High Council are not immune to surveillance, as Councillor Vena discovers when she discusses treason with one of her colleagues, Renis. She is denounced by the new Council President, Maylin Tekker, and condemned to the Timelash. But before sentence can be carried out, she snatches Tekker's amulet of office and flings herself voluntarily into the vortex.

The amulet is more than just a symbol of office, it is also the key to the planet's power system, and its retrieval is vital.

Vena's journey down the time corridor takes her to Inverness, Scotland towards the turn of the nineteenth century, but on route she passes through the environs of the TARDIS and is spotted by the Doctor and Peri. Concerned for the woman's safety, the Doctor steers his ship back to the corridor's source. He is astounded to find himself back on Karfel, a world he visited while still in his third incarnation, and cheerfully accepts Tekker's offered hospitability.

Tekker intends the Doctor will retrieve the amulet, and has Peri taken prisoner as a guarantee of his compliance. Reluctantly the Doctor agrees and follows Vena to Inverness, where he finds she is being looked after by a young writer named Herbert.

Herbert is incorrigibly curious and stows away aboard the Doctor's time machine on its return trip to Karfel.

Meanwhile, assured of the Doctor's obedience, Tekker decides to dispose of Peri by feeding her to the Morlox – savage beasts which dwell in the caves beyond the city. There she is rescued by a group of rebels, headed by Katz and Sezon, who, after questioning her, draw courage from news that the Doctor, once before the saviour of Karfel, has returned.

Peri's rescue is short-lived. Admiring her tenacity and quick-wittedness, as well as her physical beauty, the Borad instructs she be recaptured and brought to his sanctum, where he has a use for her.

That use, the Doctor discovers, is participation in a genetic engineering experiment. Breaching the sanctum's defences he finds the Borad far from the white-haired old man seen by Karfelons on their broadcast screens. Half his face is that of a young man, the Borad as he was. The other half is the head of a Morlox, a combination the result of an accident years ago which genetically combined the two creatures. As a hybrid, the Borad found his intelligence and his life-span considerably expanded, hence his wish to conduct the same metamorphosis on Peri, turning her into an ageless companion for the lonely dictator.

Delving further into the Borad's motives, the Doctor learns the true reason why he is inciting a war with the Bandrills. The Borad wants the Karfelons destroyed that he might repopulate the planet with mutated life forms based on the Morlox.

Launch of the Bandrill attack galvanises the Doctor into action. Though a blend of technical ingenuity and brinkmanship diplomacy, he ends the life of the Borad (and his clone) and negotiates an end to the war.

His last job is returning Herbert back to Scotland. Peri is concerned he might misuse the knowledge he has gained from the future, until the Doctor produces Herbert's calling card, bearing the legend, *H.G. Wells*.

The guest star in 'Timelash' was Paul Darrow, who had featured once before in a *Doctor Who* story ('Doctor Who and the Silurians') but long before his rise to fame in the other BBC hit science-fiction series *Blake's 7*. Interviewed about playing the oily, fawning Tekker, Darrow admitted to liking the part because it gave him an opportunity, 'to go really over the top', trying to match the extrovert eccentricities of Colin Baker's character.

Production of this serial was not entirely trouble-free. After the show had been fully recorded and edited, it was found that episode two under-ran by more than five minutes. Hastily Eric Saward wrote a 'padding' scene, featuring only the Doctor and Peri set inside the TARDIS. This scene was then shot during recording of the subsequent show, 'Revelation of the Daleks' and edited into 'Timelash' shortly before transmission.

REVELATION OF THE DALEKS (Serial 6Z) by Eric Saward.
Director: Graeme Harper

The return of Graeme Harper to direct a Dalek story was a prospect relished by all long-term fans of *Doctor Who*. At last, after years of watching the once shiny silver machines degenerate into blackened hulks, battered by years of church fete openings and indelicate handling, the promise of a whole new set of Dalek casings seemed the answer to a prayer. As press photo-call pictures showed the four new machines being wheeled out of the workshop, resplendent in their cream and gold livery, loyal viewers held their breath in anxious anticipation of Season 22's much-advertised climax.

The story surprised everyone, shocked some, confused others, but won every season poll by massive majorities. It was unconventional to the point of surrealism, graphic in its use of shock sequences, and lensed more in the style of a French art movie than straightforward TV science-fiction directing.

The full irony of the story was that the Daleks were hardly in it. The mainstay of the plot, which Eric Saward admits was a black comedy inspired by Evelyn Waugh's book, *The Loved Ones*, was Davros in his most macabre screen appearance to date.

The story opens as the Doctor arrives on the planet Necros, intending to pay his final respects to an old friend, Professor Arthur Stengos. Necros has two thriving industries. The first, a series of factories run by influential businesswoman Kara, produces cheap, synthetic protein, used to feed populations on less well-off planets. Much of the huge profit Kara reaps is due to the scientific researches of her partner, Davros.

Their relationship is totally commercial. In return for the process producing the high-yield synthesized protein, Davros receives considerable funding for further developing the Daleks. Recently, however, Kara has had second thoughts about the diverting of so much profit into the Dalek project, and secretly she is looking to hire a professional assassin to remove her company's one major cost liability.

The other big operation on Necros is 'Tranquil Repose', a resting place for the doomed but not dead. 'Tranquil Repose' exists to offer clients dying of incurable diseases the facility of cryogenic suspension,

Davros and the Daleks still unsuccessfully plotting the Doctor's downfall in 'Revelation of the Daleks'

until such future times when cures for their illnesses have been found. Those who avail themselves of his unique service are put into special storage cells, their metabolic functions slowed by deep freezing, although their 'resting' consciousnesses are kept fully educated, informed and entertained about events in the cosmos through a specially provided broadcasting service.

As cursory interest turns to serious investigation, the Doctor finds there are fundamental, unanswered questions about 'Tranquil Repose'. Why is it that no-one arriving there is ever heard of again? What is the truth behind rumours of body snatching and unexplained disappearances? And just who is 'the Great Healer' who serves as patron and apparent benefactor of 'Tranquil Repose'?

Discovery that the Great Healer is none other than Davros leads the Doctor to other grim revelations as he meets Arthur Stengos' daughter, Natasha. She and her partner Grigory have verified that most of the storage cells are empty. The majority of the 'Resting Ones' have been removed by Davros and turned into the base ingredient of the synthetic protein marketed by Kara's factories.

More recent arrivals, including Stengos himself, have suffered an even worse fate. Biologically altered by Davros, they are gradually becoming Dalek mutants. Once their minds and bodies are fully transmuted, they will become the core of a new race of Daleks, which Davros will then lead in a war of conquest against the Daleks on Skaro. His intention is nothing less than the total remodelling of the Dalek species, whom he believes to have strayed from the blueprint he envisaged at their genesis.

Aware of the Doctor's presence, Davros begins activating some of his newly created Daleks, feeling that he now has sufficient power to take direct control of 'Tranquil Repose' and Kara's factories.

But the Doctor finds he has allies, albeit from most unusual sources. Kara's hired assassin arrives in the form of Orcini, once a Grand Master Knight in his order, now a figure fallen from grace questioning the very reasons for his existence, but still with the talents and resources of an expert killer, and aided by his loyal squire, Bostock.

Then there are the Daleks on Skaro. Worried by the Great Healer's plans, two attendants at 'Tranquil Repose', Takis and Lilt, contact the Dalek Supreme, who despatches a ship to bring Davros back to face his trial.

Fighting begins and as the battles rage the casualty list mounts: Kara, Bostock, Orcini. At one point it even looks as though Davros is destroyed once and for all, but the master of tissue cloning has anticipated even the assassin's gun.

However, strong though the newly-created Daleks are, they are eventually wiped out by the superior numbers from Skaro. Davros is captured and must face the ignominy of answering to his own protégés.

The two industries on Necros lie in ruins, but the Doctor is able to suggest an alternative. On his way there he noticed clumps of a soya-bean-type plant growing. Cultivating and harvesting these plants should enable the factories to supply cheap protein from a more agreeable source than Davros had provided. As for the tired Peri, he suggests a holiday for the both of them, and knows just the place . . .

And a holiday for *Doctor Who* it was too. The end of 'Revelation of the Daleks' saw the programme beginning its eighteen-month period of suspension as decreed by Michael Grade. Part of Grade's opinion that *Doctor Who* had 'lost its direction' stemmed from the violence he had seen in the current season, epitomised by the two episodes of this Dalek story with its trail of strangulations, sword stabbings, severed legs and blown-off hands.

Director Graeme Harper stood by his work though, stating a preference for *Doctor Who*'s style of violent horror, accompanied by visible grief and suffering, to the sanitised violence of US shows like *The A-Team* (*Doctor Who*'s principal ratings opponent at this time) where characters escaped apparently unharmed from exploding cars.

The argument continued to rage for several months after the 'cancellation' and was never fully resolved. Nevertheless *Doctor Who* was demonstrably different in style on return from its break in the autumn of 1986.

THE TRIAL OF A TIME LORD – THE MYSTERIOUS PLANET (Serial 7A) by Robert Holmes. Director: Nick Mallett

A spectacular model effects sequence, reminiscent of *Star Wars*, opens the first of fourteen episodes linked under the generic title, 'The Trial of a Time Lord'.

A tractor beam of immense power shoots out from the landing bay of a gigantic Gallifreyan space station, plucking the Doctor and his TARDIS from their current location and drawing them here, where the outraged occupant finds he must answer for his adventures in time and space.

Once more, the Doctor is on trial for his life, a theme ironically applicable to the factual as well as the fictional aspects of the programme in this troubled year.

Michael Grade had made it no secret that he would be keeping a close watch on the 23rd season to see if *Doctor Who* still merited its special status as an annual series. But just as production routines seemed to be settling down after the year-long break, the shock resignation of Script Editor Eric Saward, after a heated behind-the-scenes row, hit everyone concerned with, or about, the programme's future for six.

Saward was co-architect of the 'Trial' umbrella theme as well as author of the final episode, so his departure mid-season taking with him all rights to use his script material, left the entire season without a structured ending. And worse was to follow.

The other architect of the season was Robert Holmes, writer of 'The Mysterious Planet' and contracted co-writer of the last two episodes. On Saturday May 24th 1986, Holmes died, following a period of illness. This threw a further question mark as to how the epic-length story would conclude. As summer lengthened towards autumn 'The Trial of a Time Lord' found it had no ending, and only a partially-edited middle. It did have two things in its favour though; a fully completed beginning, and the traditional Saturday evening, twenty-five minute slot *Doctor Who* had been without since 1981.

The return of *Doctor Who* to its institutional position was part of Michael Grade's bid to re-establish BBC1's domination of Saturday evening viewing. At its peak during the mid-seventies, *Doctor Who*, along with Basil Brush, the Forsyth/Grayson *Generation Game* and drama series like *The Duchess of Duke Street* were pulling audiences in excess of 14 million, totally wiping out any opposition by ITV.

Hence the 'big-budget-looking' opening model shot in 'The Mysterious Planet'. Its function and placing were specifically to grab an audience, sit them down, and make them want to watch the programme, and hopefully the rest of BBC1's Saturday output, for the next fourteen weeks.

After the model shot came the introductions. Storming into a gallery adjoining the landing bay, the Doctor finds it already set up as a Court of Enquiry. He acknowledges the jury, all Time Lords in full ceremonial robes, and is introduced to the judge presiding over these deliberations, a female Time Lord whose title is that of 'Inquisitor'.

He also meets the Valeyard, a grim-faced figure in black who is to be the Doctor's prosecutor. The Valeyard's charge is that the Doctor wilfully interferes in the affairs of others, occasioning by this attitude further crimes of greater magnitude.

The first evidence the Valeyard presents to the court is an incident from the Doctor's past. Drawing on information held in the Matrix, the Prosecutor displays to the assembly the Doctor's visit to the planet Ravolox.

As the Doctor explains to Peri, Ravolox is a world with exactly the same mass, tilt and period of rotation as the Earth, even though it is on the other side of the galaxy. The woodland forests and glades seem pleasant enough, but Peri senses a distinct 'atmosphere' about the place, a comment the Doctor dismisses as a residual effect of solar flares which ravaged the planet centuries ago.

Initially, civilisation on the planet appears to be somewhat feudal. There is the Tribe of the Free, ruled over by the warrior matriarch Katryca, whose symbol of belief is an ebony totem pole. Also on the planet are two mercenaries, Glitz and Dibber, an unsavoury pair of crooks who have come here to get the Black Light Source.

Viewing the Doctor and Peri as a combination of obstacle and competition, Glitz's first thought is to get rid of them. In the rush to escape, the two travellers stumble into a cave. To Peri's shocked amazement, the cave interior is anything but natural rock formation. There are tiled walls, a curved roof and the remains of a long-disused escalator. The words *Marble Arch* labelled over a circular emblem confirms the Doctor's theory. This is part of what was the London Underground, which means Ravolox is really Earth. But how has it come to be where it shouldn't, and who caused the fireballs that decimated the planet?

More clues are unearthed as the Doctor finds evidence of another, more advanced, civilisation living beneath the station in sterile, air-conditioned shelters. These are descendants of survivors from the solar flares, kept ignorant of the fact that there is life on the Earth's surface again by their master, Drathro.

Eventually the Doctor gets to meet Drathro who is a robot, albeit one with a reasoning intelligence. This meeting coincides with Glitz and Dibber's attempt to wrest the Black Light Source from Katryca's tribe. Their totem pole, it transpires, is the source, but neither villain suspects the true consequences of damaging that pylon. As a dangerous energy build-up triggered through Drathro threatens Earth with a second armageddon, the Doctor must fight to defeat the robot and discover the true identity of those who moved the planet. He succeeds in the first aim, but a fault on the soundtrack relayed to the Matrix masks the answer to the second.

The Doctor's interference, the Valeyard insists, not only led to several unnecessary deaths in this incident, but also came perilously close to destroying the planet the accused maintains he has an affection for.

The Inquisitor accepts the accusations, but backs the Doctor's protest that much of this evidence is circumstantial. The Valeyard smiles, and promises that the next incident will bring the Doctor's crimes much closer to home . . .

THE TRIAL OF A TIME LORD – MINDWARP (Serial 7B) by Philip Martin. Director: Ron Jones

The trial continues as the Doctor strives against the loss of memory he has suffered since his arrival on the space station. Pressing home his advantage, the Valeyard offers to jog the Doctor's amnesia by reminding him of events leading up to his summons to the Time Lord court.

The image forming on the screen is a beach on the planet Thoros-Beta, a colourful world with a red sun illuminating purple sand. For Peri, the novelty of space and time travel is starting to wear thin, and so the Doctor's excited proclamation that they are in the twenty-fourth Century, last quarter, fourth year, raises less than an enthusiastic response. She is starting to miss the green pastures of home.

The Doctor's memory is already troubled. He is holding a phaser known to have originated on this planet, and he can recall it being given to him by a dying Thordon warlord who entreated the Doctor to bring more weapons here. But why they are wanted, he cannot recall.

These worries are soon banished as the pair encounter a new monster, the Raak, as they wind their way through a series of natural caves. Surviving this ordeal, they are taken prisoner by a group of soldiers and brought before an old acquaintance, the Mentor Sil from their adventure on Varos.

Sil's latest business enterprise is in progress on Thoros-Beta. He is here to arrange a deal with the brilliant medical scientist, Crozier, on behalf of the leader of the Mentors, Kiv.

Kiv's brain, the hub of the Mentor's corporate expertise, has grown to a point where it can no longer be accommodated by his skull. Crozier's genius is in transplant surgery, and so Sil intends using this talent to transfer Kiv's brain into another donor's body, one with a large skull capacity. If the operation goes as planned, Sil's reward will be greater power and prestige within the Mentor's corporation. Conversely, if Kiv dies, so will Sil.

Crozier's experiments with anotomical engineering have not always been successful, and very often the donors have been less than willing accomplices. It is these atrocities which has brought Yrcanos to Crozier's domain. Yrcanos is a Thordon king, a flamboyant death-or-glory monarch here to avenge rumours of sufferings among his people. One of the first victims he finds is Lukoser, one of his loyal subordinates now mutated into a creature half-man, half-wolf.

At first the Doctor sides with Yrcanos, but some time later, as the Valeyard points out to the court, he apparently undergoes a personality change, and seems more interested in satisfying scientific curiosity by helping Sil's mission, rather than hindering it.

Already, accuses the Valeyard, the Doctor's presence on Thoros-Beta is precipitating events that otherwise would not have happened. The Doctor objects, but is warned that an even greater crime will be committed later through an act of gross neglect.

Yrcanos has met Peri. Curiously the bombastic monarch is enamoured by her words that there is more to life than glorying in combat and death. She tries explaining to him about the things she values, concepts which Yrcanos finds baffling though he realises there is much he has to learn about being a king. He determines that if they win through this struggle, he will ask Peri to become his queen.

Crozier's operation on Kiv is not going well. He manages a transfer into the body of another Mentor, but Kiv is infuriated when he finds he must share his mind with the consciousness of a mundane fisherman. He wants a better body, and warns Sil and Crozier of the dire consequences if they fail. Crozier had considered the Doctor as a donor, but found him ultimately unsuitable. But what of his companion?

The Doctor manages to play the role of turncoat well, so well that he is given freedom to enter the prison area to make a selection for Crozier. Once inside, however, he outwits the guards and frees the captured Yrcanos and his men. His plan all along, it seems, was to free sufficient prisoners to overcome the Mentors' troops. Now revolt is in the air and, uttering a fierce war-cry. Yrcanos charges off to wreak vengeance on the scientist.

The Doctor is still freeing others when, without warning, the TARDIS materialises behind him and he is drawn inside. The ship takes off, following the path of the tractor beam emanating from the Time Lord High Court.

Too late, Yrcanos bursts into Crozier's laboratory. The operation has already been completed and Peri Brown exists no more. Instead, shorn of hair, her body is inhabited by Kiv. Unable to accept the horror of her fate, the wounded king raises his gun and shoots the Mentor leader.

The prosecution rests its case. By acts of criminal folly, neglect and wilful interference, the accused Doctor caused the death of his companion, Peri. Stunned by these images on the screen, the Doctor realises he must now conduct his own case for the defence . . .

'Mindwarp' is arguably the strongest of the 'The Trial of a Time Lord' segments, mainly through its re-uniting of all the key elements that went to make 'Vengeance on Varos' so popular. Philip Martin wrote the script, Ron Jones re-assumed the Director's seat, and disabled actor Nabil Shaban further developed his much-lauded interpretation of Sil.

The new ingredient to this story was Brian Blessed, playing almost a 'Spitting Image' caricature of himself as the ebullient King Yrcanos. In fact, on accepting the role, Blessed had been specifically asked to portray Yrcanos as the King from *The Black Adder*, the over-the-top comedy series he had appeared in with Rowan Atkinson.

A great fan of *Doctor Who*, Brian Blessed's name has often been linked with the show, not least when, in 1980, he was headlined in *The Daily Express* as the actor succeeding Peter Davison for the title role, after a practical joke between him and the manager of the Blackpool *Doctor Who* Exhibition got reported out of turn.

The development of electronic technology enabled a small first for *Doctor Who* in this story. The newly-perfected 'Paintbox' system was employed to change the blue skies and yellow sand of Brighton beach into the reds and purples of Thoros-Beta, thus overcoming limitations previously highlighted by the use of camera filters to achieve this trick.

THE TRIAL OF A TIME LORD – TERROR OF THE VERVOIDS (Serial 7C – First Four Episodes) by Pip & Jane Baker. Director: Chris Clough

Despite the Doctor's addled memory, his powers of perception and observation are keen as ever. There is something not quite right about the evidence he has seen so far, and suspicions of a cover-up are forming in his mind.

His suggestion to the Inquisitor that data about his adventures held in the Matrix has been corrupted is met with indignation. It is an impossible concept, the Doctor is told. He must present his defence along better lines.

Allowed access to his own Data Extract, the Doctor hurries to pick out an incident vindicating his stance of moral intervention. The Valeyard is urging more haste in these deliberations, so the Doctor is not given much of a chance to examine his history.

He presents to the court an adventure set in his own future. At this time, his companion is a young computer programmer from Pease Pottage, Sussex, named Melanie Bush. Mel, for short, is ardently pursuing her aim to help the Doctor lose weight when the TARDIS receives a distress call.

Following its signal lands the time machine in the darkened hold of a spacer liner, the *Hyperion III*, as it prepares to leave orbit on a deep space voyage back to Earth. Predictably, it is not long before the two time travellers are spotted by the crew and arrested by Security Officer Rudge. He takes them before the captain, Commodore Travers who, to the Doctor's pleasant surprise, is an old friend. Respecting the Time Lord's past achievement, Travers agrees to allow him and Mel to stay on the ship, although he himself has not heard of any distress signal being sent.

Escorted to the ship's main lounge, the Doctor and Mel begin making the acquaintances of other passengers. Most prominent are Professor Lasky and her assistants Bruchner and Doland. All three are agronomists conducting researches with alien seeds, and a large area of the ship's cargo hold has been given over to their collection of pods. Also aboard are three Mogarians, humanoid in shape but needing to wear their heavy duty spacesuits constantly as they cannot breathe air.

Melanie is keen to begin investigations, but the Doctor seems uncharacteristically apathetic. He is quite happy just to sit in the lounge and allow his companion to wander off on her own.

Seizing on this point, the Valeyard again accuses the Doctor of risking his companion's life by his own neglect. The Doctor is puzzled. This version of events does not seem identical to the one he ran through earlier. Nevertheless, still concerned for his memory, he allows the extract to continue.

Mel's explorations make her increasingly suspicious of Professor

Lasky and her work. Why are the Agronomists so secretive about their work? What are they doing in the Hydroponic Centre? And just what do the seeds pods in the hold contain?

Seeking an answer to the last question first, she slips back to the hold where she is discovered by one of the crewmen. Seeking to re-assure her, he agrees to make an inspection. But as he touches the fenced off area, a massive charge of electricity from the booby-trapped gate electrocutes him. The electricity arcs around the compound, bathing it in light and causing some of the pods to hatch open. Running for her life, Mel does not see the shape of the creatures emerging.

The crewman's death is the first of a whole spate of murders and disappearances. Rudge links these deaths with the arrival of the time travellers, and persuades Travers to have them both restrained. But far from quietening down, the Commodore's problems have just begun.

The pods have hatched Vervoids, hybrid vegetable creatures with a rapacious hunger for human flesh. Creeping through the air ducts, the Vervoids are able to reach any point on the ship, following and seizing their victims when they are alone.

Neither are the Vervoids the only opponents the Doctor must face. Seeking to unmask the murderers, the Doctor finds he has been dealing with two enemies, not one. A disgruntled Rudge has allied himself with the Mogarians who are intent upon hijacking the *Hyperion* and its cargo.

Things go badly wrong when the hijack bid is made. The controls of the ship are damaged and it seems as though they are locked onto a course that will send the *Hyperion* plunging into the Black Hole of Tartarus.

The Doctor jumps into action, tackling not only the Vervoids and the seemingly doomed liner, but also finding time to rescue Mel from being dumped into the ship's furnace.

Using his ingenuity, the Doctor brings the *Hyperion* back on course. The hijack too is quashed, but the Vervoids are still on the loose. The consequences would be catastrophic if the creatures were allowed to arrive on Earth, but Travers cannot warn the authorities because the radio system has been destroyed.

Watching from their vantage point in the courtroom, the Valeyard replays the data segment showing the actual sabotage of the radio. To the entire court's astonishment, the culprit is none other than the Doctor.

The Time Lords watch the conclusion of the evidence. The main villain is unmasked as one of Lasky's assistants, who didn't want the Professor to grab all the glory of their researches into this new, cultivated species. The Doctor deduces the reason why the Vervoids stay in the dark is because an excess of light would overload their photosynthesis systems. By chance, the *Hyperion* is carrying quantities of a highly combustible metal which burns with a brilliant light. Armed with chunks of this mineral, the Doctor leads a party into the ducts where, after a battle, they end the menace of the Vervoids once and for all. The *Hyperion* is saved, leaving the Doctor and Mel free to continue their travels.

The Valeyard demands to know if all the Vervoids were killed in the attack. The answer is yes. Then, he stresses in a rising voice, the Doctor's crime is not just sabotage or murder, but the ultimate atrocity of genocide. The only verdict the court can possibly give is 'Guilty'.

THE TRIAL OF A TIME LORD – THE ULTIMATE FOE (Serial 7C – Final Two Episodes) by Robert Holmes and Pip & Jane Baker. Director: Chris Clough

With the evidence pointing overwhelmingly to a vote of guilty, the Doctor is still hanging on to his assertion that data in the Matrix has been tampered with. The Keeper is summoned, a venerable old Time Lord who holds constantly on his person the key to the Matrix portals: the only means by which anyone can enter this repository.

The Keeper confirms the impossibility of any tampering, but at that moment a new face sharpens into focus on the evidence screen. It is the Master, ridiculing the Keeper's argument by pointing out that he is illegally in the Matrix even now. Neither is he the only one guilty of illegality. The High Council of the Time Lords is equally as corrupt in its willingness to re-adjust the Matrix to suit 'official' versions of history. It was they, covering up a mistake, who almost destroyed the Earth by a storm of solar flares and transferred it across the galaxy, editing the facts in the Matrix accordingly.

But, reveals the Master, by far the greatest criminal presently in command of the Matrix is the Valeyard. Though it is difficult to accept, the Valeyard is an amalgamation of all the dark sides of the Doctor's character, somewhere between his twelfth and final incarnation.

To support his statements, the Master brings Sabalon Glitz and Melanie Bush to the space station, the former to admit his connections with the High Council on the Ravolox affair, and the latter to testify on behalf of the present Doctor.

Stunned by these shock revelations, the members of the court notice too late the Valeyard making his escape back into the Matrix.

The Doctor knows he must follow the Valeyard and defeat his future self if he is to be acquitted of the charges facing all his incarnations. This the Master knows and relishes, and is the reason why he is helping the Doctor. The prospect of both the Doctor and the Valeyard at liberty in the Universe is daunting to his plans, so if they can be brought together, one must lose from the clash. Secretly as well, the Master fears the growing power of the Valeyard and is willing to render the Doctor assistance in his quest, although from the background.

Grudgingly, the Keeper hands the key to the Doctor, and he steps through the portal.

The Valeyard's power is indeed great within the Matrix. The Doctor finds himself in a gaslit Victorian street with the sound of maniacal laughter echoing in his ears. Ahead of him a huge signboard illuminates, welcoming him to the Fun Factory. Warily the Doctor enters, to be met by a Dickensian-dressed clerk named Popplewick. The due processes of procedure must be observed, warns Popplewick, but realising he is being bamboozled into accepting the Valeyard's created reality, the Doctor rebels and bursts through the closed office door to . . .

. . . the shore of a deserted beach. A surging tide of quicksand immobilises the Doctor and the Valeyard appears before him. Like the Doctor, he realises two incarnations of the same Time Lord cannot co-exist together, so one must perish. A deadly cloud of gas starts drifting towards the struggling form of the Doctor.

Rescue is at hand from the unlikely source of the Master, who has brought his TARDIS into the Matrix. Yet, even with the help of Glitz and Mel, the Master's plan to defeat the Valeyard, using the Doctor as a hypnotised decoy, fails.

The turning point comes when the Doctor deduces the hiding place of the Valeyard's own TARDIS. Wrecking his escape route, and the source of his control over the Matrix, the Doctor finally comes face-to-face with his alter-ego as the Valeyard's domain becomes a raging inferno.

The Doctor is the survivor, pulled just in time from the Valeyard's collapsing world. Justice has been done and the Inquisitor acknowledges the Time Lords' debt to him. Promising an investigation into the conduct of the High Council, she drops all charges and the Doctor is free to leave the station with Mel.

As the TARDIS departs, the Inquisitor instructs the Keeper to have the Matrix secured once more. Nodding, the Keeper turns away, laughing to himself. It is the Valeyard . . .

This cliffhanger ending was the one finally agreed for production once the task of writing the very last episode had been re-allocated to Pip and Jane Baker. Both Eric Saward and Robert Holmes had advocated a more downbeat ending with the Doctor, as well as the Valeyard, trapped in the Matrix with no hope of escape. Such a climax would have been open-ended enough to provide either a lead-in to the next season, or a final wrap-up for Doctor Who if Michael Grade had chosen not to renew its production schedules for 1987.

In hindsight, the Saward/Holmes ending might have been better, given the sensational nature of events following the season's transmission.

Ratings for the majority of episodes were disastrous, on average less than those for imported cartoons like Scooby Doo. Neither Roland Rat nor *Doctor Who* had captured the targeted big audiences tuning in week after week to *The A-Team*, so heads had to roll.

Just before Christmas 1986, Fleet Street headlined the BBC's decision to sack Colin Baker as the Doctor. Unlike the previous five title actors, the BBC felt Baker was not popular with the general public, his presence being a hindrance towards their bid to re-establish *Doctor Who*'s substantial, regular audience that had defected since Peter Davison's departure.

Accepting this decision as final, Producer John Nathan-Turner strove to win a concession allowing Colin Baker to appear in next season's opening story, thereby setting the scene for a regeneration. Conceding the point, the BBC gave way, but by this time Baker was so disgruntled by his treatment that he flatly refused the offer.

In mid-January the *Doctor Who* Production Office appointed newcomer Andrew Cartmel as Script Editor, his first task being to untangle the continuity dilemmas posed by having to start season twenty-four with a new Doctor and a continuing companion, Mel, who has yet, historically, to meet the Colin Baker incarnation!

III The Doctor in a New Dimension

SLIPBACK by Eric Saward. Director/Producer: Paul Spencer

The concept of *Doctor Who* on radio was not entirely new when Director/Producer Paul Spencer approached Michael Grade with his ideas in Spring 1985.

Spoofs based on *Doctor Who* have studded the airwaves ever since the *I'm Sorry I'll Read that Again* team's immortal *Professor Prune and the Electric Time Trousers* saga of the late sixties. In a parody of the then current Doctor, Patrick Troughton, Professor Prune (Graeme Garden) travelled the Universe searching for ever more preposterous adventures in a pair of dimensionally transcendental time trousers (bigger inside than out), accompanied by his glamorous but expansive companion, Boobyrella (bigger outside than in) alias Tim Brooke-Taylor.

The Daleks, predictably, were rich sources of fun. John Lloyd, later of *Hitch Hiker's Guide* fame, produced a sketch outlining development of the ultimate weapon in the war against the Daleks – stairs.

Up until the mid-seventies, however, no characters from television *Doctor Who* had ever appeared on radio. That changed in the autumn of 1976 when Tom Baker and Elisabeth Sladen agreed to play the Doctor and Sarah in a schools broadcast designed to teach children about the origins of the Earth.

Backed by the Radiophonic Workshop, this half-hour programme followed the Doctor and Sarah's travels in the TARDIS as they watched the planet Earth evolve from clouds of rotating gas into the lush, verdant world of today, foiling the aims of the Megron, Lord of Chaos, along the way.

Paul Spencer wanted something more for his 1985 production. His aim was nothing less than a one hour *Doctor Who* drama serial on Radio 4, featuring the current regular cast (Colin Baker and Nicola Bryant), and preferably scripted by someone with knowledge of the TV show's format and continuity.

The story would be broken down into six ten-minute segments, each with a cliff-hanger, and slotted into a new children's magazine programme, *Pirate Radio 4*: a kind of radio *Saturday Superstore*. Each edition of *Pirate Radio 4* would feature two episodes of the *Doctor Who* story, broadcast at irregular times as a hook to keep listeners tuned in.

Grade received Paul Spencer's application right in the middle of the 'Cancellation Crisis' and so, probably with an eye to calming some of the fuss, readily agreed to the experiment, suggesting Spencer should contact the *Doctor Who* office for a list of possible writers.

With little work on the TV show to worry about since the postponement, Script Editor Eric Saward agreed to handle the script, his own writing experience having been gained on radio in the first place.

Saward's original title, 'The Doomsday Project', was changed to 'Slipback' shortly before transmission, which began on Thursday, July 7th 1985. For this production, Colin Baker and Nicola Bryant were joined by an actor already familiar to TV *Doctor Who* fans, Valentine Dyall. The face and voice of the Black Guardian, Dyall was more known to radio listeners as the infamous Man in Black from the *Appointment with Fear* series years ago. 'Slipback' was his last performance on radio. He died in June 1985, just weeks before the serial went out.

The story is set aboard a giant star freighter, the *Vipod Mor*, drifting through space on a census-taking mission sometime in the distant future. All is far from well aboard ship. The captain is ill and has retired to a lava bath for his health. His body is incurably infected with Mors Immedicabilis spores. At present they are dormant, but any excessive strain or worry will cause them to erupt and infect the rest of the crew.

The ship's computer has its problems too, seeming to hear another voice within its intelligence centre controlling the output messages. And within the ship's air ducting, a savagely powerful monster is roaming loose.

The Doctor is woken, by Peri, from a dream in which he heard a voice forewarning him about 'The Eclipse of Time'. Peri tells him the TARDIS has effected an impromptu materialisation alongside a space freighter. Examining the controls, the Doctor detects evidence of Time Spillage, caused by someone on board interfering with time itself.

He relocates the TARDIS inside the ship, unfortunately landing inside the air ducting. They are attacked and pursued by a hungry creature, whom the Doctor identifies as a Maston. With seconds to spare they dash past a closing bulkhead, activated by the computer.

The computer reports to Grant, the First Officer, the presence of an Earth girl in the ducting, and he, anxious to appease his suffering captain, gives instructions for her to be diverted here. The Computer enquires of its 'other voice' why it was not allowed to report the Doctor's presence. The voice replies that knowledge is needed from the Time Lord . . .

Peri gets separated from the Doctor and meets two more stowaways, Seedle and Snatch. These two, it transpires, are special investigators looking into the theft of priceless art treasures from worlds visited by the *Vipod Mor*. One of the names they are tracing is Shellingborne Grant.

The Doctor is captured by Grant. Concerned that the computer could not locate him, Grant suspects the Doctor is a police investigator, and admits his part in the art thefts. He escorts the Doctor to a special cell, constructed to specifications supplied by the computer. Once inside, however, a piercing noise fills the air and the Doctor hears the computer's voice change to that of the voice he heard in his dreams. This unearthly intelligence intends draining the Doctor's mind of its knowledge.

Just in time, the sound dies away. The intelligence within the computer is unimpressed with what it found, describing it as 'cluttered with trivia'. It has, however, absorbed enough knowledge to enable the next stage in its plan to proceed. Brought into being by a computer technician's error, this powerful intelligence has found the Universe in chaotic disarray. It intends re-starting the whole process again, and has already begun its task, predicting that any potential resistance from the crew will be dealt with by the infection spreading even now from the Captain.

Seedle and Snatch rescue the Doctor, re-uniting him with Peri just as the freighter begins slipping back through Time. The Maston creature devours the two investigators as the Doctor tears back to the TARDIS, intent on intervention. But he is stopped by a booming voice in his head: the voice of the Time Lords.

All this has happened before, the Time Lords tell the Doctor, and will continue to happen. The computer will pilot the ship back to the beginning of time where it will fuse with a mass of original matter. Detonation of the Ship's auto destruct will in turn trigger the biggest explosion of all, the Big Bang, from which the Universe was formed.

The Doctor admits defeat, and leads Peri back to the TARDIS. This was something he should have remembered, he grumbles, and determines to set off in search of the biggest library he can find instead.

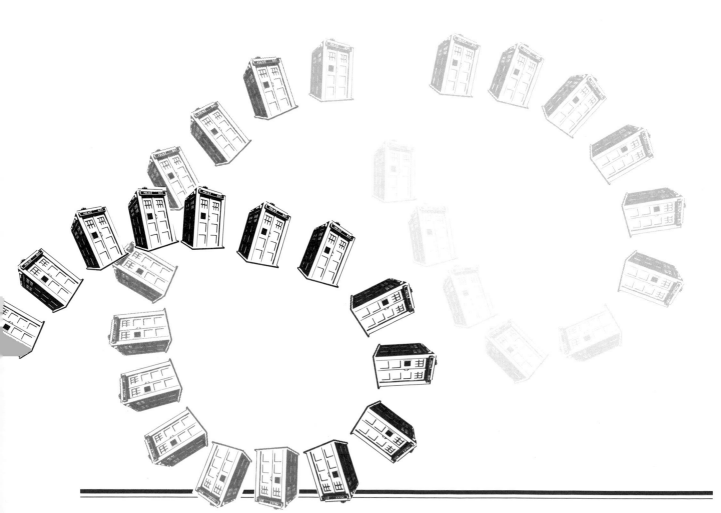